GERI'S
SECRETS

GERI'S
SECRETS

THE TOTALLY AMAZING, COMPLETELY
UNAUTHORISED BIOGRAPHY

VIRGINIA
BLACKBURN

JOHN BLAKE

Published by John Blake Publishing Ltd, 3 Bramber Court,
2 Bramber Road, London W14 9PB, England

First published in paperback in 2002

ISBN 1 904034 61 6

British Library Cataloguing-in-Publication Data: A catalogue
record for this book is available from the British Library.

Design by ENVY

Printed and bound in Great Britain by Bookmarque

1 3 5 7 9 10 8 6 4 2

Papers used by John Blake Publishing Ltd are natural, recyclable
products made from wood grown in sustainable forests. The
manufacturing processes conform to the environmental
regulations of the country of origin.

The publishers are grateful to Express newspapers for supplying
the images used in this book.

Every attempt has been made to contact the relevant copyright-
holders, but some were unobtainable. We would be grateful if the
appropriate people could contact us.

Contents

Very many thanks to
Jane Clinton, Jane Sherwood and,
above all, to Chris Williams.

1

Who's
That Girl?

The atmosphere was tense. The world's most famous pop group were gathering for an appearance on the National Lottery show in May 1998, but one of their number was missing. 'Where is she?' hissed the organisers to the girls.

'Where is she?' hissed the girls to one another.

No one knew the answer, but one thing was for sure: Geraldine Estelle Halliwell, aka Geri, aka Ginger Spice, was missing. And nobody knew where she was.

In the event, the Spice Girls went on with the

show, explaining to their fans that Geri was suffering from gastro-enteritis. Behind the scenes, though, it was far from clear what was going on, even amongst the girls themselves. Geri had been telling them for some time that she was tired of being a Spice Girl, that she wanted to quit at the end of the world tour in September, but none of the girls had taken her seriously. And they certainly never dreamed that she would just walk out, leaving them in the lurch. But as they flew out to Norway to perform two tour dates in Oslo, Geri still wasn't to be found. The awful truth was beginning to sink in. 'This is very serious,' said a source within the group's entourage, 'and the other girls desperately want to talk to Geri to find out what's going on. If she has left the group the consequences could be quite severe.'

At first, the girls tried to play it down. They went on stage as a foursome in Oslo and in the second half of the show Victoria announced to the 8,000-strong sell-out crowd, 'We just wanted to say that Geri is poorly and in bed and really she couldn't be with us tonight. But she hopes you are all having a wicked time.' Meanwhile, a note was taped to the concert hall doors. 'Geri is ill and can't be here tonight,' it read. 'If you want your money back, it will be refunded. We are sorry.'

But as the show wound down to a close,

speculation was reaching fever point. Had Geri really left the world's most successful group? Was there really to be no more Ginger Spice? The girls were a phenomenon: since bursting on to the scene in 1996, they had become the first act in pop history to have number ones with their first four singles. On top of that, their first single, 'Wannabe', and first album, *Spice*, made chart history with the highest ever European debuts in America, 'Wannabe' went to number one in 32 countries and the *Spice* album sold over 8 million copies worldwide, making them the fastest-selling new artists in the world since The Beatles. And Geri wanted to leave that?

It was becoming well known that the girls had been rowing incessantly, with particular tensions between Geri and Mel B, but no one had expected this. And no one had any idea what was really happening, not even the girls' record company. 'Geri is suffering from nervous exhaustion; she has been seen by doctors,' said a spokesman for Virgin Records. 'She is extremely tired and overwrought by the tour and has had a bad bout of gastro-enteritis. There has been a falling out between the girls but this is not the first time. Geri is very strong-minded and they have had many such arguments in the past. The truth is we simply don't know what will happen. It is possible that this could be the end but personally I find it extremely unlikely. Geri needs time to recover and there will be a big making up.'

As it happens, he was wrong. It might not have been the first time the girls had had a huge row, but it turned out to be the last. For Geri, infuriated that her fellow band members were not according her enough respect and aware that the first to leave the group would have the greatest chance of solo success – in the same way that her friend-to-be Robbie Williams found after Take That – had finally had enough. She was leaving the band that had made her into a household name halfway through their world tour and just a couple of months before they were due to appear in stadiums across America. Forty venues had been booked, one million tickets sold and the organisers of the tour were not pleased. 'We've booked to stage the Spice Girls and we want all five, including Ginger, not four or a replacement,' one organiser said.

The situation started to look desperate. 'I haven't a clue where Geri is and neither have the band,' said a spokeswoman. 'We've not heard from her.' There was even speculation, which turned out to be untrue, that Geri had split from her boyfriend Christian Horsfall and had fled the band to recover from a broken heart. Finally, a statement was released confirming Geri's departure from the Spice Girls – and, indeed, from her former life. 'This is a message to the fans,' she wrote. 'Sadly, I would like to confirm that I have left the Spice Girls. This is because of differences between us. I'm sure the group will continue to be successful and I wish them all the best. I have no immediate plans. I wish to apologise to all the fans and to thank them and everyone who's been there. Lots of love, Geri. PS: I'll be back.'

Initially, at least, the girls responded gracefully, issuing a statement in reply that was read out by their spokesman Alan Edwards. 'We are upset and saddened by Geri's departure but we are very supportive in what she wants to do. The Spice Girls are here to stay – see you at the stadiums! We are sorry to all our fans for having to go through all of this. All our love, Victoria, Emma, Mel C, Mel B. Friendship never ends.'

Some hope. In the years to come a bitter rivalry was to grow up between Geri and her fellow band members but at the time, at least, everyone was feeling traumatised, including Geri herself. 'It's as if I've just left a marriage,' she said at the time. 'It's normal that anyone who goes from one extreme to another has a period of adjusting.'

But the world was in shock, with intensive speculation as to whether the other girls could carry on without Geri, to say nothing of what the future held for the Ginger one herself. Little girls, who made up much of the Spice Girls' fan base, wept over the departure of one of their heroines and even the stock market responded to the news, with shares in EMI Group, Virgin's parent company, dropping 10p to 508p per share. As ever, though, in the pragmatic City, there was at least one voice of common sense. 'People have been looking for an excuse to mark down EMI,' said Paul Richards, an analyst at broker Panmure Gordon. 'I'd be more worried if Geri wrote all those songs and could sing and dance.'

It soon emerged that there was a reason that Geri left at the exact moment she did (although she had been planning to do so for some time): the girls had denied her the chance to be Serious Spice. The day before her non-appearance on the National Lottery show, Geri had given an interview in which she revealed that in her teens she had had an emergency operation after a breast cancer scare. She had found a lump in her breast and, though it proved benign, this had been a terrible shock. Geri's revelation provoked an enormous amount of interest – which angered the other girls, who felt that Geri was hogging all the limelight – and another request for an interview, which would have clashed with the Lottery show.

Geri had wanted to do the interview, the other

girls refused to give her time off and an impasse was reached. 'She was delighted at the positive response it [the interview] got and wanted to do everything she could to promote awareness of the disease,' a source close to the Spice Girls explained. 'But the others knew they were committed to the Lottery and didn't want to disappoint the BBC and fans.'

Breast cancer was certainly on her mind at the time. That summer Geri had read a book entitled *Before I Say Goodbye*, an extremely moving account of suffering from cancer by Ruth Picardie, who died of the disease. As soon as she'd finished the book, Geri got in touch with her personal assistant and asked her to arrange a meeting with Ruth's sister Justine. Justine later published an account of the meeting in the magazine *Elle*.

'I catch a plane to Nice and then a helicopter to St Tropez,' she wrote. 'Geri Halliwell meets me at the airport. She starts crying when she sees me, and I'm not sure what to do. So we go to lunch and then back to George Michael's house where she is hiding from the press. She talks about Ruth's book and how it changed her life, about how it made her want to leave the Spice Girls. Geri had a lump in her breast, she says, but it wasn't malignant. Why not her? Why was she saved? I don't know the answer to her questions.'

But Geri's interest in health issues and her desire

to be taken seriously might not have been the whole story behind her departure. Shortly before splitting from the group, Geri was seen lunching with the television personality Chris Evans – with whom she was later linked romantically – and from whom many people suspect she took advice. He himself was certainly interested in her departure: 'I think she left the Spice Girls at exactly the right time, before she lost her personality within the group,' he said.

Geri, like the rest of the girls, was very aware that the Spice Girls had only a limited shelf life. Their original manager, Simon Fuller, had always felt that the world tour would probably be the pinnacle of their career as a group, and so to get out just as the girls were at the very top was an extremely canny career move. Many felt that Chris Evans himself was involved, either trying to get Geri to sign up with his Ginger Media Group (and what a public relations coup that would have been – 'Ginger joins Ginger!') or at the very least advising her on a move into television. 'I wouldn't be at all surprised if she went into television,' said one insider at the time. 'Geri is quite a serious-minded person. She wouldn't be interested in some silly weather girl telly-bimbo project.' As it transpired, Geri's television career never materialised, but if that was what she really, really wanted, then she was talking to the right man.

And so, Geri walked out of the group, leading to the obvious question: what next? No one, Geri included, seemed to know. First she headed off to Paris with her brother Max in tow, and then went on to Mauritius to lie low for a week until the dust stirred up by her departure began to settle down. Next stop was George Michael's villa, Chez Nobby, in the South of France (the other girls took refuge in Sir Elton John's even more luxurious pad nearby).

There then followed a series of frenetic journeys around the globe as Geri attempted to decide what to do next, starting with meetings with Hollywood executives to talk about a part in the forthcoming movie *Charlie's Angels*, as revealed by Randy Spelling, son of Aaron who produced the 1970s television original. Ultimately Cameron Diaz, Lucy Liu and Drew Barrymore ended up starring in the film, but at the time Geri seemed to be very much in the picture. 'Geri's coming to LA later in June for several meetings about future TV and movie projects,' said Randy. 'She's going to read for Dad for the new *Charlie's Angels* movie. He thinks she'd be great. She's funny, sassy and sexy – everything an angel needs to be.'

But it was not to be. Geri's only acting experience to date had been in *Spiceworld: The Movie*, which might have been greatly enjoyable for the group's fans, but left something to be desired as far as training to be an actress was concerned. Geri fled to the South of France – to George Michael, again – with her then boyfriend, the dancer Christian Horsfall, and was pictured thoughtfully reading *Further Along The Road Less Travelled* by the American psychotherapist Dr M Scott Peck. Many believed the carefully staged pictures to be yet another stunt from her PR company Freud Communication, which, co-incidentally, also looks after Chris Evans.

Geri didn't let such speculation bother her: she bounced back and continued on her radical change of image, which first started when she left the other girls. Gone was the busty, brassy Sexy Spice, spilling out of her Union Jack mini-dress and shaking her long red hair and in her place was an almost unrecognisable Geri – sleek blonde hair, demure dark clothing and an already noticeably slimmer figure. The new image was to a great extent a response to the *Charlie's Angels* people, who had told Geri her image was too extreme. 'I felt like I'd reached the end of my panto-damehood,' says Geri. 'I was starting to look like a drag queen. I wanted to calm down and blend in.'

But not that much. To begin with, at least, it was starting to look as if Geri had made a big mistake, with industry figures queuing up to tell her that it had all gone horribly, badly wrong. 'I think she will be, for years, my standard for telling a singer why not to leave a group,' said a record company insider at the time. 'The Spice Girls made some good records, but what was she thinking?'

Another show business PR was equally scathing. 'She can never hope to recapture the Spice Girl scenario,' he said. 'That comes once every 20 years. I think it'll be TV – something along the lines of Cilla Black, though she'll have to work very hard to make such a success of it.'

As for the girls themselves, once the shock began to wear off, they were becoming less charitable towards their old band mate. Stories began to circulate that she was a very weak singer and that the other girls had to carry her. She had so little to sing by herself, it was said, that her lines were easy to allocate to the others. They themselves seemed to have emerged unscathed from the trauma and were enjoying a triumphant tour across the United States: 'The other girls don't even mention her name now,' said a source close to the remaining Spices. 'To them, Geri and that whole episode is part of history.'

There was very briefly a reunion between two of the Spices, Geri and Victoria, but it was not to last. Victoria, her then fiancé and now husband David Beckham, George Michael, with whom Geri was staying, and Geri all went out to dinner at the exclusive Le Girelier restaurant in St Tropez, with the girls greeting one another with a hug and a kiss. 'There was no bad blood between Geri and Victoria, but there was a lot of bad blood between Geri and the group as a whole,' said a Spice insider. 'They were furious and upset when she left them. They felt she had stabbed them in the back. That's why this kiss-and-make-up meeting is such a shock. I can't believe that Mel B – who had many fallings out with Geri – will be too pleased about this. But it shows bridges can be built.'

An onlooker remarked, 'Geri and Victoria had a fantastic time, laughing and joking together.'

That was until Victoria, who was then three months pregnant with her first child, saw the resulting press coverage and was not amused, saying afterwards that Geri had tipped off photographers in advance in order to make it appear that there was still the possibility of a reconciliation. It later emerged that the dinner was in fact initially to have taken place in George Michael's house and it was only after the Beckhams had accepted the invitation that they discovered it was to be at a restaurant. 'Everyone said it was a publicity stunt,' said Victoria. 'And I said, "No." But I had denied myself the truth.'

In retrospect, Geri's departure probably did herald

the break-up of the band, but then again, they were never designed for the long term. And when Geri stopped being a Spice Girl, she did it on her own terms. At the time, however, even Geri's family was unclear as to what she was going to do next. 'We were all shocked when she left the band,' said Geri's brother Max. 'She is just sort of taking time out. I don't really know what her long-term plans are. She did not tell us. I certainly think she's got the drive and charisma and potential to stay in the limelight.' Asked about whether she was interested in making a career in television, he replied, 'Who knows. It's a possibility. I think she's got options.'

Geri's stepfather Steve Parkinson was also in the dark. 'We don't know – I don't think she knows herself, really.'

And Geri's aunt Maria Victoria, who lives in Huesca in Spain, could shed no light on the matter. 'I don't know what's going through her mind, but I can imagine,' she said. 'But she is stubborn, headstrong and will not give up until she achieves what she wants. Geri has come out of nothing to be somebody. If she ends up a nobody again, we will love her just the same.'

But Geri didn't want to become a nobody again. As it started to become clear that she was taking neither Hollywood nor White City, the home of the BBC, by storm, a serious rethink was needed and by September 1998 Geri had decided to return to her singing roots. She asked Lisa Anderson, widely regarded as one of the most powerful women in the music industry – she had marketed the Sex Pistols and Simple Minds and was the first woman to head a record company, BMG/RCA – to become her manager.

'Geri decided some weeks ago that she wanted to get back into music,' said an industry insider once the announcement had been made. 'When she first left the band, she was keen to get into television and film, but she now realises her future is in music. Lisa is widely regarded as one of the most talented and innovative people in the business. Geri has hired her knowing she is the best around.'

Lisa herself was equally effusive. 'I am genuinely excited by this new challenge,' she said. 'Geri is a wonderful person with a lot of ideas for the future. I think we will make a dynamic team.' She was right: Geri went on to sign a £2 million solo record deal with Chrysalis Records, also owned by EMI.

The relationship between Geri and Lisa in fact lasted only a year – it was a meeting of opposites. Geri was young, free and single: Lisa, 45 at the time, was a married mother of two. Her husband David Campbell was a former manager of U2 but by that point in his life was content to stay at home looking after the couple's children Hereward and Hannah. Like Geri, though, Lisa was a tough cookie. Lisa received the Music Industry's first Woman of the Year Award in 1995, while earning the nickname 'Lethal Anderson' from Jonathan King when she took over the organisation of the Brits in 1991. And most of all, Lisa was very top drawer. 'Yes, I am posh,' Lisa said in an interview in 1998. 'When I started in the music business, if you had a posh accent you were supposed to hide it and talk like David Bailey. But I never got the hang of it, so I just had to be awfully posh instead.'

Lisa was not a big party person, preferring to head home to Kent. 'I hate going to parties,' she says. 'I'm always the one in the kitchen. I never have anything to say. I prefer to come home, because I have a home, and see my kids because I like them.' As for her new working relationship with Geri: 'I have record experience which is pertinent, TV experience and big show experience,' she said. 'I didn't know why Geri chose me, I didn't ask her. But I like her because she knows what she wants. She is very clear about the direction in which she wants to go. And we are going to do it together.'

It emerged that Geri was not just returning to her roots in her career – she was, for the first time, putting down some roots in her own life. Despite the fact that she by now possessed a multi-million-pound fortune, Geri had been living in a rented cottage in Hertfordshire. It was time to buy a place of her own, and she splashed out on a £1.5 million mansion close to London's Heathrow airport, which had until recently been home to a group of Catholic nuns. A further £500,000 was put aside to refurbish the property, including installing an indoor swimming pool and a tennis court.

'Geri had been house hunting for months and was staying in a rented cottage,' said a friend of the family. 'But she knew this place was for her the moment she clapped eyes on it. She was particularly struck by its history. Geri has very deep religious beliefs – hard to believe when you think of Ginger Spice in that Union Jack dress – and used to be a Jehovah's Witness. She's no longer a Witness, but is really looking forward to the peace she hopes she'll now find at home.'

The next step was to embark on a round of good works. First Geri dashed off to Uganda to film a report for Comic Relief, which was not a total success. The work went well, but Geri took some time off to go white water rafting on the River Nile (coincidentally at a village called Jinja) and was dragged under the water when the boat she was in capsized. 'My most horrifying experience was last year in Africa when I went out there for Comic

Relief. I nearly drowned,' she said. 'I have a fear of water anyway after my near drowning experience – especially fast-moving water. I thought I was going to die as I was being swirled around under water. When I watched the film *Castaway* it freaked me out – all those big waves. I even watched Disney's *Tarzan* the other day and when I saw the big waves, I was like, "Aaargh".'

In typical Geri fashion, this experience became a part of her life philosophy. She'd had a nasty experience but now she was going to learn from it and move on. 'Fear can paralyse you,' she said in an interview a year after it happened. 'I nearly drowned last year when I was making a documentary in Africa. It made me realise you have no control over your life and your time is up when your time is up. I'm OK about planes and things, but I'm afraid of feeling afraid and want to feel a grip on situations. I challenge my fear all the time because I don't like feeling afraid. Maybe I'm kind of a brave fool.'

And the experience did not put her off charitable works. Geri next whizzed off to Holloway Prison where she talked to inmates about breast cancer and then auctioned off her Spice Girls costumes, raising £150,000 for Sargent, a children's cancer charity, before rounding it all off by becoming a goodwill ambassador for the United Nations, following in the footsteps of the likes of Audrey Hepburn and Roger Moore.

This was quite a change of direction from the Sexy Spice image of yesteryear, but unfortunately one which didn't go down entirely well with everyone. Geri's speciality in her work with the UN was birth control, still a very delicate subject in many parts of the world, as she found out the following year on a visit to the Philippines. Mobbed by crowds of young women (not all of whom were entirely sure who she was), Geri told them that birth control is a 'fundamental right' to protect against disease and unwanted pregnancy: she was later denounced by a spokesman for the Philippine church. 'We do not need population control,' he snapped. 'Any effort at safe sex is utterly immoral.' There were other upsets. In a documentary about her life shot by Molly Dineen – of which more anon – Geri was pictured as being somewhat ill prepared for a press conference, with a shaky grasp of her brief. No matter, she was determined to prove herself a serious player, not merely in terms of music, but in global politics as well. Girl power had never been quite like this.

And finally, there was a return to performing. The record deal signed, Geri made her first singing appearance since leaving the Spice Girls, when she appeared at a gala to mark the 50th birthday of the

Prince of Wales. Geri had made headlines around the world when she first met Prince Charles and promptly pinched his bottom, but on this occasion she was decorum personified: first hosting the proceedings and then changing into a royal blue gown designed by Kenny Ho. Strapless and full length, it was a striking creation, although her rendition of Happy Birthday to the Prince raised eyebrows, as it bore a very strong resemblance to Marilyn Monroe's version of the same song to President Kennedy back in 1962. An unfortunate reference, said some, but the message was clear: Geri was back and now she was performing for royalty. By herself.

And so the Geri bandwagon began to roll once more. After a summer spent flitting around the world, sometimes hiding from photographers and sometimes sitting in carefully posed positions which allowed the public to see the new incarnation of Geri Halliwell, Solo Spice was ready to take up where she had left off. Relations with the girls were to worsen and a series of bizarre relationships were to follow, before Geri faced her biggest ordeal of all: a dreadful eating disorder that she has not fully conquered to this day.

But for now she had broken free of the band that had made her a household name and was ready to go it alone. And the lady herself had no real regrets. 'I don't regret leaving when I did, but I regret not having the opportunity to appear at Wembley Stadium with them at the end of the tour,' she said rather wistfully some months on. 'That made me feel a bit sad.'

On other occasions, she voiced regrets about not finishing the rest of the tour, but she had plainly had enough. Asked if she missed touring with the girls, she replied, 'I suppose it was nice, but it was still very heavy schedules and tiring – and I've always been the sort of person who takes on board the stresses and responsibility, regardless of being in a group. Most of the time I like to feel that I have a sense of control and responsibility of where I'm going. I suppose if you're in a group and if it does go wrong then you have support. The blame is shared, but then the praise is shared, too. It's nice to be praised for your own solo work – it's liberating. It may sound egotistical, but I can write about what I choose without having to think about anyone else.'

What a telling comment that was – and it provided an explanation that rang more true than any other: Geri left the girls because she wanted to have fame and praise all for herself. And Geri is not good at thinking about anyone else – hence her decision to quit when she did. The girls continued to have mixed feelings. 'I miss Geri a lot,' said Victoria a year after

GERI'S SECRETS

the departure. 'When she left, people thought there was a bust-up, but there was nothing like that. There had been tensions in the past but at the time she left it had never been so smooth. Anyway, one morning, after a plane journey, Geri just announced she wanted to leave. It was a complete shock; we couldn't understand it.

'Ultimately we had to put it down to the fact that Geri's a very spontaneous person because otherwise it was quite painful. Apart from working with her, we were very close to her. *Very* close. Now I just think back to the laughs we had and the funny times. I mean, we've been through so much together, it's almost like unconditional love. If your sister goes out and kills someone, you still love her. Whatever Geri has done, I'm still really fond of her – *really* fond.'

Geri herself felt she had grown up a lot. 'You only had to look at me in the last six months before I left to see that I was changing,' says Geri. 'What I wore off stage was completely different. When we started the band I was 21 and when I left I was 26. It's natural that people are going to grow up. There is nothing false or contrived about the way I look.

'Even if we were five angels, you're not going to get on all the time. I am in touch with some of them in a low-key way. I'll send presents to them on birthdays and births. I haven't seen their babies yet. I

27

want to address the future before I do the past. I know we'll be pals. I'm not trying to escape from being Ginger. It'll take time to change that name. You can love someone but if you're not in love with them then it's dishonest. I knew it was time to move on. There was no logic behind it. I'd given everything I had to that band. It wasn't so much of a change as a transitional progression.'

Geri was being extremely optimistic: these days there is a permanent state of hostility between Geri and her erstwhile pals (and, indeed, between the pals themselves if some current reports are to be believed), but the point was made. Her days as a Spice Girl were over. Solo Spice was on her way.

2

Look at Me

It was the moment of reckoning. Geri had tried and failed to establish a second career as an actress and so, desperate to remain in the centre-stage position she had fought so hard to attain, she returned to the industry that had made her famous: music. And the title of her debut single as a solo artist could not have been more appropriate: 'Look At Me'. All her life Geri had been desperate for attention and now that she'd got it, she wasn't giving it up lightly. Nearly a year after walking out on the Spice Girls, Geri was ready to go it alone.

'Ginger was a part of me and she still is,' she said as she prepared to unveil her new disc and her new image, a far cry from the cartoon character she had portrayed in the past. 'But you've got to understand that I was 18 when I started to wear platform shoes and it's natural that everybody changes. I was changing within the Spice Girls but nobody noticed. When I was up on stage I was wearing the hot pants and the bra because that was what people wanted to see, but when I came off stage my hair was being toned down and my clothes were changing. It was a slow process but by the time I had left it was really apparent.'

Geri was also beginning to learn that less can be more and that her new covered-up image – which was not, incidentally, to last – could convey just as much of a message as the 'bursting out all over' look of old. 'It can be just as powerful not to show breasts,' she said. 'I suppose I was saying, "Look at this but don't look at me." It's like hiding behind a suit in a bank. Everyone hides behind a costume or an outfit. If we're not sure who we are that day, we put that on and it makes us feel something.'

Sensibly, Geri tried to both dampen expectations and explain the action of the last year. 'It's not that I take myself too seriously. I am not Céline Dion and I never claimed to be,' she said. 'What I am is honest. I didn't want to do anything too contrived when I left the band because I find quick image changes a bit of bullshit and patronising. What I did was just be myself. Whatever I gave to the Spice Girls – and, you know, I used to write a healthy contribution to those songs and to the imagery in the videos – I have taken it with me and gone one step further.'

The publicity bandwagon set off. Geri flew to Sydney to launch her new career and talked openly about the experiences of the previous year. 'I've been licking my wounds,' she said. 'I've been in mourning, re-evaluating myself. But now I want to come back with a bang. I'm a great believer in facing down your fears. I'm 26 years old – far too young to retire.' And of her break with the girls she said, 'I had to leave. We fell in love, had this whirlwind romance but like one in three marriages, it didn't work. It's just like an ex-lover, you need a little bit of time to get over it. And so I was giving it that space and time. I will always have a special place in my heart for those girls. I wouldn't be sitting here without them.'

And so to the new Geri. Ginger might have remained a part of her but not for long: the video for the song showed a coffin with Ginger's name on it and ended up with Geri reborn, rising naked from a swimming pool, her bottom hidden by a slogan saying, 'Geri's back' (geddit?). She also played four characters throughout. Not everyone appreciated the imagery: Victoria Beckham had some choice remarks to make about the coffin, pointing out that Spice Girls fans tended to be very young and might well be very upset to hear of the supposed death of one of their number. Geri was unrepentant.

'What I am dealing with is four stereotypes of women, what we box ourselves into,' she said. 'One's a vamp, one's a virgin, one's a PR workaholic and the other one is a "look at me girl". The video is saying, "Who is Geri Halliwell?" Is she this one or that one, which woman? We are all of them and we are none of them.' On another occasion she said, 'I know I'm not the best dancer in the world but I like the whole character of the video – the cheekiness of it all. It's very much inspired by Audrey Hepburn's *Funny Face*. The idea is, I'm portraying the stereotyped parts of women. You're a mother, you go to work, you're a friend and you can be vampish when you go out at night. Women can fulfil many different roles. Personally, I'm somewhere between a virgin and a vamp. It was poking fun at myself and the way we are as human beings – obsessed by image. It was saying: I like to dress up and have fun.'

It was another canny move. Anyone who wants a long-term career in the music business has a very tough job ahead and so frequent changes of image, à la Madonna, are one way of keeping the public's attention. Geri knew that as well as anyone and she also understood the position of celebrity within society. 'People in the media will eventually realise that you have to be honest about who you are,' she said. 'Immortal celebrity no longer exists. The way forward is to show your imperfections. To admit, I don't really know what I'm doing but I'm trying.

'In the olden days, in the fifties, they hung out their washing and talked over the fence and said, "Have you seen what that girl's wearing at number seven?" There was their own gossip within their own community. But now that community has broken down to such an extent that it no longer really exists, we need something larger. That's where the tabloids come in. It gives us something in common to talk about, a glue.'

Geri certainly knew how to play the game, but what about the actual product? The single was to be followed up by an album, *Schizophonic*, which was described by Geri in terms that were frankly alarming. 'I think the way to describe my album and my music is Johnny Rotten meets Julie Andrews,' she says. 'When I wrote the album, I really poured my own emotion into it, whether it's down there and reflective or up there being quite outlandish. This album is one big hormonal mood swing.'

Scary stuff, but Geri was absolutely determined to make it work. She was also now promoting herself as a mature musician rather than a favourite of under-fives the world over, a transformation that came across as not entirely convincing. 'I was really frightened to admit that [staying in pop] was what I wanted to do,' she said. 'In the pit of my stomach I was thinking, Oh I really want to do that but I don't know whether I'm good enough or whether I can really carry it. You see, I am not musically trained but I've always had it in my heart to express things. I was really afraid but I am a great believer that we are drawn to what we are afraid of. I had to do this. I had no choice, because I didn't want to get to being an adult, all grown up and thinking, Why didn't you give it a go? I hope everybody loves it, but if they don't … well, I gave it my best shot.'

Geri was also keen to portray herself as having suffered since leaving the girls, a suffering that matured the creative process. 'I took my time getting this record right,' she says. 'When I left the group I just kept my head down, tended to my wounds and found out who I was again. I felt I needed a year to get my feet back on the ground. I wanted to start from scratch and say, "OK. This is where I am at the minute." I nearly drowned when I left the Spice Girls but now I just think that you can't take life too seriously. I am a very, very lucky girl and now I just try not to take things for granted and enjoy it.'

There were other changes, too. Geri's friendship with George Michael was at its peak; she had taken up the yoga that was to become such a part of her life and she had acquired a dog from Battersea Dogs' Home, a shih-tzu called Harry. 'George Michael has been brilliant,' she said. 'He gave me direction when I was feeling insecure. And I have been doing yoga and standing on my head a lot and that's really helped me. I am eating healthily and I've got a dog, Harry, because I was desperately lonely, I really was. You know everybody wants companionship. And my dog just fills the gap in my day and gives me something to love. Can you imagine how vulnerable I felt leaving that group and just standing there by myself?'

Harry was pretty brilliant, too. 'He's so affectionate,' said Geri. 'It's one of the nicest things to have. It's better than a man: he doesn't answer back, he loves you no matter what, shows he's glad to see you and admits when he's jealous.'

Geri had not, however, entirely given up on her previous ambitions. 'I'd love to do more acting,' she said. 'I think I was really crap in the Spice Girls movie but I would love to do it. And if people want it I would love to tour. I will have to wait and see how this album does. If nobody buys it and nobody wants to see me on tour, then I'll be sitting in my back garden. I just hope people join me on my rollercoaster adventure because I am trying to give something back.'

In the event, the single only made it to number two, beaten to the top spot by Boyzone's 'You Needed Me'. It was said to have been Geri's decision to pitch herself against Boyzone, and it was undoubtedly a mistake. Her album, *Schizophonic*, released a month later, did even worse: despite a £2 million promotional campaign, the album sold just 17,000 copies in the first three days of its release, massively lower than expected. Industry insiders were not impressed. 'It is a complete disaster,' said one. 'It was expected that someone of her stature would sell at least 100,000 copies. She will pick up more sales at the weekend, but so will every other artist as well.'

In the event, the album perched briefly at number four in the charts before falling back to a miserable 53. It was not the start to her career that Solo Spice would have wanted and, indeed, there were reports of a furious row between Geri and the suits at EMI.

'Think of your worst nightmare. This was it,' said a rival record executive. 'The word went round that she had marched into EMI and screamed the place down. She was very upset, saying she would leave and join another company. You get used to hearing that kind of thing from the artists, but generally they calm down.'

One problem was that no one seemed to be sure who Geri was trying to be at that moment and the audience to which she was attempting to appeal. 'EMI are launching a second phase in Geri's career and they're trying to get beyond her core market of teenybop fans,' said one media analyst. 'The album has a bit of Latin, a bit of disco, it goes right across the board. They've gone for a fairly mainstream adult market, and that's quite an intangible one. It's only really the Corrs who are doing well in it. The trouble so far is the mixed messages she's sending out. Is she an ambassador, a mainstream popstar or is she going for the gay market? That's something they've got to decide.'

The other Spices did not hide their glee. The album was 'not great, but all right', said Mel C in an interview with Q magazine. 'I find it difficult to take her as a serious artist,' she continued. 'For me she's just cotton wool. She's not a talented musician, and she's not a very strong singer. She's a great celebrity, but musically it doesn't come from here [the heart.] It's just hollow.'

Mel B – briefly known at that time as Mel G, courtesy of her marriage to the dancer Jimmy Gulzar – was even cattier. 'She wasn't one of the most best singers,' she commented ungrammatically, 'or the best dancers, but I'm sure that wasn't the whole reason why she left … I suppose it's a bit annoying when all you're seen for is your lips and your boobs.'

But Geri had not walked out of the biggest band in the world to content herself with a bit of gardening. Her first move was to part company with her manager, with the two agreeing 'to conclude their business relationship'. Secondly, she still had a considerable fan base on her side. 'She remains a source of intrigue and fascination and affection for a lot of our readers,' said John McKay, then editor of *Smash Hits*. 'I've had a lot of mail saying, "Will you pass this on to Geri?" She's inspirational. She's like a refuellable lighter – the flame won't go out.'

And indeed it didn't. Never one to back away from the limelight, Geri was now learning a cunning when it came to personal publicity that would have rivalled that of the late Diana, Princess of Wales. The previous year, while still holed up in Paris in tax exile, Geri had contacted the film-maker Molly Dineen about making a film of her life. 'She asked me if I was interested in making a documentary on her as she'd already started making a video diary of herself,' said Molly at the time. The only subject that was taboo was the Spice Girls themselves, not least because Geri had apparently been in tears when they did their final concert at Wembley. 'I did try and get her to watch the Spice Girls concert on TV, but she said, "You must be joking." She never regretted leaving the Spice Girls, but she was gutted about not appearing at Wembley with them. I don't think she was crying about leaving the group. She was in a vulnerable state because of something deeper that's going on in her.

'Geri was going through a total crisis. Ginger was a persona that Geri had created as a teenager, and that persona got famous. Geri grew up behind it and had to get out. Deep down she wanted people to know what she was like. Geri's 26, filthy rich, beautiful and has a nice house, so we shouldn't feel too sorry for her. But she has problems of self-worth.'

Molly certainly uncovered a different Geri from the one known to the public at the time. 'People look at her and think, Big knockers, sexy chick, but Geri's much more likely to be sitting at home under a crucifix reading a novel,' she said. 'She's subdued and private with lots of religious pictures in her house.'

The film, when it appeared, was a revelation. It begins the day after Geri left the Spice Girls when, in (tax) exile in a Paris hotel, Geri calls Molly to ask if she'll make a film about her life. It follows her as she travels to London, auctions off her Ginger Spice memorabilia, retreats back to Paris, writes to Prince Charles asking for his support (for what exactly is never specified), decides she wants to write an autobiography, retreats to George Michael's villa on the Côte D'Azur, and returns to her hideaway back at her dairy farm in Hertfordshire. Geri then travels to New York for a UN press conference, performs at Prince Charles's 50th Birthday Gala, visits Battersea Dogs' Home with George Michael to choose a dog, breaks down in tears and buys Harry. It ends with Geri moving out of the dairy farm house she had been living in and into a £2 million pile in Middle Green, Buckinghamshire. In a previous incarnation, the house had featured in the film *The Omen*.

If Geri had wanted the documentary to be revealing, then she certainly got her wish. As a portrait of a celebrity in search of some meaning in life, it couldn't have been bettered. 'Every weekend I start crying, because I realise there's nothing there,' she says at one point. 'Throughout the week I'm OK because I'm busy but it's the weekends that are a problem. Maybe I just want some love in my life.'

Geri gave the impression of a woman who wants fame at all costs, but who doesn't actually know what to do with it once it's arrived. It also revealed for the first time quite how badly Geri was hit by the death of her father when she was just 21 – grief that kicked off an increasingly serious eating disorder. 'I went to see him,' Geri tells Molly. 'He was lying there and his nails were black and everything was sunk. He looked like the Penguin from *Batman 2*. It's this horrible memory. I was too depressed to even commit suicide. I wanted to kill myself. I couldn't function. It was awful.'

Her increasingly isolated lifestyle was laid bare for all to see. 'People I work with become my friends,' Geri explained. 'Like my accountant, he is my mate. My other mates, they're all in Watford. I've got some really good friends, three or four. I ask them to come out but they don't. They've all got their own lives. It is incredibly lonely.' Indeed, it emerged that Geri only wanted Molly to film her because she wanted a mate. 'I was just desperate for company, that's what it was!' she said. 'I thought, I'll make you my friend. It's all been one big farce because I wanted a friend. You've been fished in because I needed someone.' Given this loneliness, it would seem her decision to leave the Spice Girls was perhaps unwise. 'Some days when we were touring and I was feeling down I'd look from backstage for a sign saying something like "I Love You Geri" and it would really help.'

Back home in Hertfordshire Geri continues, 'Did I tell you about my cosmic shopping lists? It's like wish fulfilment. Suppose you have a dream like you want a number one hit record or a new house or car, you write it down and then put it in the back of a picture frame or something. I wrote George Michael is my husband, but now he's my friend instead.'

Of her childhood she revealed, 'I always felt like the symbolic poor kid that was allowed in. I've always been told by people that I'm not good enough or I'm lucky to be here. I was always the donkey in school plays and never Mary or baby Jesus!' Now, of course, Geri was a UN ambassador. 'This is going to give my life meaning,' she said. 'It's scary, I mean I'm going to be talking about a subject I'm still learning about. But for the first time in my life I feel like I've got a proper job. I'm damn well going to use my fame for a good cause.'

The documentary touched on Harry the dog. 'Geri's friend George Michael convinced her to get a dog,' said Molly. 'They went to Battersea Dogs' Home where he got his dog Pippi and Geri got a shih-tzu called Harry. Geri called it a "shiatsu" until George said, "That's a massage, not a dog."'

The film also made much of Geri at home, where she 'drinks a lot of slimming mix' and spends time with friends and her mother Ana, who was not entirely enthusiastic about her daughter's new home. 'Depressing isn't it,' she said, pointing to a bed. 'It looks like a coffin. I don't know, it's creepy.'

Geri didn't agree. 'Everyone wants to hide,' she said. 'We all want to hide in our own shells. At the end of the day [a favourite Spice Girls phrase], if I've got enough money to live on I can just retreat. I've created this little world.'

'In many ways Geri's a lucky girl, because she has a solid, grounded family and friends who don't want to be famous,' said Molly. 'I filmed Geri sitting at the kitchen table while her best friend Jeanine dyed her roots. Jeanine was pointing out that Geri has to love herself more and that if she mixes in worlds where people aren't her true friends it will make her feel bad.

'Geri talked to me about her extraordinary plans to do a book, a record and plan a charity concert in aid of cancer. I was thinking, Oh yeah, not likely, but she's done every one of them. She's really funny and vulnerable and ballsy. I think she has a fantastic character.'

Molly did have some doubts about her famous subject. Geri's primary interest is now and always has been Geri Halliwell and over the years it has become increasing obvious that, Jeanine or no, she doesn't actually have that many friends. Geri tends to become extremely close to individuals when she needs them, but the relationships rarely last: she and George Michael fell out when she became overfond of publicity while Robbie Williams once described her as scary. All of those elements began to come out during Geri's association with Molly. There were also hints of other problems to come: 'When my father died I went completely anorexic,' she confessed on film.

'She came to me, I had reservations, I got hooked, she got pissed off,' Molly said. 'From the start I didn't know what it was about. Geri would say, "It's about ME!" And I'd say, "Yes. And?" The problem was I lacked the baggage of thinking of her as Global Icon Ginger [Molly had barely heard of Geri before the start of filming] so I slightly thought I was doing her a favour and she thought the opposite.'

It appeared to many people, including Molly herself, that Geri was not just asking to be filmed, but was asking for friendship. Begging for it, in fact. 'My subjects often let me in because they are lonely or bored,' said Molly, 'but no one before has ever said, "I want you here because I want you to be my friend," which is very true to Geri's character.

'I think the problem for Geri was that in the end it was Ginger who was famous and not her. The frustration is you want people to know what *you're* like. What I wanted to show was that what she's chasing ultimately is elusive. There's the dream, but it's empty.' The film showed a good deal of Geri sitting alone in her big empty house: 'Ooh yes,' said Molly. 'My eyes are constantly swivelling for symbols and metaphors. And she really does skate around it. So Miss Haversham.' And, she was asked, would they stay friends? 'I hope so. We've had some big rows. It's been very ugly. Sadly, I think it will depend on how this film is received.'

The documentary met with a mixed reaction. Along with Geri alone in her house, it also showed her making a mess of a rehearsal for a UN press conference, to say nothing of appearing a little vapid in her quest for fame. The psychologist Oliver James wrote, 'The nation will tonight see what it is like to be a celebrity in a way it has never seen before. The celebrity in question – Geri Halliwell, aka Ginger Spice – emerges from a television documentary as lonely, loveless, self-obsessed, attention-seeking and, above all, despite her millions of pounds and global fame, massively insecure.'

Another reviewer wrote, 'Geri lives her life in fame's empty bubble and she knows how lonely it can be with only a few self-help books for company.' No matter: the film had certainly achieved one aim. Geri was all over the headlines again.

And so the real offensive began. Suddenly Geri was everywhere: one minute attending Sir Elton John's White Tie and Tiara summer ball and the next performing at Party in the Park for the Prince's Trust. That latter date took place in July 1999, a couple of days after David and Victoria Beckham tied the knot: while not entirely upstaging her erstwhile flatmate, Geri certainly held her own. Barefoot, permed and sporting a raunchy new gypsy image, Geri cried, 'Have you missed me? I just want to be loved.' The crowd roared approval. 'You know how to make a girl feel wanted,' Geri replied.

There were more sightings of Geri in the company of Prince Charles: 'Geri made a special effort to see the prince as they had no time for a chat at the Party in the Park where Geri was performing for the Trust,' confided a gleeful friend.

And Geri had more projects in the pipeline. A second single, 'Mi Chico Latino', was set for release in August 1999, with her autobiography *If Only* coming out a couple of months later. And it was beginning to occur to people that Geri had a good deal in common with one

Robbie Williams, someone else who left a massively successful five-member group – although in his case, not entirely of his own volition – and who also had rather a shaky start to a solo career. 'Geri's not dissimilar to Robbie,' said a music industry insider who knows them both. 'If you speak to either of them, sometimes you think, You're a stupid, whingeing pain in the neck. Other times you think, God, you are smart.

'You just can't cast her as a stupid pawn. She has a pretty acute understanding of market shifts and movements and she does know what the game is about. Like Madonna, she's a manipulator and manipulatee. Madonna isn't much of a singer or a dancer but her genius is as a voracious consumer of other people's styles and Geri has some of that. She can be a real pro in the way Madonna is. Sometimes she hits, sometimes she misses but her instincts are spot on.'

This was high praise indeed and there were further indications that Geri was not going to disappear from the scene. 'She's not Brain of Britain, but she's incredibly streetwise,' said a friend. 'She's a fighter.' The friend was right: 'Mi Chico Latino' gave Geri her first solo number one and Geri, unsurprisingly, was said to be thrilled. Solo Spice was well and truly on her way.

'I do love Latin music, that's why I wrote "Mi Chico Latino",' said Geri. 'My mother's Spanish and it's always been a strong influence in our house. It's kind of a metaphor – take me back to my sweet life, where is my sweet life? That song can operate on many levels. It's about if you've tasted happiness or inner calm, then you lose it, it can be frustrating. I know I can write a good pop song but singing a whole album by myself, I was unsure whether I could do that. It's been great for my self-esteem doing it. I think it's regarded as a good pop album, a smart one. Pop music doesn't have to be crap. You can find some depth in my songs – they're multi-dimensional.'

There were still some stirrings of doubt amongst the powers that be at EMI, however, not least because of that gypsy appearance. Geri had by now cultivated two images since leaving the girls: first as a sober type ideally suited to being a UN ambassador and now as a wild Latin chick. 'You can see they're panicking at EMI,' said a gleeful record company rival. 'If the other images had worked, there'd be no need to change them. The last time we all saw Geri, she had huge boobs and was wearing a Union Jack mini-skirt. Now she is saying, "Please take me seriously."'

In actual fact, Geri the gypsy was beginning to want to be viewed as a sex symbol again, but even this was not enough to placate her critics. 'Sex appeal is good for a guy but not for a woman,' asserted one industry insider. 'It worked for Robbie [Williams] but has done nothing for Geri in her solo career. If you are male you can lack talent but if you have sex appeal you will still sell. We see it all the time. But if you are a girl, you have to make damned good records and have a good voice.' The other Spice Girls were delighted: by now they were reportedly referring to their former band mate as Geri Hasn'tdonewell.

But they spoke too soon. Geri was not giving up on anything and despite industry sniping about her image changes, she would have been well aware that pop's greatest survivor, Madonna, has constantly changed her image from the moment she first strode out on stage. There were other fears though: many believed that, especially in light of the split with Lisa Anderson, Geri had decided that she didn't need a manager and that she was able to run her career on her own (as indeed, the Spice Girls had done when they sacked their own manager, Simon Fuller, a few months before Geri left). There were also worries that the documentary had left her dangerously over-exposed. All these fears were groundless, however, not least because Geri knew how to grab a publicity opportunity – and milk it for all it was worth.

3

Ginger Melody

Geri was becoming a genius at media manipulation. She might have been a run-of-the-mill singer, but when it came to keeping herself in the newspapers, no one could top her. That flair for publicity was becoming increasingly obvious and it was about to be needed: Geri was squaring up for a battle royal with her former band member Emma Bunton. Both were releasing singles towards the end of 1999 and there was no way that Geri was going to lose that particular race. It was war.

In what could almost be seen as a trial run for what was to come, Geri garnered yet more headlines when she appeared on *TFI Friday* with Kylie Minogue, herself something of an expert in the art of inspiring headlines: the two began to arm wrestle and then suddenly started kissing. 'Kylie is a brilliant kisser, but she hasn't made me turn,' said Geri afterwards. 'I could never go out with a girl smaller than me!'

Chris Evans was in seventh heaven. 'It looked like the arm wrestling would end in deadlock,' said a thoroughly overexcited *TFI* spokesman. 'But all of a sudden they both leaned forward and gave each other a full-on snog. No one in the audience could believe it – two of the world's sexiest women kissing in front of their eyes! Chris was gobsmacked but absolutely loved it.' You can bet he did. What's more, Chris was about to play a large part in Geri's life – albeit for a very short time.

It started with a kiss – but not the one with Kylie. In the run-up to her next single, 'Lift Me Up', Geri joined her new friend Chris Evans for a drink in his local and ended up kissing the ginger one, and what a happy coincidence that was. Quoth Geri, 'The song is all about how we need someone to lift us up out of a bad mood.'

All well and good – and, of course, Emma had a new single out, too, a cheery cover version of Edie Brickell's song 'What I Am', performed with the pop band Tin Tin Out. 'It's quirky, melodic and brilliant,' she chirped. And what riveted the world was that the singles had the same release date: 1 November 1999.

Although Emma had yet to realise it, she had a battle on her hands. It was not enough for Geri that she had left the Spice Girls and was beginning to carve out a solo career, it was also imperative that she should defeat her erstwhile friends. As Gore Vidal once remarked, 'It is not enough to succeed. Others must fail.'

William Hill realised its importance: they offered 2/1 on Geri making it to the top slot, putting Emma at 5/2. 'It had to happen,' said an industry insider. 'Once the girls started releasing solo singles it was inevitable they would come head-to-head. This is Geri's third single, while it's Emma's first. But her single is really catchy and looks like it could go all the way.'

A spokesman for Emma tried to put a good spin on it. 'There's always competition in the charts,' he said. 'Emma's single is a great record and we're very confident.' As yet, though, no one had any idea quite how determined Geri was to ensure that she, and not Emma, got her number one.

The first casualty in this latest instalment of Spice wars was, of all people, the Queen. On the day of her single's release Geri was supposed to be attending a reception at Buckingham Palace in aid of the Prince's Trust: instead she chose to spend nearly an hour at the HMV store in London's Oxford Circus, signing copies of 'Lift Me Up' in front of 2,000 fans. 'I'm keeping the Queen waiting,' said Geri to the ecstatic crowd. 'I was supposed to be at Buckingham Palace an hour ago, but I'm keeping her waiting because I wanted to see you.' She went on to ask her fans to pray for a hit. 'I'm here for the fans,' she said. 'Without you I'm nothing. I owe it all to you.'

Gennaro Castaldo of HMV was a witness to the proceedings. 'Geri is in a Spice war with Emma but she is trying to play that down,' he said. 'It is Emma's debut single. She does not have an album out and if anything is going to swing it for her, it is that. Geri already has an album out and many people who have bought that may not want to buy this single. But Geri is winning the publicity war. She has been on more TV programmes and done more interviews. Every record she signs and sells here today will help her to be number one.'

He was spot on there. Geri was making headlines with every move she made, even revealing at one point that she was almost lured into a secret sex orgy with a group of Arabs in Marbella. But, conscious perhaps that she hadn't won yet, Geri was careful to play the battle down, complaining that it was unfair of the record companies to make fans choose between the two, all the while carefully emphasising the fact that while Emma's single was a cover, hers was an original. 'I really, really care about my fans,' she said in a newspaper interview that could be used in a master class about how to do down your opponents while managing to appear loving towards them.

'When I left the Spice Girls, I thought everything was going to be taken away from me. I didn't know where my career was going. I didn't know if anyone would stand by me, but they did. When you think you're going to lose something it makes you appreciate things. I appreciate every single person who has bought my records or who has just willed me to do well – I've really felt that. When I put my music out I write to make people smile and to touch them.

'I still share my fan base with the Spice Girls and it's very sad to make anyone choose. It's like choosing between two parents and that's very unfair. It makes me angry. On the other hand, this is a very hard industry to be in – it's so volatile. One minute you're in and the next you're not. I wish Emma all the luck in the world. I remember the original and I think she's done a great copy. I've got two B-sides on my single because I believe when you buy a single you should have value for money – not just eight versions of the same song. I know what it's like to be poor and it's a lot of money to part with. I don't expect my fans to part with that money for nothing – I want them to buy it because they love it. "Lift Me Up" is a proper song with feeling.'

This was a sensational start to Geri's campaign, but at this stage in the proceedings, the race was still too close to call. The day after the single's release, Geri was just fractionally in the lead with sales of 26,868, while Emma weighed in with a very respectable 26,200. With just over 600 singles separating them, it was clearly going to require serious tactics to ensure that number one slot … and Geri still had a very strong card indeed up her sleeve. Chris Evans.

It was just a few days after the release of Geri's single that the rumours started to circulate: the two most famous redheads in show business were in love. Actually, they weren't just in love, they were considering getting married. No one seemed to be entirely sure when the romance had started (and even at that early stage, cynics noted they had the same PR company) but it seemed they had hit it off very well indeed when Geri appeared on Chris's television show and were now head over heels about each other. The fact that the relationship coincided with the single's release was just the most extraordinary twist of fate.

And then the publicity onslaught really began. A 'friend' said the couple were 'inseparable soul mates who are planning their lives around one another. They are both saying that this time it's special and they are going to make a real go of it. They are very much in love.' Geri was spotted having a drink with Chris at his local. The couple went to a private dinner party and were, according to reports, all over one another. Chris gave Geri a piggyback. Geri was spotted having another drink with Chris at his local, this time accompanied by Ant of Ant and Dec and *TFI*'s Chris Worthington, more commonly known as Worthers. 'The funniest moment came when Geri and Chris took Worthers's clothes off and sent him out in to the street!' chortled an onlooker, who may or may not have been Matthew Freud, head of Freud Communication.

Rather than taking months to develop, as most relationships do, this one matured within a matter of hours. There was a serious blip when Geri was heard bemoaning the fact that she didn't have a boyfriend – 'I haven't even had a nibble recently' –

but a swift recovery later in the day when it emerged the couple were to wed. 'Ginger Splice!' yelled the headlines.

There was another blip when it was revealed that Chris had also been chasing another woman – one Emma Bunton. 'I've had nine calls from Chris,' she revealed. 'He rang over the weekend asking me out for a drink but I refused' – and then a serious comeback in the form of Chris's radio show on Virgin the following morning.

Geri was on it, of course, as was a fake vicar. 'Do you take Christopher-Virgin-Radio-owning-Evans to be your publicity-seeking husband?' he enquired of Geri.

'I will if it helps me to sell more records and get to number one,' the blushing bride replied.

Then came Chris's turn: 'Do you take Geraldine ex-Spicey-Halli-soloartist-well to be your popstar wife?'

'Only if it gets me in the papers,' said the bashful groom.

Pausing only to have another drink with Chris at his local, Geri rushed off on a tour of newspaper offices to talk about her very private happiness. 'I've never been happier,' she said. 'Whatever happens on Sunday [chart day], I've never been happier. Everything's come together and it's fantastic. Chris is great and very sweet, a fascinating person. I'm very content. I'm a bit stressed but it's all been worthwhile.'

Was it conceivably possible, she was asked, that the relationship was just a big publicity stunt? 'I get enough publicity anyway,' laughed Geri, 'and so does he.' Under intense pressure to admit it, the couple admitted it.

'We are a couple,' they said.

Chris also spoke in rather hurt terms about the odious amount of publicity they were attracting. 'It's private,' he explained. 'There's been so much hype about me and Gezza at the moment but that's to be expected. I don't want to talk about our feelings. Everyone who thinks it's all hype is going to end up with egg on their faces.'

Finally, on the eve of the charts, Chris gave an emotional interview about his new love. 'I hope it goes on forever,' he announced, cracking open a bottle of champagne. 'You only have to look at us to see how happy we are. We're both having a ball. I really like her, we're having a great time together. At the moment it's all about having fun, but who knows where it will lead. Hopefully it will go on forever.'

Tragically it was to last but a couple more days, but Chris seemed blithely unaware of the cruel fate that awaited him. He was, however, greatly hurt by suggestions that the whole thing was a fake. 'We first met 16 days ago and since then we've been everywhere together. If people thought it was a fraud or a set-up, we must be very bad at our jobs, because it's a miracle nobody caught us out. We've been to every restaurant and bar, even feeding the ducks in Hyde Park. All this stuff the other papers are saying about us doing it to publicise Geri's new record just makes us laugh. And that's all it does. We didn't even know the Spice Girls had a book launch this week – no one told us.'

Emma Bunton didn't stand a chance. Geri clocked in a number one with Emma right behind her. 'I'm absolutely gobsmacked,' Geri announced. 'I'm the happiest girl in England. I've got the biggest grin on my face.'

Emma was gracious in defeat. 'I'm really happy for Geri,' she said. 'She did really well and congratulations were in order. I'm very thrilled to get to number two with my debut single. It's been a lot of fun.'

The 'relationship' tottered on for a couple of days, with Chris pictured carrying a sloshed Geri into his house after a celebratory party (and it clearly had occurred to no one that this would result in a rush of 'Lift Me Up' headlines, great heavens, no!), until Chris was caught canoodling with an old flame.

The pair were said to be holding crisis talks in Geri's Berkshire mansion, but sadly it was all over for love's young dream: Chris decided it was getting 'too heavy' and he 'needed his own space'. Geri, meanwhile, was said to be 'devastated', an emotion that seemed a little out of place alongside her earlier declaration that the relationship was 'nothing to do with me'. And so ended the greatest love story since *Romeo and Juliet*, with a scarcely less tragic ending, made only just bearable by the fact that Geri had got her number one.

As for the big question, did they or didn't they? the answer is almost certainly yes. Consider this. When Geri accidentally bumped into Chris with his real popstar wife Billie Piper in Los Angeles in spring 2002, it was clearly an extremely uncomfortable encounter for all concerned and came to an abrupt end, which it would not have done had nothing happened between them. Certainly those who were close to her at the time thought that she – not he – had taken it a little bit too seriously and actually got involved. Others still said that Chris and Matthew Freud had cooked up the scheme between them and forgotten to tell Geri. As for Geri, she recently revealed what brought the relationship to its very abrupt end and there are no prizes for guessing who was at fault. The media.

At least Geri still had George Michael to rely on. The friendship was going from strength to strength as Geri herself admitted. 'Ours is not a celebrity friendship,' she said. 'I can't stand that "Hello darling, lovey, lovey" kind of stuff. We're both famous and part of the music industry. But we've both lost a parent, both come from Watford, both have a Mediterranean parent – and were both ugly kids who blossomed!'

The two did indeed have far more in common than you would have thought from their very different appearances (and musical output). Geri was devastated by the death of her father Laurence in 1994, when she was just 21 and had yet to hit the big time. Equally, George was inconsolable after his mother Lesley Panayiotou died of cancer in 1998. Geri's mother Ana Maria, meanwhile, was a Spanish-born cleaning lady, while George's father Jack was a Greek immigrant. Both went to schools in Hertfordshire, both were not the prettiest kids in the class and both found fame early on with a band which went on to split up.

But it was the fact that George is nine years older than Geri which really helped. She looked up to him as a mentor, while he saw her going through some of the problems he had faced early in his career. (Geri had also idolised him as a teenager, sticking his posters all over her bedroom wall.) And she could trust him. 'He sees through me,' Geri said. 'I share my doubts and fears with him. He said, "There's no rush, nobody's going to forget you. If what you are doing is good it will stand the test of time." I play him things but it is like taking it home to your parents, desperately wanting their approval. He's brutally honest – sometimes I walk out with my head in my hands and sometimes I'm going, "Yes!"'

Geri first met George when she was still a member of the Spice Girls, after she heard an interview in which he talked about the death of his mother. 'Nobody wants to talk about death,' Geri said. 'Then I heard George talk about losing his mother. I was a fan. I thought I was going to marry him, I was so drawn to him. I gave him my telephone number, gave him big eyes and tried to flirt with him, thinking I had a chance. How wrong was I? I got second best and we became best friends.'

And, of course, George came to Geri's rescue when she walked out on the girls. 'When I left the group he invited me to stay for three days,' said Geri. 'I stayed three months. I don't know what I'd have done without that guy, he was an absolute angel. To begin with he didn't know me that well, but I had nobody. I was so lonely. I needed someone to give me a cuddle and say it's all right. George and Kenny were everything to me, the moral support I needed to get through that time.'

The admiration was mutual. A couple of years earlier George gave an interview in which the subject of Geri came up. 'She's one of the most remarkable people I've ever met,' he said. 'I really think she was the Spice Girls. No disrespect to the others but let's be honest, who were you looking at when you saw a Spice Girls performance?'

The Millennium saw Geri in fine fettle. She had kicked off the proceedings by throwing a £200,000 Millennium party, attended by, amongst others, her still-best-friend George Michael – 'Geri's the only person who has the guts to throw a party like this,' he said in the run-up to the event. 'I don't know anyone who's planned anything. I think most people are staying at home' – and the new year was marred only by some more spats with the girls. In January it was revealed that, with a fortune of £25 million, Victoria was the richest of the Spices, but the others all had at least £20 million in the bank. Geri was left trailing behind with a paltry 19.6 million.

Then Victoria had a go at her former friend when talking about the Chris Evans affair: 'I wouldn't go to the *Sun* dressed as a schoolgirl with my boobs out and talk about my relationship,' she sneered in a reference to one of the more unlikely pictures of Geri that appeared in the course of that very special week. She picked up the theme again in her television show, *Victoria's Secrets*, in which the following exchange took place with Sir Elton John:

Sir Elt: 'Do you see Geri much any more?'

Victoria: 'No. Not really.'

Sir Elt: 'Isn't that a bit of a shame?'

Victoria: 'It is a shame but I think she's turned it into a war in a way. I mean, when they had single out together – her and Emma – she did as much as she could.'

Sir Elt: 'But isn't that what this business is all about?'

Victoria: 'Yeah but I wouldn't go to the *Sun* dressed as a schoolgirl with my boobs out and talk about my relationships.'

Geri rose above the fray, proving yet again that when it came to publicity, she had lost none of her touch. She donned hair extensions and an extremely revealing green jungle-printed Versace dress and grabbed headlines all over the world when she appeared at music radio station NRJ's annual awards ceremony in Cannes. On that occasion she even managed to outclass Elizabeth Hurley, who was wearing an equally revealing red two-piece gypsy outfit, but who, said commentators, lacked that certain 'oomph'.

There was a temporary cessation of hostilities when Geri went to court in February to support her former friends. And given that the court case very briefly reunited them, it was ironic that the problem was actually caused by Geri's departure. It centred on a deal with Italian scooter firm Aprilia, which had sponsored the girls' 1998 tour, and which signed the girls up to promote a range of scooters aimed at teenage girls. The only problem was that shortly after that signing, they found themselves with a quartet on their hands rather than a five-girl band.

It was the girls themselves, though, who provoked the action by suing first, when they launched a claim for £212,000 in unpaid sponsorship and royalties. Aprilia promptly countersued for misrepresentation, saying they had presented themselves as a five-piece outfit when they knew full well that Geri was about to leave (and indeed, she left three weeks after the contract was signed). The case was to establish when they knew Geri was going to leave and whether they should have signed the agreement. 'Aprilia would just have put it down to something that had gone wrong, just written it off,' said Susan Barty from CMS Cameron McKenna, who was representing the company. 'But they were forced to counterclaim when the Spice Girls sued them.' Geri was not a party to the action and just turned up, she said, to support the girls.

A clearer picture began to emerge of the final days of the fivesome. 'At the back of my mind I wanted to leave but I didn't know whether I was brave enough to do that – leave the security of such a big band,' said Geri. 'So the reason I was drip-feeding the idea [to the other girls] was to see if I was brave enough. So there wasn't one defining moment when I consciously made that decision. One part of me wanted to stay but the other half said it was time to go. What one wants to do and what one does are two different things.'

It emerged that Geri had first told the girls that she was thinking of leaving in March 1998. 'I do not think they took me seriously,' she said. Then later on in Milan she repeated her desire to go and of the band's reaction she said, 'I think it was possibly disbelief, a mixed reaction and still not taking it seriously.' It was 'an emotional thing among the band. We wanted private time to possibly resolve it. We wanted to come to terms with it first and then make it public. It felt kind of better to do it at the end of the tour.'

The advertising photographic session for Aprilia picturing the five girls with the scooters took place in early May and Geri agreed that she knew the company was investing a lot of money in their association with the band. But it was not uppermost in her mind because, 'when you are an artist, you are an artist'. Why didn't she tell Aprilia, the tour's sponsor? 'It was more an emotional occasion, I wasn't thinking about the practicalities,' Geri replied. The girls eventually lost the case when they were found guilty of unintentionally but unlawfully misrepresenting themselves as a five-girl band when they signed the deal and, despite various appeals, were ultimately forced to pay out £1 million.

There was, however, a lighter moment when a DJ Geri had worked with in her early days as a dancer himself got into the charts. Des Mitchell from Birmingham, who has been a DJ at the BCM dance club in Majorca for more than a decade, saw his first record '(Welcome) To The Dance' go straight into the charts at number five – and that at the ripe old age of 42. 'Geri was a good pal,' he said. 'She was great fun and it's wonderful I've now hit the charts as well. I still can't believe it. I worked with Geri for a year and a half and got on with her really well. She was really good fun, a fantastic person and great to be around. Back then she was small and attractive. Now she's just wonderfully cute and attractive.'

Geri also perked up when the Brit Award nominations were announced: she found herself nominated for two while her erstwhile band mates could only muster one nomination between the lot of them. There was some excitement, though, when it turned out that the girls were to be honoured with a special Outstanding Contribution Award. Would Geri accept the award with them? The girls (four of them) put out a statement. 'The Spice Girls started out as a five and we feel this award is in recognition of the great achievement of all five,' it said. Brits host Davina McCall entered the fray. 'Geri should go up with the girls to collect it,' she said. 'She's been a great part of the whole thing.'

In the event, Geri put in an eyewatering performance. She came on stage at the Brits between two huge, inflatable legs – yet another symbol, apparently, of her 'rebirth' since leaving the girls. She then strutted down a huge Union Jack carpet, a reminder of that scene-stealing dress a few years earlier, followed by four overweight women pushing shopping trolleys containing men. Overlooking the proceedings was a 20-foot sign reading 'girl power' – the Spices' mantra, coined by none other than Geri herself. 'The shopping trolleys represent people thinking they can buy happiness,' said a spokesman for Geri – although other commentators suggested that they really represented the other girls using their fame and wealth to attract men. She then proceeded to dance around a lap dancing pole, singing her latest single 'Bag It Up', before ripping her shirt open.

And no, Geri did not accompany the Spices on stage to receive their award. 'It was inevitable that Geri would do her best to steal the show and get all the attention,' snapped a Spice insider, while Geri herself explained she had let the others go on stage to collect the award alone because, 'I think it would be wrong to join in. I left two years ago.'

The other girls were not impressed and suggested the prancing around between women's legs was a ploy to disguise the fact that Geri could neither sing nor dance. 'I thought it was quite vulgar,' said Sporty Spice, aka Mel C. 'I think it's a great song and it sounded really good, nice and loud. But she's sort of hiding behind all that because she's not talented. Geri can't sing and she can't dance either.'

That may well be true, but 'Bag It Up' made it to number one anyway, providing Geri with her third solo number one. 'I'm absolutely thrilled,' said an ecstatic Geri. 'Counting my time with the Spice Girls, this is my tenth number one. To have three number ones and a number two on my first solo album is just a fantastic feeling. I would like to say thank you to all of my fans who have stuck by me and helped to make it all possible. I'm one very happy girl today.' And the success was all the sweeter as her former best friend-turned-nemesis Mel B had managed only eight stays at the top slot – and only one on her own.

Geri's ambition to be an actress was still burning away, as well. In May she went to Cannes to sign a deal to star in a £7 million movie called *Therapy*, about a young professional woman who falls in love with her therapist. 'Geri can add a lot of her own personality to the role without actually playing herself,' said director David Green, who also directed the film *Buster*. 'I don't want her to play Geri Halliwell, but I don't want her to stretch into serious Chekovian or Ibsenian drama.'

That was just as well, not least because the film was never made. Despite the initial excitement, the company behind the film, September Films, was unable to raise the cash to finance the project. 'There's been no progress,' a spokesman for the company admitted some months later. 'There hasn't been any development on the film.'

There were three problems: the timing, the script and the star. As far as timing went, it was all wrong.

Another film, *Honest*, a gangster comedy starring three of the All Saints, had recently been released and was a complete and utter flop (deservedly, say the few people who actually saw the film). Film industry bosses were thus cautious, to put it mildly, about another film involving someone from a girl group. 'The timing of the film couldn't have been worse,' said an industry insider. 'If *Honest* had been a huge hit investors might have looked more favourably on a movie starring a popstar. Instead it confirmed their worst fears.'

Then there was the minor matter of the script. The story involved a young, nightmare boss (Geri) who regularly reduced her assistants to tears. On the advice of her colleagues, she investigates a number of therapists, settles with one, falls for him and then discovers he's involved with her sister. Unfortunately, it didn't go down well with everyone. 'It's appalling, a hackneyed load of rubbish that might have made a reasonably amusing half-hour sitcom but wouldn't work as a feature film,' was one of the kinder comments.

And then there was the minor matter of the star herself. Geri had failed to light up the screen in *SpiceWorld: The Movie* (although neither, it must be said, had the other girls) and had so far got nowhere in her attempts to become an actress. This did not make her ideal for a starring role in a film. 'Geri Halliwell may be a big star, but she's not a proven box office draw,' said a source within the film industry. 'She's also not even a proven actress. It would be a huge risk for a movie company to invest in, especially as the budget is high for a British film.'

It was at around this time that another extraordinary Halliwell story surfaced, only this one concerned Geri's sister Natalie. It emerged that she had formed a strong friendship with Nick Leeson, the rogue trader who brought down Barings bank. The two had known one another since their teenage years and had exchanged letters during Leeson's incarceration in a Singapore jail. The friendship, though platonic, was said to be becoming increasingly close.

'Natalie has been a tower of strength to Nick,' said a friend. 'Nick has been through the wars and Natalie has helped him to cope. Natalie has always been the rock in Geri's life. A similar relationship has started to develop between her and Nick. He feels he can trust her. It is not a romantic relationship, they just get on very well. When he returned to Britain last July he met up with Natalie a month or so later and got on very well. They go out and speak on the phone regularly.'

It was also around this time that Geri's changing

shape began to alarm onlookers. Even at her most voluptuous, Geri could never have been called fat, but it was becoming increasingly apparent that she was losing a drastic amount of weight. Reports surfaced that she had cut out all carbohydrates and was eating a protein-rich diet. George Michael cropped up yet again: Geri had spent two weeks with him and Kenny at their home in Los Angeles and their numerous dinner dates had apparently meant that Geri had piled on a few pounds. Experts, however, warned that this kind of diet could prove to be extremely dangerous for anyone's long-term health and warned Geri that she was risking making herself ill. Geri shrugged off criticism. 'Geri feels great at the moment and reckons the diet is working fine,' said a friend. 'She wants to get a little more trim and feel confident about herself. Her weight does fluctuate and she tends to put it on around her face.'

Geri had been plagued by eating disorders for some years now, but denied her problems had resurfaced. And at that stage, at least, no one wanted to pursue it because there was a happy event in the family: Geri's mother Ana Maria married Steve Parkinson, her boyfriend of eleven years standing. The wedding took place at Durrants Country Club in Croxley Green, Hertfordshire, in front of 100 guests (including George Michael) and the bride shimmered in a silver satin gown designed by Maggie Heyburn. 'She'll look stunning,' said Maggie. 'She's a lovely, sweet lady and I'm just so happy for her.' Ana's granddaughter was a bridesmaid, her two grandsons were pageboys and her daughter provided security – bouncers patrolled an eight-foot barrier to keep out prying eyes.

Geri and George arrived in a chauffeur-driven Mercedes with blacked-out windows, as befitted such important guests, but it was not to be long before Geri found her next best friend in the music business. For she was planning a holiday in St Tropez with another musical star who was becoming even more famous than she was. His name was Robbie Williams.

4

Summer Lovin'

To cynics, it was déjà vu. Geri Halliwell had something to promote – the paperback edition of her autobiography – and Geri Halliwell had a new high-profile boyfriend – Robbie Williams. Robbie had something to promote as well, if it came to that: a new single, 'Rock DJ'. The two had been caught sneaking off together for a holiday in St Tropez. 'Robbie and Geri: It's Love' roared the headlines as the ex-Spice Girl and the ex-member of Take That frolicked amongst the sandcastles.

'It's love,' one of Robbie's 'pals' was quoted as

saying in a newspaper. 'We haven't seen him like this for years. He's been saying he thinks he's fallen in love with Geri. He has had a lot of one-night stands but he believes there could be much more to this. They make a perfect couple and have fallen for each other in a big way. It's very unusual for Robbie to go on holiday with a girlfriend and it shows the depth of feeling. Geri is a lovely girl and they have a lot in common. They are on the same level and Robbie's found someone he can really talk to. Obviously it's early days and the pair won't be saying anything public about it yet. They just want to get away and enjoy each other's company. He says she excites him and he is full of it – he is buzzing.'

The pal might have spoken too soon. The pair were indeed on holiday with one another, staying in a villa in St Tropez, and their relationship was far deeper than the farce with Chris Evans, but it was not a romance. Both tried to play down the rumours. 'They are friends and are together in France, but there is no romance,' said a spokesman for Geri, while one of Robbie's people added, 'They have been good friends for ages.' Certainly it was obvious what drew the two together. An acquaintance of both commented, 'Geri and Robbie have known each other for years. They are both with the same record company and get on really well. After all, they have so much in common. They were both in massive bands and they both left to form hugely successful solo careers.'

The 'are they or aren't they' speculation did neither any harm, though, and kept both firmly positioned on the front pages. And so, with the eyes of the world upon them, Geri and Robbie continued to cavort in front of the cameras. One day Geri would be practising yoga as Robbie looked on, the next they would be splashing around in a swimming pool. Outings on motorbikes and speedboats followed, with numerous excursions to the beach. Every minute of every day was accounted for in the pictures that followed, with Geri and Robbie seemingly blithely unaware that the whole world was watching their sojourn in the sun. Others were not so sure. 'It's a lovely villa,' said a neighbour living near by. 'But there are all sorts of vantage points it can be seen from, so I wouldn't recommend it to celebrities trying to avoid the limelight. If you actually wanted to be photographed, however, it's absolutely ideal.'

One person who agreed with that analysis was Victoria Beckham. Talking about the rather repellent video for 'Rock DJ', in which Robbie strips off first his clothes and then his own skin, she commented, 'It's probably been done to get it banned and get attention. It's like bringing out an album and saying "Bollocks" all the way through it. Sometimes it can be fun to do things like that. Sometimes it can be boring. Same with all of these people who start a new relationship the week their single comes out. I'm glad I'm out of all of that. I'm surprised people fall for it. But if Geri and Robbie are happy together, I'm really happy for them.'

She may have been ecstatic for them but she didn't stop there. Some years earlier, Robbie had briefly been out with Mel C but behaved, by all accounts, indifferently and left her very upset indeed. All five girls, revelling in their new-found girl power, proceeded to snub him – and now here was Geri, collaborating with the enemy. Victoria couldn't stop herself. 'I don't know whether it's love but I know he loves himself,' she snapped. 'I'm sure they'll be talking a lot about therapy together. I just hope she knows what she's doing.'

Mel C was more succinct. Geri was 'talentless' and Robbie a 'cabaret singer'.

And for a couple who were just friends, the two were certainly getting on exceedingly well, as one photographer testified when he saw them together. 'Robbie and Geri were kissing and cuddling on the boat,' he said. 'They were very lovey-dovey. They spent the day on the beach, then went for an ice-cream together. They were laughing and joking all day.'

Needless to say, 'friends' were only too eager to shove their oar in and warn Geri off Robbie, not least because of his reputation as a ladies' man. 'Geri is really very sensitive, while Robbie is a real Jack the Lad,' said one. 'She hasn't given in to him yet – and she says she's not going to. Geri knows Robbie's really handsome and she knows what he's like with women. Even so, I don't think she realises what a Romeo he is. She's been told to beware of him because if he does have his way with her, what are the odds of him staying with her? Despite what people think, Geri was really cut up over the Chris Evans romance. She was very hurt and it took her a long time to get over it. She's been told Robbie's just a more handsome version of Chris. And if she was hurt then, she'd be devastated if Robbie broke her heart.'

Sure enough, the two promptly managed to have a lovers' tiff. Out to dinner in a restaurant called La Madrague, the couple bumped into the hypnotist Paul McKenna and his manager and erstwhile fiancée Claire Staples. Robbie spent much of the evening commuting between the two tables, eventually angering Geri because he was talking so much to Claire. She marched over to Claire, thumped her on the back and then marched back to her own table. She then marched back and the following exchange took place:

Geri: 'Fucking stand up.'

Robbie: 'No, leave me alone.'

Geri: 'Robbie, c'mon, stand up.'

Robbie: 'Fuck off!'

Geri burst into tears and ran off back to her table, while Robbie, Paul and Claire left. 'Geri was clearly distraught and was being consoled by a friend, but Robbie seemed to want to get out of the place as quickly as he could,' said an eyewitness to the fracas. 'As soon as Geri saw Robbie leave, she ran over to a couch opposite her table and started sobbing loudly. She put her face down on the table and put her hands over her head and stayed in that position for a few minutes. A lot of people were staring at her but she didn't seem to care. Eventually she got up and went to the ladies with her pal. She carried on crying and then threw up in one of the loos. She was in such a terrible mess no one could console her. She just went ballistic.'

Geri returned to the villa alone, while Robbie continued partying elsewhere. Claire was horrified to find herself in the middle of it all. 'It was a misunderstanding. Geri thought there was something going on when there wasn't,' she said. 'I've known Robbie for years – we're always bumping into one another. I can't believe Geri thought something was going on. Nothing was going on and I'm sorry Geri was upset.'

She soon recovered and the pair were back on the

Top: Geri's childhood was tough but her huge personality shone through. *Left*, with her father Laurence and *right*, with her Spanish mother, Ana Maria.

Bottom: Geri loved the camera from an early age. Here, she is pictured with big sister Natalie. The two are still close.

The Wild Child. Pre-Ginger, Geri was desperate to get her face known and worked as a model.

Top: Geri with the Spice Girls and their former manager, Simon Fuller. He was later sacked by the girls, and rumours of power struggles between Geri and Mel B. were rife.

Bottom left: That dress, those awards! Geri performing at the Brits.

Bottom right: Look at Me! Geri gives the crowd what they want.

Always the performer.

Top: Geri as a teenager in Magaluff.

Middle: The sleeve of the controversial video that the Spice Girls wanted no one to see: Raw Spice.

Bottom: You've come a long way…Geri performs with a host of Gingers at GAY in London.

In happier times...*Top*: The Girls having fun at a press call.

Bottom: Ginger and Baby have a quiet moment together before a Spanish TV appearance.

Top: Geri and the Girls promote breast cancer awareness. Geri is close to the cause, having suffered a couple of scares herself.

Bottom: Oh Geri, where art thou? Her solicitor drops the bombshell that she has left the Spice Girls and the dream is over.

Geri's causes.

Top left: It was Ruth Picardie's book on her fight against breast cancer that touched Geri and inspired her to campaign for breast cancer awareness.

Top right: Out with the old…Geri auctions off the infamous dress for Cancer Research.

Bottom: Geri arrives to carry out her duties as a U.N. Goodwill Ambassador. Her mission was to raise awareness of women's health and reproductive rights.

Top: Despite her admiration for Margaret Thatcher, Geri appears in a Labour Party Election broadcast.

Bottom: Geri chats to Prince Charles at a dinner to celebrate the 25th anniversary of the Princes Trust.

beach again, frolicking about as if nothing had happened. And finally, the true nature of the relationship began to emerge: that they were friends, just friends, who were more than well aware of the publicity to be garnered by two famous young popstars canoodling with one another on holiday. Robbie was the one who first let the cat out of the bag. 'Geri wouldn't go out with me because I'm too much of a slag,' he said a couple of weeks later, after finishing a concert in Cologne, Germany. 'We have been having such a great laugh reading all the things said about us. We are not boyfriend and girlfriend and we are not in love. We are two people who have been through the same thing.'

He continued on this theme in an interview. 'We haven't slept together or kissed,' he said. 'I like her an awful lot and don't want to ruin the friendship by it becoming more than that. She's a really nice girl who I can't mess about. I've done that in the past and I want to grow up. It's very difficult because she's a beautiful, sexy, fantastic personality but she's just my mate. I'm still sowing my seeds. If I had a daughter I wouldn't allow her to go out with the person I am, but I'd allow her to go out with the person I'm going to become.'

Except that that wasn't the whole story, either. In another interview it turned out that he did want to be involved with Geri after all. 'It's not for the want of trying,' he said of their non-relationship. 'She just wanted none of it.'

Most of the time, that is. Robbie, who is something of a blabbermouth, revealed yet another detail about whatever it was that was going on in the summer. At a concert Mr Discreet boasted, 'I have been on holiday and you'll never guess who with. She was in the Spice Girls. I was also in the Spice Girls. I've been in two of them.' He then dedicated his song 'She's The One' to Geri adding, 'I shouldn't have said that. I've got a big mouth. Don't tell Geri.' A year later, in fact, he retracted. 'I must come clean, I have to make amends to Geri,' he said. 'We've never slept together and that's the truth. I kind of made it up as a joke. It's just me and my loose mouth.'

Geri herself clearly saw Robbie as another of her celebrity support systems. 'In life we all need people to give advice and a shoulder to lean on. They don't have to be famous or role models but George offered me help when I needed it and gave great advice about the music business. I don't claim to be the best singer in the world. I like to make people smile. I write songs that everyone can sing along to and there is always a good melody. I hadn't enough confidence to go it alone and George gave me that. He did really encourage me. Robbie and I share something in common, too – he left his band and I left mine, both to go solo. No one else can know what it feels like to leave a band. We have been friends for a long time. We bonded when I spent time with him after a warm-up gig he did in Watford, where I'm from. I think Robbie is a lovely fella.'

And needless to say, even this wasn't the full story. Rumour was linking Geri to another man – and it was, of all people, George Michael's boyfriend Kenny Goss. Geri, Robbie, George and Kenny had all spent some time together in France and now Geri and Kenny were spotted arm in arm in Los Angeles. Next they were seen cuddling. Kenny had attended Geri's 28th birthday party in St Tropez without George, and now here they were in the States while George was stuck recording in London. 'They're all three friends together,' said a friend of George, eager to dampen the speculation. 'George isn't jealous. There's no romance. Geri and Kenny are just enjoying time together. It's what friends do. George would be there if he wasn't busy.'

But still the rumour mill rolled on. Geri and Kenny might not have been in a relationship, but friends believed that she was smitten with the handsome Goss and that George did not like the growing closeness between them. Geri herself merely described Kenny as a great friend she liked to go shopping with.

Meanwhile, Robbie was still on the scene. And just

in case the situation were not already complicated enough, Robbie muddied the waters still further when he decided to out himself at a concert in Paris and announced that he was in a relationship with his songwriting partner Guy Chambers. 'Guy and I have been in a steady relationship for three years now, so this is my coming-out party,' he quipped. 'I am now officially known as Roberta Williams.' He followed that one up by getting drunk at the MTV awards in Stockholm, eventually foaming at the mouth and keeling over, leading to speculation that Robbie had returned to the hard living that had marred his past.

But at least he still had a friend to rely on. At the beginning of 2001, Robbie had a new single out, 'Supreme', and so it came as no surprise to absolutely anyone when he turned up in Gstaad in Switzerland, on holiday with Geri. The two were pictured ice skating, with a wobbly Geri clinging on to Robbie. 'I didn't know they were on holiday again, but as I said they are friends, that's all there is to it,' said Geri's rather resigned-sounding spokesman. They certainly were sticking together. Next stop on the world tour was Los Angeles where, in between shopping with Kenny, Geri found time to support Robbie: she was pictured dropping him off at a meeting of Alcoholics Anonymous. She's my 'guardian angel', said Robbie. He's my 'rock', replied Geri. Almost inevitably, there was speculation that they were to record a duet. They didn't. 'We are just good friends … who have the occasional shag,' said Robbie.

Geri did not take it well. 'She was absolutely furious when she found out what Robbie had said,' revealed a friend. 'Last night Robbie tried to patch things up by claiming he had never slept with her. Geri's refusing to even speak to him. She's put up with Robbie's comments before, but this has sent her over the edge.'

How could they top this? Easily. It turned out that the two of them spent much of their time strolling around Robbie's flat naked. 'The pair of us are not bashful about our bodies,' Geri explained earnestly. 'He's always pulling his trousers down and I'm always pulling my top up.' And she wasn't so furious that she was incapable of fuelling speculation about the relationship still further when presenting Robbie with a Brit Award for best solo artist. 'According to the press he's been giving me one. Now I'll do him a favour and give him one,' she explained sweetly, embracing a rather unimpressed-looking Robbie. He did give her a hug though – 'He's very male,' said Geri. 'He's very healthy. He's a very talented artist and he's got the biggest heart. My dearest friend Robert Williams.'

In fact, it was very nearly Geri herself who stole the show. Wearing an outfit that revealed she was slimmer

– much, much slimmer – than she ever had been before, Geri was clad in a gold butterfly top, white micro mini-skirt and white boots, showing off masses of tanned midriff. No one as yet realised, however, that Geri was now on the verge of becoming seriously underweight.

Geri and Robbie's relationship couldn't last, of course, and it didn't. Just two months later, in April 2001 – just before Geri released her single 'It's Raining Men', part of the soundtrack for the film *Bridget Jones's Diary*, and her second album, *Scream If You Wanna Go Faster* – there were reports that all was not well and that Robbie was beginning to feel rather hemmed in. 'Robbie's head is in a whirl,' said a friend. 'Geri is very strong-willed. He likes her enormously but also enjoys his own space.'

It may well have been Geri who decided to back off, for the truth of the matter is that Geri – consciously or not – does tend to see her friends when she needs them and then forget about them the rest of the time. It wasn't just Robbie who was unhappy about the way things were going: George Michael was also said to be less than pleased with his former protégé. 'He feels Geri is using their friendship to sell records and he doesn't like it,' said a friend. 'George has told friends he seldom hears from Geri or sees her unless she is plugging something. Then when she wants to publicise her latest record or book, it's "George this" and "George that". She seems to constantly mention his name in interviews. He feels very hurt. He thought they had a genuine friendship – like two normal people. But now he's not so sure. George has been a fantastic friend to Geri over the years and he has supported her through some tough times. But now he feels a bit miffed.'

Pop music commentator Rick Sky believes there was a further reason for the break-up of the relationship: namely, that George wanted to preserve his privacy. 'In my opinion, the disintegration of her close friendship with George Michael was down to the fact that he is an extremely private person,' he says. 'She is not. The difference between them is that George's career is boosted by publicity and Geri's career is based on it. George has a very close circle of friends and hates his private life getting out, which is why he felt betrayed by Geri when she started talking to the press about it. I doubt they will ever get that close again. In a recent interview, George Michael was asked, "Is Geri offended by the fact you continually push her out of your video [Shoot The Dog]?" George replied, "No, not at all. I spoke to her about it and she's very cool about it as I knew she would be." I'm not sure I believe that. Geri Halliwell doesn't have a life of her own. She lives through the media and even admits it herself. She often confesses to having very few genuine friends. It's quite sad really.'

George was not alone in feeling betrayed – the four remaining Spice Girls could have empathised there. Robbie Williams was also having his doubts, as he revealed later that year. 'She's a demonic little girl,' he snapped. 'When her career started happening again, she became a different person – making these mad, impulsive decisions. Before she was working, she was OK, mad but good mad. But she turned into this demonic little girl playing with dolls and a tea set. She started speaking like a psychotic child and she developed this possessed look in her eye. It was genuinely scaring me. It was around that time I realised our friendship wasn't what I thought it was.' And did he miss her? 'No I don't,' said Robbie firmly. 'I'd be lying if I said I did.'

And now for the big question: did they or didn't they? Yes, according to Robbie. 'We slept together,' he says. 'I don't think we find each other physically attractive. It wasn't really a sex thing.'

Geri didn't agree – that they'd slept together, that is. According to Geri, the couple had once spent a night in the same bed but nothing had happened and that was that. And to date, the friendship would appear to be over. There was one brief moment of reconciliation, though, in May 2002, when Robbie discovered that

Geri was being treated in an Arizona clinic for her eating disorder. He rang her and sent her a bunch of flowers. Said a source close to the singer, 'He's proved that he has a big heart.'

Of course, what was really on Geri's mind at the time was promoting her new single and her new album. 'Her affair with Robbie Williams was an interesting one,' says Rick Sky. 'It certainly kept the media interested. About the only thing that was certain about the whole affair was that they both had an agenda to sell as many records as possible.'

And indeed, Geri was giving interviews right, left and centre, wearing increasingly revealing clothing (and onlookers were beginning to notice that due to her extreme weight loss, there was increasingly little to reveal) and plugging her new album for all it was worth, although in the event its highest chart position was number five.

In one interview, she gave a run-down of all the tracks on the album. George Michael's misgivings turned out to be very well founded indeed: talking about one track, 'Shake Your Bootie Cutie', Geri burbled, 'I wrote this with Greg Alexander from the New Radicals and it's inspired by a Ricky Martin concert. There's a rap on it that's so Wham! – George hasn't heard it yet but I'm sure he won't mind.' And then, of course, there was her cover of the Weather

Girls' classic, 'It's Raining Men', which featured in the *Bridget Jones* film. 'I loved *Bridget Jones*,' said Geri. 'So when they asked me to do this for the film, it was like a gift – and such a great excuse to put legwarmers on! It's fun.'

It was also fun to bask alone in the limelight, without four other girls sharing the praise. Geri didn't just want to be a star: she wanted to be a solo star and she was relishing every minute of it. 'I'm trying to let go of the end result, but I'm fucking proud of this album,' she announced. 'I know you're not supposed to seek outside approval but … I'm starting to feel a bit respected, which is unbelievable. I was always instrumental in the Spice Girls but I never knew whether anyone got it or not. You could scream it from the rooftops but it's all in what people perceive you to have done.'

She certainly was feeling confident about it all. 'Last year I was in complete denial, "Fame does not exist",' she observed rather unrealistically. 'Before I'd really embraced it and because I was ashamed of it I went to the opposite end and hated it. Now I've found a happy medium. I am ordinary but, like Nelson Mandela said, "Don't shy away from your extraordinariness." I'm glad that I'm famous. If God wanted me to be an accountant, He would have made me good at numbers, but I'm shit at maths.

'But I think I'm good at writing pop songs. Sometimes I question that. The song "Feels Like Sex" for me is like a *Carry On* film. Whether you're 80 and like bin bags, sellotape and wellingtons or the missionary position. Even if you're into just kissing, whatever your thing is, it doesn't matter. Also no one's done a song about sex recently. Hello? I talk about three things at the end of dinner. Diets, sex and men. And pooing, but that's too much information.'

One group of people who were less than impressed by the new album, though, were road safety campaigners outraged by the cover of the album – and, ironically, Geri had been banned for driving for six weeks and fined £400 in March after she was caught driving at 60 mph in a 30 mph zone. 'She puts herself in your hands for justice to be meted out to her,' said Nicola-Jane Taylor, Geri's solicitor, after telling the court that Geri wanted to be treated like anybody else. 'She is very, very sorry. She appreciates the gravity of the charge.'

She didn't appreciate, though, that she was about to run into more controversy, for once unwittingly. The cover of the album showed Geri on rollerskates holding on to the back of a speeding Cadillac and safety groups were not pleased. 'This seems to be very irresponsible behaviour for someone like Geri Halliwell,' said Jane Eason of the Royal Society for the

Prevention of Accidents. 'We are very concerned about kids playing with rollerskates, micro scooters or skateboards anywhere near roads, never mind hanging on to the back of cars. We had a lot of problems a few years ago with the film *Back To The Future*, where similar tricks were used. Considering Geri Halliwell has only recently been banned from driving, I think it is very wrong of her to encourage this kind of thing.'

She was not alone. Mary Williams, a road safety campaigner, was also feeling decidedly tight-lipped about the album cover. 'Geri is an icon for young children and our worry is that kids will be tempted to copy her. I would have hoped Geri and her advisers would have had a little foresight into the possible consequences of such a message.' Geri was clearly taken aback by the fuss. 'It's amazing the cover is being taken so seriously,' said a spokesman. 'It's just meant to be a bright, fun image. My advice is, don't try it at home.'

'It's Raining Men' was the first single to be released from the album. Geri was asked why. 'OK, firstly I don't take myself too seriously,' she said. 'Second, it's really nice to be asked to do things, sometimes. This film is going to be great. I went to see a playback last week and it looks fucking brilliant. When [producers] Working Title got in touch with me and asked me to do it I had loads of ideas for it. It's fun. It's camp. I loved singing it. I played it to my target audience last week – a female friend who loved it. Then a gay friend who's a dress designer and he went mad over it.'

And so to the premiere of *Bridget Jones's Diary*. The film certainly was a gift, in more ways than one. For a start, Geri, like many other single women in the country, could relate to Bridget in a big way. 'At the moment, I'm very much a singleton,' she said. 'I have so many Bridget moments. It's in the way I talk about boys, food, exercise, dieting and just about everything else. The movie is so funny, so witty, and I'd definitely say it's the best performance Hugh Grant has ever done – he is very sexy as a villain.'

And while Geri might not have been the greatest singer in the world – her version of 'It's Raining Men' certainly bears no comparison to the original – she was becoming seriously adept at her own publicity. The night of the premiere of the film was a case in point. As its three stars, Renee Zellweger – clad in discreet black – Hugh Grant and Colin Firth made their way into the cinema, Geri, dressed in a backless turquoise dress by Julien Macdonald, bounded across to the huge crowd of fans waving a spare ticket. 'Who wants to be my date for the evening?' she yelled. The crowd went berserk and Geri picked 14-year-old Edward Spencer as her escort for the night.

'We were in the crowd and I could hear Geri

shouting,' says Edward, a boarder at Oakham School in Rutland. 'So I pushed myself to the front, just as she was asking, "Who wants to come in with me?" I yelled at the top of my voice, and I couldn't believe it when she picked me. She helped me over the barrier and took me inside. I think she thought I was a lot older than 14 and she looked shocked when a reporter later asked for my age.

'In retrospect, it was probably all just one big publicity stunt. But if it was attention Geri wanted, it certainly did the trick. The press went crazy and photographers wouldn't leave us alone all night. I've never been a big fan of hers or the Spice Girls, but luckily she didn't talk too much about her music. She nudged me when her song came on in the film, though. Later, she gave me her autograph, with a note saying "Thanks for being my date. Love Geri."

'I got into the party afterwards at the Mezzo restaurant in Soho with my sister. We stood near Geri who was sitting on the sofa nibbling on sushi all night. She was joined by a female pal and they were giggling and chatting among themselves. There were loads of free drinks, delicious food and even an ice-cream parlour, but Geri asked a waiter to get her peppermint tea. At the end of the night, I remember her berating her minder because it was too late to get food back at the hotel. She looked good to me, but maybe a little too skinny. If I gave her a big cuddle, I could probably snap her in half.'

The next day, Edward was besieged by the media, among them a television team who persuaded him it would be a good idea to join in a press conference at the Dorchester Hotel organised by Freuds, the PR firm which was publicising the film and Geri's career. It was at this point that his 15 minutes of fame proved well and truly up. Freuds, which had been only too happy for him to help them generate headlines the previous night, was having none of it. 'I'm sorry, we know nothing about you being here and you're going to have to leave,' he was told. 'I have never been in touch with them or Geri since – although they did send me a goody pack full of Geri and *Bridget Jones* merchandise as a way of saying thanks,' he said.

Geri saw it differently. In a television interview with Ant and Dec, the following exchange took place.

Ant: 'At the premiere for *Bridget Jones's Diary* it was reported you took a fan along as your date. What actually happened?'

Geri: 'A girlfriend was meant to come with me and she couldn't at the last minute so I had this spare ticket in my bag. Do you remember *Charlie and the Chocolate Factory*? Well I just thought, how cool would it be if I turned up and said to someone, "Do you want to come?" I just saw this little guy there and his eyes were all shining and I said, "Do you want to come with me?"'

Ant: 'Was he over the moon?'

Geri: 'He certainly was! He was a bit gobsmacked. He had a great time.'

Dec: 'Did he buy you a hotdog or anything?'

Geri: 'No, he didn't actually.'

Dec: 'What a lousy date!'

5

New Geri

An election was on the way. The formidable Labour spin machine was rolling into action, determined to give Tony Blair a second election victory and creating a series of party political broadcasts designed to keep him at Number 10. In one of those broadcasts, a slim – very slim – young woman is seen making cups of tea for pensioners to Labour's campaign theme tune, 'Lifted' by the Lighthouse Family. It was all well and good apart from one small point – Geri had not always supported the Labour Party. In fact, back in 1996, it was none other than Geri Halliwell who had saluted

Margaret Thatcher as 'the first Spice Girl'.

'We Spice Girls are true Thatcherites,' she said in an interview with *The Spectator* when the girls first became famous. 'Thatcher was the first Spice Girl, the pioneer of our ideology – girl power. Mrs Thatcher is Godmother Spice.'

Not any more she wasn't. These days, it appeared, Geri was firmly on the side of the Labour Party and a great admirer of Tony Blair. 'I think he has done a lot of good work in the last four years,' she said. 'Cherie Blair and I have worked together for Breast Cancer Care and I think she's also fantastic, a great role model. We all need good parenting with love and guidance and I think Tony and Cherie are great examples to us.'

The compliment was returned big time. 'We're very glad to have her endorsement,' said an emotional Labour Party spokesman. 'Geri is not a Labour Party member but she is very clear in her support for Tony Blair's government.'

He spoke a little soon. It isn't often that the mighty New Labour publicity machine finds itself playing a part in someone else's agenda, but then it isn't often that New Labour runs up against anyone like Geri Halliwell. Just as she did when she was first starting out, Geri was having to live off her wits. She had to keep herself in the public eye and one step ahead of the other Spice Girls because, given limited musical ability and, so far, a complete lack of success in establishing an acting career, that was the only way she was going to keep her career afloat. And so when Cherie's people approached Geri's people or vice versa, Geri, who could spot a publicity opportunity even blindfolded in a dark room, did not hesitate. New Geri and New Labour were the ideal fit.

And so, as ever when Geri got involved in anything, rumour and counter rumour began to circulate about how this slightly bizarre pairing had come about. 'I believe Cherie mooted it to Geri, but I think it was suggested first by Tony,' said Jonathon Hackford, who looks after Geri's interests at Freud Communications. 'I'm not sure. I mean, Cherie suggested it originally to Geri, but I assume Blair had already suggested it to Cherie and asked her to ask Geri.' And how, exactly, had Geri and Cherie come to be such good friends? 'They don't hang out at each other's houses,' said Jonathon. 'So I suppose it was in an official capacity.'

One newspaper suggested that Geri – or Cherie or Tony – might have come up with this brilliant wheeze the previous month when Tony met Geri at the *Daily Mirror*'s Pride of Britain Awards. *Mirror* editor Piers Morgan says that Geri demanded an introduction to the PM. 'She said she quite fancied him and wanted to talk to him,' he said. 'So Geri chatted to him for about 40 minutes and they got along famously. They talked about everything. I'm sure she put her hand on his thigh ... she asked him all sorts of things. She says anything for a laugh.'

And so should we assume that Geri would be voting Labour? 'You'd have to ask her, but I imagine she'll be voting for him, bearing in mind she's done the party election broadcast,' said a slightly fraught-sounding Jonathon. 'She would vote. Come to think of it, absolutely she'd vote for him. I'm sure.'

He was wrong: Geri wasn't voting for anyone. The reason was simple – she was not on the electoral register, sparking an absolute outcry. What right had Geri to tell people how to vote when she had no intention of going anywhere near a polling booth herself? 'I am not telling people who they should vote for,' said Geri, displaying, it must be said, a certain lack of understanding about the point of a party political broadcast, 'but I do want people to realise how important it is to have a vote and have their say.' And she wasn't registered, it appeared, because of worries about a stalker after her flat had been broken into earlier in the year.

The Labour Party was clearly a little embarrassed. 'It is a personal matter for Geri and we feel the same about all people who endorse our party,' said a Labour spokesman, adding that the party was aware that Geri had not registered.

What was less clear was whether the party was aware of an interview Geri had given just a couple of months earlier, in which she was asked if she regretted talking about Margaret Thatcher. 'No,' said Geri firmly. 'At the end of the day my father was a Conservative and all I remember are the good bits. The greengrocer's daughter made good. How inspiring was that? That meant anything was possible. That's what I admired. I didn't know anything about the miners' strike, but I do admire anyone who has a strong set of beliefs.' Result: Geri 1, Labour Party 0.

What Geri's appearance in the Labour broadcast really meant, in fact, was that Geri was and is prepared to do almost anything to stay famous. 'Geri's career is not so much to do with music as being Geri Halliwell,' says Rick Sky. 'She has created a product that is basically herself and in the past that has sold very well. What she is careful to do is keep the public interested, whether that is through shedding her clothes, dating other celebrities, or talking about her eating disorder. This is a girl who could have been a television presenter or an actress, the point is she is famous, and that has always been her main aim in life. Her primary talent is her burning ambition.

'Geri's obsession with fame and publicity is the reason she is willing to starve herself to look like a seven year old. She may look like a scrawny child in real life, but in front of the cameras – which are notorious for being cruel – she looks fantastic. And that's all that counts to her. As long as she looks sexy in her videos it doesn't matter what real people think. Geri is a media sponge. She soaks up everything she reads and hears, from self-help books to diet tips and old Hollywood movies, and then pours them back out to anyone who will listen. If you study her interviews, it's hard to ignore the continuous stream of quotes she's ripped off from others. Being clearly so fascinated by celebrities explains why she is so keen to be one herself.'

There was a very big downside to celebrity, though, as Geri discovered after that break-in earlier in the year. In March, Geri returned home from visiting Robbie, who was on tour in France and Belgium, to discover that her £600,000 rented flat in Notting Hill had been broken in to: £80,000 worth of personal possessions, including a necklace bought at auction and once owned by Elizabeth Taylor, her computer and personal photographs were taken, while graffiti was daubed on the walls. The thieves clearly guessed the identity of the flat's owner and the damage was as much malicious as designed for personal gain. Furniture was trashed and blackcurrant juice sprayed around the furniture and carpets.

Geri was devastated and moved straight into a hotel. 'Geri has been really shaken up by this,' a friend said. 'She doesn't want to go anywhere near the flat. It's in a terrible mess – it's a good job she wasn't there at the time, judging by what this person is capable of doing. She is not taking any chances and has someone with her at all times.'

It turned out that the thieves had managed to get past four security locks, a CCTV camera and a burglar alarm to break in but it then emerged that it was a coincidence they had chosen Geri's flat. 'Police believe there is nothing sinister about the break-in,' said Jonathan Hackford. 'It looks as if it was a simple burglary. The raiders didn't even know who lived in the flat until they were inside. Naturally, Geri is very upset, as anyone would be when they are burgled, but she's coping fine. She is staying in a hotel until the mess is cleared up and the damage is repaired. I don't know when she will return to the flat. It's in such an appalling mess.'

Geri never returned to the flat. She moved into the Lanesborough Hotel and even today, when she's in London, she tends to confine herself to hotels. The robbery clearly took its toll. 'It made me feel very vulnerable,' she said. 'It was really horrible. I opened the door and my trainers were at the bottom of the stairs. I thought, Why are they there? When I went upstairs, all my washing was thrown around the flat. It was everywhere. I feel that I am very very lucky in a way because I could walk away from what has happened and did not have to stay at home. Some people come face to face with an attacker and that would just have been the end of everything for me. I was lucky because I did not disturb anybody and I have enough money to go and stay in a hotel.'

She also had enough money to hire a minder, which she duly did. But even this was not without ramifications, when it emerged that the minder in question, Steve Marshall, had appeared in a raunchy film which in turn put an end to his 17-year career in the police force. The film in question showed Steve cavorting with two women dressed as Father Christmas on Television X – The Fantasy Channel and ended with all three naked. A disciplinary hearing was launched and Marshall resigned from the force before it was held. 'Steve was well aware that he had been caught literally with his pants down,' said a fellow policeman. 'He didn't wait to find out what would happen to him.'

Questioned more closely, the City of London

police, where Marshall worked as a constable, became tight-lipped. 'One of the breaches of our code of conduct is anything likely to bring the service into disrepute,' a spokesman said. 'That would cover any behaviour that the public does not expect of a policeman. If an allegation is made, a disciplinary inquiry would be held and the Commissioner would decide what action to take after any hearing. He [Steve] resigned of his own volition.'

Geri's people were not amused. 'Geri wouldn't want to talk about this,' one snapped. 'We have no comment.'

And shortly after the burglary she put her other property, the mansion in Berkshire, on the market for £4.5 million. She and Robbie were still extremely close – so much so that Geri had originally based herself in Notting Hill to be close to him. What's more, Geri's people had had to dispel rumours that after the break-in she would actually move in with him, so there was a great deal of speculation that she would buy a new place in the area. 'Geri still wants to buy in Notting Hill – to be near Robbie,' said a friend. 'But as a result of the break-in, she's going to make sure her new home has the most up-to-date security equipment on the market. It will be absolutely topnotch. Despite the break-in, Geri does love that part of London and obviously she wants to remain as close as possible to Robbie. But if she doesn't find anything she likes she will also look at homes in Hampstead.'

There were other reasons to sell the house. It had always been an odd choice for a single woman, given that it would have been much more suitable for a family, and Geri did not spend much time there. 'She has not been at St Paul's [her Berkshire home] since the end of last year and she wants to be back in London so she can base herself near friends,' said a source close to the star. 'She did love living there but it has become too impractical for her to realistically keep it on.' Another friend confessed it hadn't been right for Geri. 'She has not spent a lot of time there and when she did, she found it incredibly lonely,' he said. 'It looks like a dream home but the truth is that Geri was never happy or comfortable there.'

The house was certainly one that was fit for a popstar princess. After buying what she referred to as 'my *Gone With The Wind* house' for £2.5 million, Geri had spent hundreds of thousands of pounds doing it up. She had got the builders to create a white marbled, pillared hallway, with marble, wood and stone floors. The dining room was red, most of the other rooms were cream and there were chandeliers everywhere. Geri herself had a huge bedroom on the second floor with views out over the garden – all 17 acres of it. There was also a gym and tennis courts. 'She is very determined and what she wants, she usually gets,' said a friend. 'Geri is set to make a huge profit on the house.' To date, however, she hasn't. At the time of writing, the house is still on the market, at a reduced price of £3.5 million.

There were lighter moments, however. That year also saw the release of a documentary called *Raw Spice*, shot in the days before the girls hit the big time. It had been lost for some years and had only recently come to light. 'I hardly recognised myself and Robbie and I laughed so much about it all,' she said. 'It felt like I was watching a different person but it's also great closure about that experience.'

And there was more excitement on the cards. Geri was preparing for another publicity onslaught – and this one in the name of a good cause: entertaining our boys – the British troops – in Oman. Godmother Spice must have been proud.

Operation Ginger, as it came to be known, was announced in July. Geri, as well as Steps and Bobby Davro, would be flying out to entertain the troops. 'We are delighted that Combined Services Entertainment (CSE) have been able to sign up such big names,' said the Ministry of Defence statement. 'These shows will be a massive boost to everyone's morale after a few weeks' exercising in the desert.'

She was to entertain 7,000 troops. 'Once we had Gracie Fields, now we have Geri,' said the CSE. 'It's a matter of who is available and who expresses willingness. Artists who have performed recently include The Stranglers and, of course, Jim Davidson is a great supporter.'

The concerts were to take place in October, and it soon became apparent that the military had no idea what they were up against. This was actually to be Geri's very first full solo show and so, along with the normal superstar demands, Geri was also so nervous that she banned all press coverage. Those normal superstar demands were causing some problems, too. Irons, ironing boards, clothes racks and even computers with full access were to be expected, but there were also reports that Geri was demanding air-conditioned tents for herself and her entourage, and that fridges be stocked with soya milk and fruit juice. In addition, she insisted on staying in a different wing in the Hilton Salalah hotel from her fellow stars on the tour, Steps. Nor would she board *HMS Illustrious* while they were there.

'The woman is a nightmare,' grumbled an army officer. 'It has been quite an eye opener trying to look after her and cater to her every demand. It was great when she originally agreed to do it, we thought it would be a good reward for the men who have been working so hard. But the feeling among a lot of us now is that it's all been too much effort for what it's worth.'

A spokesman indignantly denied that Geri was being difficult. 'Geri is being very brave,' he said.

Steps were clearly getting fed up, as well. 'Steps are not an argumentative bunch,' said a spokesman. 'We were there to do a show, not worry about soya milk. It's not clear whether there was any argument, but if there was then it's a bit sad. Steps have met Geri before. There's never been a problem. I haven't heard anything bad about her.'

The MoD was not so sanguine. 'It's been a nightmare to plan all of this,' said a spokesman. 'There's more friction here than there is between our regiments.'

There was also behind-the-scenes panic when it was realised that Geri's concert would clash with the World Cup, in which England was playing Greece. The concert was postponed for nearly two hours, sparking off yet more grumbling from all parties involved.

But, ever the professional, Geri soon started larking around for the cameras. Clad in a tiny white bikini, she and a group of soldiers frolicked off the surf in Salalah before Geri, egged on by her companions, chased Wing Commander Mark Smith through the waves, drenching him in the process. There were more antics for the camera, until Geri was at long last ready to step on stage. Wearing a khaki battle dress, which barely covered her behind, and accompanied by backing singers wearing Union Jack bikini tops, she announced, 'Hello boys. This is my first time, so be gentle with me. I hope I dressed appropriately.'

The men, who had driven for eight hours through the desert to see the concert, were delighted. 'All the guys got a kick out of being in the glamour world of rock 'n' roll, even though it meant sweating buckets in the searing heat,' said Private John Mackay. 'It was a welcome break from all this tension flying around.'

There was another outbreak of tension back in Britain, though, when it emerged that Geri was being paid to do the concerts – and the total bill for the shows came to over £550,000. That was against an average cost of £6,562 for most shows put on for the troops and it came out of the welfare budget, which also covered the costs of soldiers phoning and e-mailing home. Geri had been paid £80,000, which sparked outrage from, amongst others, Dame Vera Lynn. Dame Vera had entertained the troops in World War II: she hadn't been paid a penny, she said, and nor should any other wealthy performer.

Tory defence spokesman Bernard Jenkin agreed.

'Wealthy performers like Geri should sing for free,' he said in December 2001. 'While I was out there, soldiers in Oman were denied the chance to phone and e-mail loved ones at home as they were told the welfare budget was all but spent. I think it's fairly obvious why. What would have happened if these troops had gone to Afghanistan? They would have been unable to contact home. These figures leave me absolutely speechless. When I first asked to see them I was told they were far too complicated to put down on paper. Now, nearly a month later, they have been released quietly.'

In fact, the exact cost of the show was £550,055 – almost ten times the cost of the most expensive troops shows in places such as Kosovo and the Falklands. Tales of Geri's demands resurfaced, while it was said that she was paid much more than the other performers. A source close to Steps said, 'Steps' performance fee was nowhere in the region of Miss Halliwell's. Hers only came to light as it was extraordinarily high.'

And one member of Steps, Ian Walker commented, 'Geri insisted on being treated differently from us. She wanted to be on a much more elevated level.'

Meanwhile Bobby Davro, who only appeared at one performance and who usually charged between

£10,000 and £15,000, was said to have cut his fee. 'I assume Bobby's fee wasn't very much at all,' said a source close to him.

Jonathan Hackford hastily spoke out, claiming that the other two acts had also been paid £80,000. 'Geri walked away £20,000 out of pocket,' he said. 'She subsidised the trip with money from her production company. Geri had eight dancers and twelve costume changes. She was determined to put on a first-class show for the troops.' And of complaints that while Steps and Bobby Davro were out in the desert meeting the troops Geri was posing for pictures wearing a bikini on the beach he retorted that she had spent an entire day, 'travelling in a Chinook helicopter along the supply routes, visiting troop hospitals and supply depots, none of which she was contracted to do'. It was an occasion – a rare occasion – in which Geri's instinct for publicity had rather let her down.

And it turned out that the other girls had neither forgiven nor forgotten her behaviour a couple of years earlier, either. The Spice Girls as a group have never officially split up, but they have been drifting apart for some time now and, by the end of 2001, they were all but over. There remains, however, the possibility of a reunion tour – but as a foursome and not a fivesome. Emma Bunton made that quite clear in an interview at the end of the year.

'We've discussed touring as a four-piece but never getting Geri back for it,' she said. 'I've seen Geri a few times since she left and everything's cool now. But I found it really hard when she left. I'm a very loyal person and I just felt she shouldn't have been so disloyal. Obviously I don't hang out with her but we have seen one another. But so much water has gone under the bridge now and we're big enough and old enough to just get on with it.'

But for Geri it was business as usual: she had plans on the go – lots of them – and was running around, keeping her profile as high as it ever was. By this time she'd lost so much weight that she appeared to have shed about a third of her body size: it was, she informed us, through yoga. And as surely as night follows day, that announcement was followed by the appearance of a yoga video, *Geri Yoga*. Geri was trained by Katy Appleton, yoga teacher to the stars as well as another well-known instructor, Kisen (who also brought out a yoga video.) 'Yoga has taught me that a healthy mind and a healthy body are integrated,' Geri said. 'It's made me feel good and it can make you feel good, too.'

In fact, Geri was becoming near evangelical on the subject of her new obsession, crediting it with helping her lose 28 pounds in weight. 'I've tried everything to stay in shape, exercising down the gym since I was 17,' she says on the video. 'I've run for miles and been on every diet there is. But now, taking my nature and disposition into consideration, I'm convinced it has to be an "inside job". I had to get a healthy mind first. Yoga has taught me that a healthy mind and a healthy body are integrated. It's all about loving yourself.'

According to Geri, yoga was even responsible for curing her eating disorder. 'You could call me a happy foodie now,' she said. 'It's no secret that I've suffered from raging disorders for the past ten years. My disorder was about not wanting to take responsibility for my life. Every time I had a problem I would turn to food. Now I eat three meals a day whether I'm hungry or not.'

Geri had initially been introduced to yoga after meeting the Britpack artist Sam Taylor-Wood at one of Sir Elton John's parties. Sam had previously suffered from cancer and had used yoga to help her through: Geri thus decided to try it out shortly after leaving the Spice Girls. One of her teachers was Kisen, who had also taught Sam.

'When I met her, she was in a pretty bad way,' he said. 'She had big chunks of fat on her thighs and her neck was quite short and almost tucked in to her body. Her whole body was quite solid and dense. I could see she was quite unhappy. The split from the

Spice Girls had obviously affected her emotionally and mentally. Within six months I could see the change in her. She became more articulate, lost weight and the density of her body was reduced. About nine months after I started teaching her she showed me an advance copy of her "Chico Latino" video and said, "I look like a babe." And it was true. There was a radical difference.'

Of course, it was not only yoga that was making Geri look so different: she was again having severe problems with food. Kisen admitted as much, when he spoke of her protein-only diet and said she would eat only packets of processed meats throughout the day. And he provided an insight into the loneliness of the celebrity lifestyle. 'I saw a side to Geri that the rest of the world didn't know about,' he said. 'She does have all the trappings of fame but that's not where the true richness of life is to be found. You can create your own prison. You can live in a big, beautiful house, but when it has high walls, security guards and an alarm system linked directly to the police station you can become a prisoner. It taught me a lot about the stresses and strains of public life.

'Geri was incredibly generous. She used to let my children have the run of her house and I have lovely memories of my middle son, Joseph, teaching her to rollerblade on the tennis court. She only ever treated me with courtesy, kindness and hospitality. At the end of our first class together, she broke down and cried. At that time, I don't think she realised how vulnerable she was. She realised she was under enormous pressure and the yoga acted as a key to open the floodgates. Those tears represented her repressions and hidden fears.'

But Geri did not want to lose her status as a celebrity, no matter what the strains might be. Next stop on the Geri-go-round was, for one afternoon at least, a stint as an agony aunt. Geri went off to launch a new sex education website, 'Like It Is', aimed at reducing teenage pregnancy rates and developed by Marie Stopes International. 'This site gives frank information, but in a way that is appropriate and safe for young people,' said Geri. 'I fully support any initiative that improves knowledge and protects young people from crisis pregnancies and sexually transmitted infections. Dealing with the peer pressure to become sexually active is even harder. I remember the massive pressure to lose one's virginity – everyone else seemed to have done it.'

That done, Geri, who had just fallen out badly with Robbie, found a new best friend – an even more unusual choice than those who had gone before. She was none other than Nina Campbell, the 56-year-old society interior designer, who met Geri through her daughter Alice, a celebrity PR girl. Geri, who had been living in hotels since the break-in, went to live with Nina and seemed to find in her a mother figure-cum-confidante. 'It's just like being youngsters and sharing a flat,' said Nina.

'I suppose it is rather odd. I find Geri's company incredibly stimulating. She is a very sweet person. Last Saturday night I went to the opera at the Albert Hall and then I went to a gay club to see Geri sing her new single. The opera was fantastic, but seeing this young person make 3,000 people happy was a really new experience for me.' That was not all that had changed. 'I've lost two stones in weight and Geri is helping me get fit,' said Nina. 'Hopefully she gets some home comforts and family life with us.'

The papers could not believe it: 'The Odd Couple', proclaimed the headlines. And indeed, the two women could not have been more different: Geri came from a dirt-poor background and, as we will chart later in the book, was so desperate for fame that she started her career as a topless model. Nina, on the other hand, had a well-heeled background in Belgravia and came out as a débutante. Twice divorced, she started her career with John Fowler, of Colefax and Fowler, before going on to decorate for the likes of Rod Stewart, the Queen of Denmark and the Duke and Duchess of York.

Of course, rumours immediately ran riot about Geri's behaviour during her stay at her friend's flat. 'In our circles, it's best not to shout across the table at a guest, "Hi, how much does your dress cost?" sniped one of Nina's friends. 'And maybe she shouldn't have told another guest to stay off the dessert as, "It's full of sugar and you're big enough already."' Others cattily said that given Geri was dating Bobby Hashemi – of which more in a later chapter – the founder of the Coffee Republic chain, it showed she wanted to move up a step socially. 'Since meeting Bobby and getting into his polo playing circles, Geri has decided it's time for her to move up in the world,' bitched one 'friend'. 'She's meeting all sorts of frightfully well-to-do people and is desperate to fit in. It's just a matter of time before she'll be trying to set up matches with [Prince] Charles. She likes to think he is a pal anyway.'

Nina ignored the sniping from her friends and took Geri's advice when it came to a pantomime she was appearing in that Christmas, *Alice in DecorLand*, for the British International Design Association. Nina was playing the part of the Queen of Hearts and, along with getting the top dress designer Tomasz Starzewski to design her costume, she turned to Geri's voice coach for help in learning how to sing. The result caused uproar and only served to strengthen the unlikely friendship.

And finally, Geri seemed to take comfort from the church. She signed up for a ten-week guide to Christianity called the Alpha course, a series of 90-minute meetings held at the Holy Trinity Brompton Anglican Church in London. Another participant spotted her halfway through: 'This course has been running for seven weeks now. Geri's been attending now and again but hasn't been at all the meetings. We sit around and discuss religious issues and Jesus. It's very informal. Geri blends in and appears to be comfortable during the meetings. She likes having a break from the spotlight.'

She needed one. Despite a year in which she was rarely off the front pages, the public finally seemed to be tiring of Geri. In a poll conducted by the news website Ananova, Geri was deemed the most media-hungry celebrity of 2001, which just goes to show that while you can fool some of the people some of the time, you certainly can't fool everyone all of the time. It was time for a period of quiet and Geri did just that – for about a week.

6

Waxwork Spice

It was January 2002 and Geri was furious. The reason? Madame Tussaud's was making a waxwork of her – and Geri, who was by now about a third of the size she had been as a Spice Girl, felt she looked too fat. She had had three sittings for her waxen image, but every time she saw the waxwork in progress, she felt they'd made her bottom, waist and thighs too big. 'Every time she sees the work in progress she has gone ballistic and accused us of getting her sizes wrong,' said a Madame Tussaud's insider.

'Geri says we are making her look fatter than she is and she isn't happy. Every time Geri has a sitting she says she has lost more weight and that we should change our model accordingly. We have repeatedly taken measurements of her and they are correct but she still insists that the model makes her look fat. Her constant demands for change are driving the model-makers up the wall.'

It seemed that the trouble began when the model-makers showed Geri early clay impressions of her likeness. 'She wanted to be re-measured and was keen to have reductions on the bottom, thighs and waist,' said the insider. 'We checked her measurements and those of our model and there wasn't any difference. But she still insisted it was too fat. A lot of people here wish we had never bothered with her.'

In the event, a waxwork of Geri went on display in Madame Tussaud's in summer 2002. But it was a measure of quite how serious Geri's eating disorder was becoming when she even thought an effigy of her now tiny frame was too fat: it's common for sufferers to see distorted images of themselves in the mirror – but in the form of a waxwork? But still no one realised how ill Geri was becoming: commentators spoke admiringly of her super-slim figure – a figure that Geri was only too happy to show off. At the NRJ awards in Cannes in January – the French equivalent of the Brits – Geri was determined to upstage fellow performers Britney Spears and Kylie Minogue.

Geri sang a French version of her hit 'Calling' while giant fans blew her white chiffon clothing into the air, revealing a completely flat stomach and a tiny pair of white knickers. No one commented on the fact that the stomach was almost flat enough to be concave: instead everyone picked up on the fact that Geri still wanted to get into the movies. 'I still love doing my music but I really want to concentrate on getting a film role by the end of the year,' she said, although still no firm projects had been lined up.

In fact, when she was not being obsessively exhibitionist, Geri's behaviour was becoming increasingly bizarre. There were reports that she was taking Harry the dog into meetings and then even practising yoga in front of bemused record executives. 'It is very odd seeing a dog shown to its seat and then having to put up with its wind problems during serious discussions,' said one EMI executive with commendable understatement.

This was not the only occasion on which Geri raised eyebrows. After one interview at a television studio, Geri asked if she might stay behind and do some yoga: given permission, she launched in to a 45-minute session as the equipment was packed away around her. 'She only stopped when someone eventually told her we had to leave the studio,' a bemused eyewitness reported. On yet another occasion, Geri acted in an even more unusual manner. 'She just started charging round in circles with her personal assistant following behind trying to take notes,' said an onlooker. 'Then suddenly she started screaming at her PA, "Get me some protein, now. I need protein."'

But still no one clicked what was really wrong – instead, they were riveted by another bout of the Spice Girl versus Geri show, yet again initiated by the redoubtable Victoria. In a television documentary, *Being Victoria Beckham*, she lashed out at her old friend, this time for not offering support when her husband David was enmeshed in a bogus kiss-and-tell.

'All the other girls phoned me and were really, really supportive,' Victoria said. 'Geri knew how that would have made me feel. I was very, very surprised she didn't call. In my mind, that's when I said, "That's that." Laying it on with a trowel, she then proceeded to announce that she was sure Geri regretted leaving when she did. 'She doesn't know our children,' said Posh. 'It must be very lonely for her. It must be very, very lonely.'

As if that were not enough, it emerged that Victoria had written a song, 'Watcha Talkin' About', which was about none other than Geri. It certainly made her feelings about her old band member clear, with some of the lyrics as follows: 'It started when the fame and the fans kept coming in, and then you changed on us. Then you told us you were cool and we were wrong. When I call you on the phone you act like you ain't home. You're checking your caller ID. Why are you getting fake on me? I remember talking to you constantly, we had a ball, but now it's "Let's do lunch."' It might not have been Shakespeare, but it certainly brought the message home.

Geri was not letting it get to her. She continued to attract attention with pretty much everything she did. February saw her in Singapore, where she was to perform at a charity concert before the Singapore Masters tournament – convenient timing, given that it was the time of the Brits in Britain and Geri hadn't been nominated for a single one. She was, however, looking forward to the gala concert, chirping, 'They'll get the full monty – a range of songs old and new.'

Gamely, Geri had a go at golfing, but even the presence of Nick Faldo, who was coaching her, failed to impress onlookers. 'She didn't seem to have any co-ordination,' said one. 'Nick was patient, but even he couldn't make her a golfer overnight.'

Geri's next move was to raise eyebrows in a big

way: she muscled in on Hollywood royalty in a determined bid to be noticed. At the Los Angeles BAFTAs, Geri put on her usual suggestive performance, prancing around in hotpants and a bowler hat. She went a little too far, though, when she coaxed the veteran actor Sir Ben Kingsley on to the stage, before sitting on his knee, plonking her bowler on his head and cooing a Marilyn Monroe song in his ear. The audience, which included Steven Spielberg, George Lucas, Carrie Fisher and Harrison Ford, clearly did not quite know how to react, but their astonishment was as nothing compared to what was to come.

Some of the guests were part of the original cast of *Star Wars* and were present for a reunion. Geri managed to squeeze in to a picture being taken of Harrison Ford, Carrie Fisher and George Lucas, and while it may be one thing to upstage Renee Zellweger at the première of *Bridget Jones's Diary*, it is quite another to upstage possibly the most successful actor of his generation when he is reunited with colleagues on one of the most successful films ever made. 'It was like she was desperate for attention,' said one onlooker: on that occasion, at least, Geri did herself no favours at all with the film world.

She also managed to upset Bulgari. The jewellery

giant hired Geri to open their new £43 million store in Moscow for a six-figure sum, but the performance was not an unqualified success. In her speech Geri talked at some length about herself and her views on the new Russia: she forgot, however, to mention Bulgari. After dinner, she then sang a number of songs including 'Wannabe' and 'It's Raining Men': some present felt that her act lacked sparkle. Bulgari's official comment was, 'We like to mix various peoples and styles' but off the record they were said to be disappointed.

'Bulgari were not entirely happy,' said a source. 'They didn't feel they got value for money. It is safe to say that she will not be asked back.'

And then, on top of that, Geri was briefly and inadvertently reunited with her old flame Chris Evans. Chris and his young bride Billie Piper turned up in Los Angeles in March and checked in to the very fashionable Sunset Marquis hotel. Two days later Geri hit town and, unaware of who else was in residence, checked in to the same hotel. This led to an extremely awkward moment when, inevitably, all three bumped into one another on the sun loungers the next day. A rather shocked Chris blurted out, 'Hey, how are you? How long have you been here?'

Geri, looking equally stunned, managed, 'Er, hi, how are you?' And that was pretty much it. Chris and Billie moved sunbeds soon afterwards, with all three continuing to look shaken for the rest of the day.

Geri is someone who acts on impulse and then regrets it, and who is constantly seeking out a new look and is never satisfied with her appearance. So it was no surprise that her next move was to have her two tattoos removed. After leaving the Spice Girls, Geri had an eight-pronged star tattooed between her shoulder blades and on a later occasion added a little black jaguar in the small of her back, 'because my dad used to sell Jags and it reminds me of him'. Now she wanted to be tattoo free. 'I have changed,' she said. 'It's time to get rid of them and move on.'

She emphasised the point by pulling down the back of her dress at a post-Oscar party in Los Angeles. 'Look at these,' she said to a friend. 'Say goodbye to them. It's the last time you're going to see them. I'm having both tattoos lasered off. I hate them. I've been to see Cher and I asked her how she got her tattoos taken off. I'm going to her doctor.'

The Geri bandwagon rolled on: her yoga tape had turned in to a bestseller; there were reports, later denied, that she was going to star with the Scottish actor Alan Cumming in a new sitcom; and it turned out that she had to knock another £1.5 million off her home, which meant that the asking price had fallen from £4.5 million to £3 million. And still the attempts to build up a film career continued. By the summer all sorts of rumours were circulating, starting with one that Geri was to star in a film called *Semper Occultus*, as a Lara Croft-style secret agent. She was said to be 'extremely excited' about the possibility.

'There's quite a buzz about this project and Geri is the person the producers want as the lead,' said a source close to the film-makers. 'The title, Semper Occultus, is the motto of MI6 and means Always Secret. Geri would have to fly to locations in Spain, South Africa and Paris to shoot the big scenes. Luke Goss and Nick Moran have been mentioned as possible villains. There is also some talk of getting Sean Connery or Roger Moore to play the role of M as the big shot MI6 boss.'

Another possibility was a role in the sequel to *Charlie's Angels*. The film would feature a character called Nora, an evil British woman who is out to get the three angels. 'She's desperate to get it and has been pulling out all the stops for Columbia Tristar bosses to sign her,' said a studio source. 'She's told executives she is perfect for the role because she's British. But to be honest they want someone who's an established actress and plainly Geri isn't.'

Television has always looked like an option for Geri and in the summer of 2002, along with songwriter and all-round musical genius Pete Waterman, and Louis Walsh, manager of Westlife and Boyzone, Geri appeared in the third series of *Popstars* as a judge. Initially, at least, it was hoped that Chris Evans would also be participating. 'It'll make great TV because they're sure to have it out with each other on screen,' said a source. 'Geri has never forgiven Chris for dumping her.'

In the end Chris decided not to join in, but Geri came under fire from various quarters, nonetheless. Sporting a new haircut – a fringe – she returned to these shores just before her 30th birthday, having spent much of the proceeding year in Los Angeles, and promptly seemed to upset almost everyone, despite announcing 'I will be honest but with compassion.' One who found her less than compassionate was Carol Lynch, a curvy size 16 singer, who went on the first day of auditions and left, furious, because Geri called her fat. 'I am proud to be size 16 but I don't think it went down so well with her,' said Carol, 19, a shop assistant from Basildon, Essex. 'When I went in I sang Brandy's "I Wanna Be Down" and Pete Waterman and Louis Walsh were like, "you've got a good R&B voice" and "larger than life personality". But then Geri added sarcastically, "Yeah, VERY larger than life."'

Carol was not impressed by this. 'I was never a fan

of hers before as I don't think she can sing, but I don't think she has a right to comment about my weight. I'm not going to eat and throw it up in the loos for anyone. She's a 30 year old with the body of an eight year old and there's nothing attractive about that and it's not sending out the right message.'

A spokesman for the show tried to calm everyone down. 'Geri said that Carol was larger than life, she had a huge voice and larger-than-life personality. She absolutely said nothing about Carol's physical appearance.'

The next upset came from Geri's co-judge, Louis Walsh, who was less than tactful when talking about Geri's qualifications for the job. 'She won't know about finding a singer because she is tone deaf,' he announced. 'All the Spice Girls are tone deaf and that's why their solo careers failed. Geri has no talent, can't sing or dance and – like a lot of the kids who audition – is desperate for fame. She did that Turkish TV show and these kids will have tried stuff like that too. She is just very glad and grateful to be on TV.' All completely true, of course, but not necessarily a reason that Geri should not be a judge. After all, if she can do it …

A third album will come out in 2003 and that could make or break Geri's career. Even here, however, there is confusion. Geri had wanted to work with Pete Waterman, her co-judge and the man who made Kylie Minogue into a singing sensation, but the two have yet to confirm any plans to work together. Insiders believe they probably won't. In fact, this year has been difficult for Geri. Her old friend George Michael finally admitted that, yes, it was Geri's quest for publicity that had driven them apart.

'The truth, the real truth is that Geri's a lovely girl and in some ways she's a remarkable person,' he said. 'But it's very difficult to maintain a relationship with a person who lives for the press. Not in a bad way, she's kind of a victim of it. It's very hard to hang out with someone who loves the press when you spend your time running away from them. We haven't fallen out.' And of Geri's now notorious appearance at the Brits the previous year he added that she did not take his advice. 'You can imagine Geri coming to me and saying, "I'm going to turn up at the Brits walking out of a big fanny and it'll have a Union Jack on it." Obviously I'm gonna go, "Don't do that!"'

George was not the only person to be getting tired of Geri's non-stop quest for publicity. Asked about Geri and Robbie, none other than Sir Elton John had his say. 'I think it's too much – the publicity and everything,' he said. 'I think Robbie knows that and I think that's why he went to LA, to get away from it all.' (This was before a naked Robbie was pictured frolicking with Rod Stewart's ex, Rachel Hunter.) 'He's a smart lad and he seems to be getting on the straight and narrow.' And of Geri's quest for publicity he added, 'Maybe Geri is a bit like that. More so, I think, than Robbie but that's because Robbie's more talented than Geri is. He is in the paper all the time, but I think it's beginning to piss him off. She does not have as much talent as Robbie ... she seems to have gone publicity mad.'

Geri, however, had more to worry about than criticism from the elder statesmen of rock. She was not well and the truth about her condition was about to emerge. In her autobiography, *If Only*, she had written at some length about having an eating disorder, but it was widely assumed she had conquered that particular problem. She hadn't. At the end of April, Geri checked in to the Cottonwood de Tucson clinic in Tucson, Arizona: her bulimia had returned. 'I can confirm our clinic treats eating disorders like anorexia and bulimia and other eating issues,' said the clinic's Michael Martell.

Of course, it should have been obvious to everyone for some time that something was wrong: at 5'1, Geri by this time weighed about seven stone, and was thus a good 10 pounds underweight for her height. She had also described her battle with

133

bulimia in *If Only*. She wrote about how she would binge her way into the new year, eating everything in the cupboards at home; she'd go to the supermarket and be eating food as the checkout girl rang up the total, eat Mars Bars in the car on the way home and end up with her fingers down her throat trying to bring it all back up again.

Anyone with that background, who quite suddenly and quickly lost an enormous amount of weight, was clearly in trouble. But in the distorted world of show business, in which women are expected to have the body of prepubescent boys – occasionally with a huge pair of breasts added on – Geri had attracted praise for losing so much weight. The disease was back with a vengeance, though: there were reports that Geri had been seen scrabbling through rubbish bins to eat the cake she had earlier thrown away.

And it could not have been more ironic. Geri had seemed to be leading an ultra-glamorous lifestyle: flitting around the world, staying at luscious villas and mixing with the most famous show business stars in the stratosphere. All the time, behind the scenes, she had been binge eating and making herself sick. 'It was awful to see,' said a friend. 'She's built a huge career on being the fittest woman in showbiz and now this. Like all celebrities trying to keep slim, she has a love-hate relationship with food and was advised that she needed help. The problem wasn't out of control, but she felt she could benefit from advice and counselling. Geri recognised she was on a potentially hazardous path.'

You can say that again. In their most extreme forms, eating disorders can be fatal and Geri was clearly much, much too thin. She still did not realise it, though, turning up to the clinic with four suitcases full of revealing clothes. They were promptly taken away from her. 'A great deal of her wardrobe was unsuitable,' said a member of the clinic's staff. 'This is a male and female facility and we urge women not to dress in what we call sexy clothes. We don't allow low tops that show cleavage, shorts or anything that reveals a bare midriff. In accordance with clinic rules all her possessions were checked and some of her clothes were put in storage.'

The extent of Geri's problems became clear when, a few days after her arrival, it emerged that she had extreme difficulty eating in front of anyone else. 'She had several calm but serious exchanges with senior staff and said she was particularly concerned about eating arrangements,' said a source. 'From the outset she had discovered to her horror that she was expected to eat with other patients, choosing from a self-service cafeteria with lots of food.'

In the event, Geri did not stay long at the clinic, not least because of the cafeteria. 'The fact is she knows what she wants and Cottonwood unfortunately wasn't set up to provide it,' said a friend. 'She wasn't in any way a prima donna. She simply explained very politely that she wasn't happy and would be leaving. Geri is sure Cottonwood is a fine place – it just wasn't for her.'

That it wasn't. A source inside the clinic said there were problems right from the start. 'She took one look at the eating arrangements and knew she wasn't going to be staying long,' he said. 'She couldn't accept that someone in here for counselling on binge eating was expected to eat with other patients, choosing from a self-service cafeteria.'

It was beginning to become clear that Geri had never really conquered her problems with food – the only surprise is that she was ever as voluptuous as she was in her incarnation as Ginger Spice. Actually the problems had been there all along, but she sought to make light of the situation. 'Geri appreciates the irony of leaving because of the restaurant set-up,' said a friend. 'She may have bulimia, but she also has a fantastic sense of humour. Geri has sought treatment elsewhere and has become a bit of a therapy enthusiast. Let's just say she knows the 12-step programme backwards. Her bulimia recurs every couple of months. It can be sparked by all manner of issues and usually involves bingeing. The problem never develops any further because Geri is so aware of the warning signs and always acts quickly to sort herself out again. She usually does this through therapy. Geri doesn't just attend eating disorder classes. She thinks she has a lot to offer group therapy sessions dealing with all manner of problems. These other sessions help the group and help her conquer her other demons at the same time.'

It must be said, the other girls were not overly sympathetic. In 2001 Victoria had already blamed Geri for starting her off on an eating disorder when the girls were still sharing a house together in Maidenhead: now it was Mel B's turn to make her feelings known. 'Geri talks about her eating disorders in her book and there's a lot of women out there who suffer,' she said. 'I've never experienced anything like that but from her point of view, she's gone a little too far. It's bad representation. She fell out with George Michael because of food. He had filled his fridge with a load of food from this really posh place when she went to stay at his house. But she got rid of all the food and he went ballistic. She doesn't eat food, she just looks at it. She just drinks water.'

And by this time Geri was beginning to look as if

she was only 6 stone, rather than seven. Experts on eating disorders began to express serious concern. 'Geri has been building up to this for years,' said slimming expert Sally Ann Voak. 'She took one look at herself as the Spice Girl in the Union Jack dress and decided she wanted to be slimmer and fitter – and she has been taking it too far ever since.'

It now emerged that Geri was only eating fruit, fish and vegetables and, despite numerous health warnings from experts, was having multi-vitamin jabs to make up her nutrient intake. 'I believe she has been dieting and exercising for so long that she cannot eat normally,' said Sally Ann. 'If this is the case, as soon as she tries to eat properly, her body will start storing fat and she will feel gross. Bulimia sufferers then punish themselves by throwing up. If she wants to see her old age, she has got to start eating normally. Girls are emulating her figure, buying her video. They believe her when she says she is healthy.'

But Geri isn't healthy, she isn't healthy at all. She has a serious illness which she has yet to conquer and which is undermining her long-term health. And while she still shines in front of the unforgiving camera, in real life she is now painfully thin and has a battle on her hands if she wants to get over it.

The difficulties are obvious. Her old friend and

current rival Victoria Beckham is also too thin – when she's not pregnant – and given the competition between them, Geri might well not wish to be seen as one pound heavier than Victoria.

Her eating is the one area of her life over which Geri has control. This is a reassurance when her future career is looking uncertain, no films are in the offing and a great deal hangs on the performance of her third album. She has fallen out with George Michael and Robbie Williams, her two greatest friends since leaving the Spice Girls, and she has yet to find a long-term partner. She is also considering a move to Los Angeles, possibly the worst place on the planet for anyone who has trouble with their body image to live.

And Geri's problems are far greater than have so far been realised by the wider public. On her yoga video she says, 'For breakfast I have a really large bowl of porridge. It doesn't have to be skimmed milk. It can be semi-skimmed milk or full fat. I'm not frightened of fat at all. My lunch – whether it's potatoes, chicken or fish – can be grilled, even fried. I wouldn't eat a potato a year ago because I thought it would make me fat, which is crap. Some occasions I eat red meat. Occasionally, I even eat chips. It sounds mad, but before if I had one chip, I'd want to eat the whole house. I'd want to eat two plates of chips. I could never eat a normal portion. I had to re-learn eating behaviours.'

So there you have it: Geri binge eats and is compelled to assert that she is not afraid of fat at all, a substance which it would not occur to most people to fear. Add to that the fact that Geri had to leave a clinic because she couldn't eat in front of other people and you have a woman with a fully fledged and very harmful slimming disease. In fact, it is only now that the full extent of Geri's problems are coming to light – and the problems are very much more severe than anyone has previously realised.

7

Seriously Skinny Spice

*It's not what you're eating –
it's what's eating you*

Geri Halliwell has suffered from eating disorders for a very long time. The real problems began with the death of her father when she was just 21, but even before that there were signs that all was not well. And in those pre-Spice Girls days, Geri had chosen the worst possible profession for someone with a fixation about their body image: glamour modelling. 'When I was 18 I did nude modelling,' she said. 'The rejection, the self-esteem-damaging effects of the endless auditions were terrible. And my father dying when I was 21 made it worse. Bulimia and anorexia are about not feeling in control in your life; it's not so much about your body as how you feel inside.'

The problems really began, however, when Geri's father Laurence died, just six months before she joined the Spice Girls. Geri says her father's death not only gave her the burning ambition to succeed as a popstar – but also triggered an eating disorder that would remain with her for years. Talking about the *Raw Spice* documentary, she said, 'The thing for me, personally, was looking at myself because my father had died six months before that and I saw a girl in so much pain. You know the way I was like, "I want it now" because I was so conscious of the fact that I was going to die now. I saw the pain in my own eyes. I don't believe I would be where I am today if my father hadn't died … although I became anorexic.'

A bereavement is, in fact, exactly the sort of event that can tip a sufferer into eating too much or too little. 'It's not uncommon for a traumatic event in an individual's life to trigger an eating disorder,' says Steve Bloomfield of the Eating Disorders Association. 'Often, when a relationship breaks down or there is a death in the family, an individual will control their food intake in order to shift the focus from the real problem. It's a way of dealing with depression and not facing up to reality.

'There is a high incidence of eating disorders among

people in the public eye, largely due to the fact they are up against intense scrutiny from the public and the media. Being constantly in front of the cameras can be stressful and creates a great deal of pressure. The idea that unrealistically slim bodies are being hailed as "perfect" is pretty tragic. It almost certainly has a part to play in the increase in eating disorders in this society. But on the other hand, talking about the problem like Geri Halliwell has done brings it out in the open and makes a lot of sufferers feel like they are not alone.

'Anorexia nervosa is a refusal to maintain body weight over a minimum normal weight for age and height. It is characterised by bouts of extremely controlled behaviour but is often linked with sporadic bouts of purging. Bulimia nervosa is characterised by recurrent episodes of binge eating, which can often mean raiding the fridge and kitchen cupboards for absolutely anything from vats of ice-cream to half-cooked pizza. It illustrates a loss of control and, almost immediately afterwards, the sufferer will be overcome with a sense of guilt and despair and go to desperate lengths to rid themselves of such feeling – i.e. purge themselves.

'Few sufferers, however, can be neatly placed into one category and it is not uncommon for one person to experience both, at different stages in their life. Often eating disorders are supplemented by strict exercise regimes. A severe reduction in food intake can cause a reduction in the amount of oestrogen produced in females, which in turn cause a loss of sexual appetite.'

The problems really kicked in around 1994, when Geri first joined the Spice Girls. Each adopted a specific persona which, in part at least, was based on their appearance. 'Our characters became more and more cartoon-like,' said Geri. 'My hair became redder, my lipstick brighter and my outfits more outlandish. Mel C wore tracksuits and did backflips on demand; Mel B's untameable afros grew even wilder; Emma wore pigtails and baby doll dresses and Victoria acquired 25 pairs of Gucci shoes.' And as the girls became increasingly famous, Geri became increasingly depressed and bulimic. 'Nothing could describe how out of control I felt,' she said.

The other girls were aware of Geri's condition – indeed, Victoria was beginning to share it – and at Christmas of 1994 Geri and Mel B, then very close friends, booked a package holiday to the Canary Islands. Mel was extremely concerned about Geri's problem with food and tried to help her eat sensibly by ordering proper meals – she herself found it incomprehensible that Geri considered food the enemy. In contrast, Mel had always been relaxed about what she ate. The girls spent Christmas Day on the beach, with Geri and Mel becoming closer friends than ever. Geri describes it as one of the best Christmases of her life.

Back in Maidenhead over the New Year, however, Geri was all alone again. The other Spice Girls were spending it with their families, leaving Geri on her own at a time when most people were celebrating together. The sudden onset of depression meant only one thing for Geri: food. She celebrated the New Year in the worst way possible. In her autobiography she writes: 'Ever since Dad's death I'd been treading water. Each time I stopped, I started drowning.'

Geri writes that she felt exhausted, lonely and out of control. She met up with her half-sister Karen and finally confided in her, effectively admitting to her – and herself – that she had a serious eating disorder and needed help. She was admitted to Watford General Hospital's psychiatric ward in early January 1995. She had told the doctor she couldn't stop bingeing and throwing up and they gave her a bed. In there, she felt calm instead of feeling frightened. Clearly she relished being given so much intense attention.

But after two or three days Geri realised the doctors weren't going to be able to help. She claims no attempts were made to analyse her problems and discover the cause of them: the doctors simply put her on Prozac and monitored her diet. Just as she stepped out of Arizona's Cottonwood Clinic, Geri walked out of Watford General only days after entering. She also came off the Prozac which 'made her feel numb' and 'stole her creativity' soon after. It was back to reality – or that which the Spice Girls were beginning to know as reality.

At this stage Geri was going for months without overeating, then finally giving up, bingeing and bringing up her food again afterwards. 'The release I'd feel after being sick after a food binge was enormous,' she recalled. 'All the anxiety of the previous months was suddenly washed away. This must be how alcoholics feel when they finally succumb and open that bottle of whisky.'

A friend who worked with her in the Spice Girls recalled Geri's problems a couple of years after she left the group, when she was running around with Robbie Williams. 'Geri's a control freak and that's why she's looking so good now,' she said. 'She used to keep her diet and fitness together for so long, then collapse into a binge. It wasn't really control – it was staggering from one crisis to the next. You've only got to look at how often she changes her image to know that inside she's probably in turmoil. I'm not at all shocked that she and Robbie have hooked up and she's helping him to overcome his alcoholism. It's another thing she can control.'

Ironically, because of her curves, Geri was not just

known as Ginger Spice but also as Sexy Spice, a sobriquet that looked all the more appropriate when Geri wore a plunging red sequinned gown to the Brit Awards in 1997 and, quite literally, fell out over the top. Her response was magnificent: 'Everyone's seen them before,' she said.

Behind the scenes, though, it was a different story. Show business types, never the most gentle and forgiving of people, were calling her fat. For a girl who had started to have trouble with food when she was in her late teens, this must have been devastating. Nor was she the only one of the girls to suffer: Victoria went on to develop an eating disorder – she blamed this on Geri – and Mel C is, to this day, criticised for weighing too much. Asked if the Spice Girls were guilty of encouraging young girls to be too slim, Mel once said, 'I think we were victims of it, well, Geri and I were. I think overall the group had quite a healthy difference in shapes and sizes and the other three girls were just naturally the shape they were. Maybe I'm guilty of putting pressure on little girls who loved Sporty. But if so, I was a victim of previous people who defined how I thought I had to look to be accepted in the pop world. Perhaps it was the case of the victim becoming the perpetrator, which is a pattern you often find.'

Geri herself became a perpetrator, according to

Victoria Beckham. 'Geri would say things such as don't put sauces on food, low-fat things were just as good and I could try not eating quite so much,' she said. 'The trouble is, when you start thinking like this, it's hard to stop. I changed from someone who was dieting to lose a bit of weight to being obsessive. I was shrinking and the excitement at getting thinner took away the hunger.'

A friend of Victoria's confirmed this. 'The one thing Victoria did say, though, was that Geri Halliwell played a big part in her problem. The bigger the Spice Girls became, the more obsessed Victoria was with weight. She'd been chubby as a teenager and didn't want to go back there. Geri battled against both anorexia and bulimia and the trouble was that Victoria listened too much to Geri without realising just how much damage she was doing to her own body.'

Geri was horrified. 'Eating disorders are very, very contagious,' she said. 'I wasn't healthy around that time we were all living together and I feel sad that my behaviour had an input on anybody else's. I would hate to think I would inflict my eating habits on to anybody.'

Unfortunately, Geri's eating habits were, if anything, about to get worse. After she walked out on the girls in 1998 her dramatic weight loss began, but even when she confessed to eating disorders the following year in her autobiography, no one seemed to realise that the incredible shrinking Geri might still be suffering from her illness. It was all down to a healthy diet and yoga, we were told: Geri herself was fine.

But finally doubts began to surface. In 2000 it was reported that Geri had embarked upon the crazy (and dangerous) no-carbohydrate diet that was then all the rage. Geri's people insisted she felt fantastic and the diet was working well. Health experts were not so sanguine, pointing out that carbohydrates are a vital part of a person's diet – but still Geri persevered.

By the end of the year, the situation was becoming serious. Geri was spotted attending a meeting of Overeaters Anonymous, whose motto was 'It's not what you're eating – it's what's eating you', despite the fact that she was by then only about seven stone. 'She kept her head hung low and hardly anyone appeared to recognise her,' said someone else present at the meeting. 'Most of the crowd was overweight. Geri was the thinnest person there. Each member discussed their problem, how they overcame the urge to eat and how they hoped to help others fight the battle. Geri kept her eyes on the carpet as she listened. She didn't offer her own story.'

She had, however, previously confessed, 'I'll never be naturally thin – I really have to work hard at it.' And she had also joined in the Overeaters mantra which said, 'God grant me the serenity to accept the things I cannot change, courage to change the things I can and wisdom to know the difference.' That particular battle was going to be a very difficult one to win. 'Like alcoholism, an eating disorder is something you never really recover from completely,' said a spokeswoman for Overeaters Anonymous. 'In an ideal situation you should go to meetings all of your life.'

Lee Redman, services manager of Overeaters Anonymous, says, 'The only requirement for membership is a desire to stop eating compulsively. All are welcome who have this desire. If a meeting doesn't have a few people looking great in it, I would certainly question whether recovery was present. I need to know the programme works. We cannot judge a person's outsides. We have no idea what it is like for them. I have worked with women who appear to be small or fit and they are absolutely insane and live in great pain and despair. It isn't the outside, the weight, it is the powerlessness that brings us together and the solution that the Twelve Steps of Overeaters Anonymous provides. Remember, our food is but a symptom, we suffer from a spiritual malady. There are many anorexics and bulimics that have found release from the horrors of this disease through OA. I am one. I have been abstinent from my bulimia for over 19 years. It is only by the grace of God and the Fellowship of OA that I can say that.'

Geri was beginning to realise that her eating

disorder, while triggered by her father's death, was also a sign of an obsessive-compulsive personality. She was also now claiming that she no longer dieted and merely avoided certain foods. 'I can't allow myself to diet ever again,' she said. 'I don't eat white flour and I don't eat sugar and I can't eat chocolate, which is really hard sometimes, but what I do eat is generally healthy – potatoes, fish – but I think about what I eat on a daily basis. I'm a compulsive, addictive person. When I put down food I go out shopping. It could be shopping, sex, exercise, music, I can obsess about anything.'

And no matter what else she was doing in her life, the subject always returned to food. 'You can't triumph over eating disorders so fast, of course I have to deal with it day by day,' she said in an interview with a German newspaper. 'But I am trying to look after myself better now. I try to eat healthily and not to bolt it down. And I don't throw up after eating or go for days without food any more. I have good friends who look out for me. It is a bloody hard process and I will probably never be perfect with it. But I have learned to talk about my feelings instead of stuffing myself with food and, later, bringing it back up.

'There are of course many women who thought I was just right before and would happily have swapped with me. Everyone says I am thin now – before, they used to say I was fat. But now I like myself. I have found my centre. The most important aim is to be happy inside. And although you cannot be happy every day, I am OK. I see on these old photos from when I was first with the Spice Girls that I was unhappy, because my father had just died. I barely notice how I looked, rather I remember how I felt. For me it is now kind of a freedom not to have to squeeze myself into trousers any more.'

However, her habits were becoming increasingly unhealthy. A smoker for years, Geri seemed to have graduated to chain-smoking in order to stay slim. Like many others obsessed with their weight, the former Spice Girl is said to have taken to 'puffing away like a chimney', according to fellow diners at London's Nobu. Chain-smoking is popular among those concerned with their weight, especially young women.

Geri lost 28 pounds in 18 months, which was too much (and too fast). Yet she would continue to say that it was yoga that had helped her achieve her new slim-line shape. In June 2001 she said in an interview with *Marie Claire* magazine, 'I love yoga because it doesn't matter what size or shape you are. Saying that, I'm a hypocrite, because I stand in front of the mirror with weights and try and get cute abs.' All well and good, but the effect of this was rather ruined when staff revealed that all cakes and sweets had been banned from the set of the photo shoot.

Poor Geri. Like so many people with eating disorders, she veered all over the place when explaining what was wrong: one minute she was saved by yoga and the next she was admitting to forcing herself to be sick – when she was eating at all. What remained constant, though, was an obsession with food and her own appearance. 'I have to work out as I put on weight easily and I lose it easily,' she explained in another interview. 'I've abused my body for the past ten years with my eating disorders. It's horrifying. Everyone has that "Does my bum look big in this?" syndrome, but it's how far you take it. I've gone from anorexia to compulsive overeating. When I have a healthy mind I can say, "Yeah girl, you look great."'

And it's a sad indictment of our times that Geri had an overwhelming response from the public when she admitted to her problems. 'The hardest thing for me to achieve in life is balance,' she said. 'My parents were such extremists and that's what I learned from them. Other people have read my book and said, "That's me! I put my finger down my throat, that's me! I binged on food, that's me!"'

If Geri herself recognised that there are many other young women around with eating disorders, then it should have come as no surprise that commentators were becoming increasingly concerned not only with what Geri was doing to herself but with the way in which she was influencing others, especially young children. In March there was a furore when a magazine called *Celebrity Bodies* appeared on the street, designed to give your average woman the body of a young boy – although that's not quite the way the magazine put it. It contented itself with boasting, 'For the first time, all the star diet, fitness, fashion and beauty secrets you want to know are in one magazine. And we don't just tell you what they do, we show you how you can do it, too.' And guess who was on the cover? Yup – one Geri Halliwell.

Health campaigners were outraged, saying that the magazine was specifically aimed at very young girls and could cause considerable problems. 'If the magazine is not aimed at young girls, why do they have a Spice Girl on the cover?' demanded Michelle Elliott, head of children's charity Kidscape. 'The 18 to 25 year old grew up with Geri Halliwell and her new figure is not normal. Why not put the more curvy and natural- looking Kate Winslet on the cover? Magazines like this are unrealistic and encourage dieting that is very harmful, particularly to young women's fertility, which can be drastically affected if a girl becomes too thin.'

She was not alone in voicing her concern. 'The self-esteem of young women is adversely affected by images of non-standard body shapes, particularly on models and actresses,' said Steve Bloomfield of the Eating Disorders Association. 'These people have the time and money to spend on personal training sessions and medical attention, so they can take their diet to the extreme, unlike mere mortals like you and me.'

Even Tessa Jowell, then Minister for Women, had her say. 'It's grim,' she said. 'It will add to the torment that 15-year-old girls already feel.'

It's a fair bet that Geri was feeling some torment herself. Eating problems aside, yoga was not her only form of exercise: she was running six miles a day, power walking uphill and seeing the Norwegian physiotherapist Torje Eike for help in working out a plan for keeping her trim. She was also regularly visiting the Integrated Medical Centre in London for advice on nutrition and homeopathic remedies and was said to have cut out all carbohydrates from her diet. There were also rumours that she'd had liposuction to deal with particularly stubborn pockets of fat.

Geri was, however, going through one of her periods of denial. In May 2001, she gave an interview in which she claimed that her bulimia was now a thing of the past. Asserting that she now ate three meals a day, she said of her new routine, 'I started changing my diet and fitness routine based on how I was feeling at the time, but I had no idea what the end result would be.

'I would gradually alter things or cut things out of

my diet. I'd try to abstain from eating compulsively and got to the position last December where I was having three regular meals and maybe an occasional snack.' Asked if she ever thought she looked too thin, she said she tried not to 'give that sort of thing head space'. And then came a hint of quite how bad the situation actually was. 'My body image can be distorted because of the disease I suffered, so it's best not to examine all of this for my own sake,' she said. 'I'll try to avoid looking at pictures of myself. I leave it up to my stylists and if they think I look OK, I don't worry. For me, what it comes down to is cream cakes. One bite's too much and a thousand is not enough. I can't eat one, I have to eat five. I'm taking this one day at a time. Everyone's got their thing – their addiction – and mine's sugar.'

In another interview with DJ Steve Wright, Geri was more upbeat than ever. 'It's no big secret that I suffered raging eating disorders and I've been on that yo-yo dieting thing of going up-down, up-down. But finally I seem to have cracked it. I eat carbohydrates, I eat porridge, mashed potatoes, sausages and I eat fat. I have lost quite a few pounds, but I'm one of those girls whose weight has always fluctuated. I'd eat a whole loaf of bread and two packets of biscuits and then go down to the gym and try to burn it off. After, I'd go and stuff my face with chocolates. It was ridiculous. It's been finding that balance which is so difficult. I wouldn't want to lose any more weight, though, because I wouldn't want to look like a skeleton, now would I?'

If only it were as straightforward as that. Just a couple of days after that interview, it emerged that Geri was being given injections of vitamins straight into the bloodstream to make up for her avoidance of food. Geri's people sought to play this down. 'She's under an incredibly gruelling schedule and vitamin injections are par for the course for many artists,' said a spokesman. 'Geri would not take anything that would harm her. I imagine that you would have to be taking them a lot before they would start harming you. She's healthier and happier than ever.'

Unfortunately, some in the medical establishment did not agree. 'For a healthy person to be using intravenous vitamins is bizarre and irrational,' said Catherine Collins, chief nutritionist at St George's Hospital in Tooting, south London. 'Under medical supervision, small amounts of injected vitamins and nutrients are beneficial to people with nutritional disorders. But for someone leading an active, healthy lifestyle, a balanced diet and maybe a multi-vitamin tablet would be sufficient. High levels of vitamins and minerals can cause all sorts of problems including liver damage, nausea, dizziness and even have neurological effects.'

Claire MacEvilly of the British Nutrition Foundation agreed. 'Vitamin injections are an extreme and dangerous fad which has come from the US,' she said. 'It's not very popular over here, yet, and hopefully won't take off.'

Even Geri's old friends in the Spice Girls were beginning to worry. 'I have had problems with obsessive training and eating behaviour,' said Mel C. 'It's very worrying, but I think she looks phenomenal – I just hope that she's healthy. I still love her to bits – we all do. We all care a great deal and just hope she's OK.'

And so it went on, until Geri ended up in the Cottonwood Clinic, thinner than ever and with her problems no more resolved than they ever have been. Her appearance has become an obsession, something to be tended to and clucked over with every last bit of energy she has. Geri never wanted to be famous just for being in the Spice Girls, she wanted to be famous in her own right. The problem is that although she has achieved solo success, it has been wrapped up in the public fascination with her appearance and Geri does not want to return to where she once was. She once revealed that, 'I used to have two wardrobes: one for when I was feeling skinny, one for when I was feeling fat. There was no in-between. So when I started to lose weight and wear more of the skinny clothes, I didn't believe I wouldn't swing back up again. But eventually I did it and now I've started to give things away, which is a good feeling.'

Those are hardly the words of a woman who has come to terms with a serious problem and has managed to recover from it. And although it was as the voluptuous Sexy Spice that Geri got the attention she craved from men, it is as Skinny Spice that she wants to continue. And she is not alone: in June 2002, a study by Surrey University revealed that children as young as seven are beginning to worry about their appearance. Up to half the girls aged between seven and 12 were unhappy with their figure, wishing to be slimmer, while a third of boys in the same age range were affected. 'It is surprising how many young children are aware of their body shape and size at such an early age,' said Dr Helen Truby, the psychologist in charge of the study. 'It was believed children didn't develop an adult ideal till puberty.'

Not for the first time, Geri found herself cited as one of the children's more unhealthy role models (as was Victoria) and as such a cause of children dieting too quickly, too much and too young, but the reality is that Geri herself is as much a victim as those children who wish to emulate her. Had she received universal praise for her figure in the guise of Ginger Spice she might have finally learned to live with her curves and even grow to enjoy them, but she didn't: she was told in some quarters that she was fat, and that hurt.

And there is the question of control. Show business is one of the most difficult industries to survive in over the longer term and there is still a big question mark over how long Geri can continue to strike out on her own. Her solo career has been only moderately successful to date and it's hard to imagine Geri Halliwell two decades on still belting it out from the heart. Nor has her acting career yet materialised. It is entirely possible that it will but, like so many of us in less glamorous careers, Geri has only a little bit of control over the future direction of her life. She does, however, have control over what she eats (control of a sorts, that is) and it is that feeling of control that holds so many other overeaters back, as well.

Most of all there is a fundamental lack of confidence that has plagued Geri all her life and which shows no signs of going away. 'Geri is massively insecure,' says clinical psychologist Oliver James. 'She appears to be someone for whom fame itself is more important than what she is famous for. She appears to have very few friends from her pre-Spice days. Her main companions seem to be her siblings and her mother. She seems to be pursuing fame in the hope that it will provide her with the love and sense of control that were missing in her childhood. She claims to have invented the phrase "girl power", yet feels out of control, despite appearing in charge of her life. You cannot help but feel sorry for her.'

True enough, but on a more optimistic note, Geri is in some ways remarkable. From a very unhappy childhood she's clawed her way to a place in the national consciousness, a place she might well have achieved whether or not she was in the Spice Girls. And she's young, rich and attractive, with the resources of the world at her feet should she finally want to deal with her eating disorders once and for all. Let's hope she does. It would be a shame if, having conquered the world, Geri herself was finally brought low by that which we all need to sustain us – food.

8

It's Raining
Men

The great irony when it comes to Geri's eating
disorder is that the cause of all this was a man –
her father. Girl power may have been Ginger Spice's
maxim, but that's not to say men didn't matter. It was
the motto that defined the Spice Girls and paved the
way for their rise to super-stardom but it didn't define
every area of their lives. And the slogan also
epitomised a younger, more carefree Geri than the one
we know now: a flame-haired vixen who wore six-
inch platforms and bright red lipstick. But that Geri
was in fact quite as troubled as the current version of
Geri – and quite as unable to work out her problems.

Without the influence of men, girl power and Ginger Spice would never have existed. Later in the book we tell the real story of the men who created the Spice Girls and started them out on their road to fame, but men have always been an integral part of Geri's life. Geri is a man's girl. She was close to her father and her best friends these days – including Robbie Williams and George Michael – also tend to be men. And men are important in her private life, as well. Geri has had long periods of celibacy – not least because she wanted to guard against the possibility of a kiss-and-tell – but the desire is still there to find Mr Right. And at the time of writing, it looks possible that she may have done so, in the form of Damian Warner, a fellow addict of a different kind. Until now, though, her romantic history has been as complicated as the rest of her life – and that is all because of the man Geri loved first and most. Her father.

It's a widely held belief that a woman's relationship with her father determines the way her future relationships with men will work out and Geri's father was more like a fellow playmate than an authority figure. That might be the reason she tends to look for security and so wants her relationships to develop too quickly, which in turn scares her boyfriends away. In this she's the opposite of Victoria Beckham, who came from a rock-solid background and has since managed to develop a rock-solid relationship. 'He [her father] spoke to me like an old mate he'd met down the pub, and I treated him like a silly boy who should have known better,' she once said. 'I don't think he had any idea how a father should behave because he had no role models. His father had abandoned him and his stepfather had never been particularly close.'

There were flaws in his personality and Geri was the first to admit it. When Molly Dineen comments on a picture of him, saying admiringly, 'He looks like a lovely man,' Geri is quick to add, 'He wasn't completely lovely, but he was sweet in his old age.'

Laurence and Ana Maria split up when Geri was 9 and still at junior school. He moved out to a high-rise council flat in Garston, a rough area of Watford, where Geri would visit him once a week to help clean the flat and listen to his rambling stories. Many of the problems she had later in life – from severe bouts of depression to the period of anorexia that got so bad she was checked into Watford General's psychiatric unit – are attributed to her strained relationship with her father. But this did nothing to deter other suitors. Geri was an attractive child, just as she was to become an attractive woman, and men were drawn to her right from the start.

Her first proper encounter with men came in her late teens, as she later recalled in her autobiography. Indeed, at 16, Geri would appear to be going on 26. Friends from Watford Grammar remember her as 'smart, sassy and gregarious'. But she still had a lot to learn. Sex was a subject her mother rarely discussed openly, instead adopting a traditionally Spanish approach: 'You must be careful of boys because they make you pregnant,' she would warn. Geri might have looked physically mature, but inside she was still inexperienced and cautious about learning any more.

For this reason, when a tipsy Geri – fresh out of secondary school – found herself fumbling in a car park with a 21-year-old friend of her sister Natalie, Andy, she froze. The couple had been to Natalie's 20th birthday party and Andy was giving her a lift home: in time-honoured fashion, Andy parked somewhere discreet and chanced his luck. Geri was having none of it. She allowed him to touch her breasts before scrabbling for the door handle and bolting. Andy: O, Girl Power: 1.

It was only a matter of time, though, before Geri, a hyperactive schoolgirl, was disobeying her mother and staying out all night at raves. Friends, however, believe that beneath the veneer of sophistication lurked a nervous child. Even as an adult Geri, who admits to having an unhealthy obsession with toys and who spends hours roaming through the children's sections of American department stores, has avoided allowing herself to really grow up.

'I'm still 13 in many ways,' she says. 'Emotionally, I'm so underdeveloped but in other ways I'm overdeveloped.' On another occasion she admitted, 'I've been through so much, in some ways I feel a like a 60-year-old woman. But then other times I'm just like a child. I think it's important to always keep the child alive within.' Perhaps this explains her apparent ambivalence towards sex, not to mention an occasional reluctance to commit in an adult relationship – a condition almost certainly made worse by her bulimia.

Geri waited until two months after her 17th birthday – 1 October 1989 – to lose her virginity and describes the event as 'memorable for all the wrong reasons'. Toby was a pale and pasty ex-public schoolboy with a posh accent, whom she had met at a rave in Hertfordshire. After dancing until dawn in 'a muddy field somewhere' he took her back to a borrowed bedsit in west London. The earth may have shook, but not in the way it is supposed to – the trains running past made the windows and the cups in the sink rattle, as she told in her autobiography. Later, Toby admitted he was in love with a girl called

Tamara. It was not an auspicious introduction to the world of romance.

Months later Geri fell in love properly for the first time and it was to prove an unmitigated disaster. The man concerned was called Niam, and she met him at one of her regular haunts, the Café de Paris in London's Leicester Square. The attraction to Niam, who was older than her and sported George Michael designer stubble, was immediate. Niam came from one of the notorious tough clans on the South Oxhey estate in Watford and, unfortunately, also had another girlfriend.

Geri has a tendency to over-romanticise her relationships and this was no different. She went home that night fantasising about gangsters and their women. If Niam was Bugsy Malone, then she wanted to be his Tallulah, she wrote in *If Only*. It was this rampant imagination that was to be the root cause of the failure of many her relationships to follow. Geri was a dreamer, as she has been since childhood. She admits as much herself. The only trouble is that Geri was not always very good at differentiating between fantasy and reality, which would cause problems in the years to come.

The inevitable soon happened: one of Geri's friends spotted Niam with his supposedly ex-girlfriend. Geri decided to issue him with an ultimatum: instead she ended up begging him to stay. Fortunately, perhaps, Niam left her.

Geri's next boyfriend was the polar opposite of Niam: kind, caring, gentle and – above all – there at her every whim. Sean Green, a 20-something businessman from Watford, would ferry his ambitious 19-year-old girlfriend in her racy crop tops and buttock-skimming hotpants from one audition to the next. He would constantly reassure her that she was good enough – better than good enough – that she was brilliant. And it was exactly what Geri needed. She yearned for someone to keep spurring her on, to tell her, 'Today's the day you're going to hit the big time' or 'This audition is going to be your lucky break.' After all, said Geri, no one else was going to.

Sean had rugged Irish looks, dark hair and piercing blue eyes. It was easy to see what Geri saw in him and she also became extremely attached to his family, with whom she stayed in their large Rickmansworth house. 'It was a typical Irish Catholic family. His mum cooked me porridge every morning and made me proper dinners,' she later recalled. But, alas, the relationship was not to last: Geri, like Groucho Marx, had decided she didn't want to be a part of any club that would have her as a member. Sean was besotted, Geri wasn't, and she went on to end the relationship.

Nevertheless, the wounds took some time to heal. While Sean may have been cast to one side in her mind, she clung on to the memory of his family home. It had been a sanctuary for Geri – somewhere she associated with love, warmth and security. And it was that which inspired her to create her own proper home years later, a sprawling country house in Middle Green, Hertfordshire. And in an interview with *Smash Hits* magazine in 1996, she remarked, 'Although you don't feel like you're ever going to meet anyone again, I don't recommend going on the rebound. Throw yourself into your friends and having fun, it can be a really positive thing.' It was certainly a theory that worked for Geri. Except, instead of throwing herself into friends she dived straight into her career – head first.

Men were pushed to one side for a couple of years while the girls got going, but that didn't stop Geri pontificating on the subject of love, albeit very much in the context of girl power. 'The mistake we girls make is we give up too much for our relationships and it's only when you're single again that you start to rediscover parts of your personality which become conditioned by a relationship,' a breathless Geri once said. 'When you are going out with someone, you become half of a person and I think that we expect too much and give too much to our relationships. Breaking up can be really rejuvenating.'

It was around this time, in 1996, when the Spice Girls already had three number one hits under their belt, that Geri met Giovanni Laporta, a double-glazing tycoon from Watford. The pair had been introduced in late-December at a Christmas party thrown by a relative. Giovanni, then 28, a well-respected local businessman, had been a friend of the family for years. What's more, he was wealthy enough not to be after her fortune. He may have been in a four-year relationship at the time – with a 24-year-old hairdresser named Kirsty Almond – and even had a 6-year-old daughter from a previous fling, but neither factor prevented the two from getting together.

'We met, started chatting, and got on extremely well,' he says. 'She was not particularly difficult to get to know, in fact she was refreshingly honest for a world-famous popstar. We are very similar. We are both headstrong, ambitious and stubborn.'

It was also not to last. Geri had quite suddenly become extremely famous and now had a schedule that was taking her all over the world, with very little time to concentrate on personal relationships. Rather more ominously, perhaps, she was also showing a great deal of interest in what was written about her.

'She was obsessed by the newspapers,' says

Giovanni. 'It would have been hard not to be. Every morning she would run out and pore over them one by one, to see what had been written about her. If anyone was nasty about her, she was seriously affected by it.' The situation was not helped by the fact that both Geri and Giovanni were extremely stubborn by nature, with neither prepared to budge. The couple split, although Giovanni still talks fondly about his ex. 'She is a very special girl with a smile that lit up the room,' he says. 'But she wasn't all looks and no brain. Geri was really smart and knew exactly what she wanted.'

What she wanted included a faithful boyfriend and Geri was not pleased when she read about his secret rendezvous with former girlfriend Kirsty in one of the tabloids. She was furious – and subsequently denied ever sleeping with Giovanni. 'But instead of confronting me about it,' says Giovanni, 'she left without ever knowing the whole truth. The newspapers manipulated the situation I was in to make it look like I was having an affair, when I wasn't.'

Whatever the truth of it, Geri didn't waste time, penning a note to her ex to tell him it was all over. 'Dear Gio,' she wrote, 'I want us to still be friends. I think it's better for both of us to do our own thing. G.'

'She is a sharp girl,' says Giovanni. 'A lot of people underestimate her intelligence. These days, we see each other out every now and then, but we never stop and talk. I am confident we'll patch things up eventually, but the papers said a lot of really hurtful things and Geri doesn't forget in a hurry.'

By mid-1997 Geri was beginning to learn just how restrictive fame could be. She had very little time to meet someone new and, even if she did meet someone special, how could she be sure they wouldn't run to the papers the minute things got messy? She had already been the subject of numerous kiss-and-tell stories and the idea of being splashed across the front pages with yet another virtual stranger was too much to bear. So, she continued on the Spice Girls conveyor belt: meeting fans, blowing air kisses to a crowd of onlookers, smiling cheekily for the cameras and then going back to her hotel room – alone.

That was until New Year's Eve 1998, when Geri and her sister Natalie found a fairytale castle in County Wicklow, Ireland, to rent for the holidays. The owner was living in a separate wing of the castle and had invited guests to stay for the weekend, a group which included a young polo player called Jamie Morrison. Geri fell for him straight away. In fact, as she was to do again, she rushed into the relationship rather too quickly.

Geri was so smitten that, the following month, she flew out to Zurich to stay with Jamie for a romantic weekend in St Moritz. The pair went ice-skating together and drank hot chocolate. They looked, to the papers, like a couple in love. 'Geri Loves Mr Polo' screamed the headlines.

But, in what was to become a pattern in Geri's life, the affair was over before Valentine's Day. 'My Christmas romance syndrome had struck again,' she confided. 'Jamie was lovely, but he was only 21 and we had little in common.'

Things began to look up in February 1998, when the Spice Girls embarked on their European tour. Geri was, once again, besotted – this time, with her very own Spice Boy: a young backing dancer called Christian Horsfall (or Storm, to use his professional surname). The atmosphere on tour was very close knit, with everyone involved spending hours rehearsing and performing, before relaxing together in the evenings. Geri – like Mel B, who was becoming involved with the dancer Jimmy Gulzar – thought she had met her man.

And indeed, in 24-year-old Christian, Geri had at last found a man who could relate to her. After all, he knew what it was to get up on stage every night in front of thousands of screaming fans. The pair were reported to be 'inseparable' in the following weeks during the tour and, when they returned, Geri showed her devotion by visiting his Grimsby home to meet Mr and Mrs Horsfall, Christian's delighted parents.

The relationship seemed to strengthen. When she quit the band that summer – in May 1998 – Christian was the first to jet out to keep her company while she hid out at George Michael's south of France villa, which made it all the more unexpected when they split up a couple of months later in July. Geri was devastated, not least because it was only a matter of months before Christian began dating rival girl band singer Shaznay Lewis from All Saints.

There were other men in her life, though, in a manner of speaking: a dog (Harry), gay friends (George and Kenny) and children (her nephew Alastair). But rarely was there a stable boyfriend. Between 1998 and 2000, as we have already written, Geri was linked to two men: Chris Evans and Robbie Williams. Both affairs were conducted in full view of the cameras and happened to take place at the very time everyone involved had something to plug. Few could honestly believe Geri had found her love match. It all seemed too contrived.

As for a boyfriend, Geri claimed all she was doing was cyberdating. She admitted to logging on to Internet chat rooms to look for virtual love whenever she had some free time. She would convince herself that this was all she needed, saying, 'That's safe sex, isn't it? They ask me what I look like and I tell them I'm quite little, with blonde hair and big boobs – a bit like Geri Halliwell.'

This lonely and cautious approach to life was a far cry from the happy, bubbly, confident girl who had pinched Prince Charles's bottom a couple of years earlier. It was the final nail in the coffin for tired old Ginger Spice. Still, fans were desperate to see the return of fun-loving Saucy Spice – and would believe almost anything. In December 2000, Geri met Steve Nash, a US basketball ace. She was spotted lunching with the giant £3-million-a-year NBA defender, giving the papers enough reason to assume she had met her love match.

She hadn't. Here were the facts: Geri had been in the States solidly for three months while she worked to complete her second solo album, due out in the spring. She had become a regular at Mavericks' games and had even been spotted wearing the Canadian-born player's No 13 jersey. She would make trips to watch the slam dunk star and afterwards the pair would be spotted together at one of the city's restaurants.

Friends said the pair's friendship had 'blossomed'. One friend commented on their height: 'The difference is striking … but people always say size doesn't matter,' while another said, 'They seem very happy indeed together and that's the main thing.'

Everyone wanted to believe Geri had found true love. Readers enjoyed speculating on the so-called romance. But the pairing was unlikely, as Nash himself made clear. He had been seeing someone else the whole time, saying 'We're just having fun.' They really were just friends, with only the hopelessly optimistic (as far as Geri's romantic future was concerned) linking the two together.

In March 2001 Geri finally put paid to the Robbie fling rumours and revealed on Channel Four's *So Graham Norton* that she was 'not getting any'. The singer told Norton she was 'abstaining' from sex for a while – and this just a week after Robbie had apologised for giving the impression he was sleeping with Geri. 'You can tell I'm not getting any, I just can't stop talking about it,' said Geri brightly.

By an extraordinary coincidence, Geri was at the time promoting her new single 'It's Raining Men'. The irony was lost on no one, least of all Geri. 'I'm abstaining from sex for the minute,' she repeated on another occasion, for the benefit of those who hadn't heard it the first time around. 'Yes, I've decided just for a little while.'

She continued on a similar theme weeks later, stepping off stage from a raunchy live performance of 'It's Raining Men' in Manchester to pronounce herself 'a sort of slim, shady character'. She added, 'When I go up on stage, that kind of hip-gyrating thing and all those little sexual moves that go on are not actually me. Deep down I'm not actually like that. I would freak.'

One song on *Scream If You Wanna Go Faster* is called 'Feels Like Sex'. But even that, according to Geri, was not really about sex. Explaining the lyrics, 'If the mood is rude, then you've got the right attitude, you better get down, you don't have to get undressed, just because it feels like sex,' she said, 'You know when you get on top of someone, but you keep your clothes on? To me, that's sexier. For me the anticipation of what's to come is far sexier, and it's safe sex as well.'

Sex, rather like Geri's boyfriends, had become something she talked a lot to the press about, but not because she was getting very much of it. Geri – the only Spice Girl with a past that involved soft porn magazines, topless magazines and go-go dancing – had, rather ironically, become a born-again virgin. She spoke out again about her 'years in the sexual wilderness' in 2001, in an interview with GQ. 'Although I understand sex for the sake of sex. It could and it can satisfy me but the problem with women is that our organs are on the inside, so sex is more internalised and emotional. And I do feel sorry for men.'

Talking of her celibacy she added, 'It wasn't enforced. But I'd rather have a meal than a cracker. Without going into detail about my sex life, I believe in quality not quantity. I go in fits and spurts. All or nothing. Anticipation and imagination are everything. Sex is in the head.'

But there may have been more basic reasons why Geri had been turned off sex – namely, her eating disorder. Steve Bloomfield from the Eating Disorders Association points out that those who are underweight lose their sexual appetite because of a lack of oestrogen produced by the body. Geri's body mass was by now massively below average – at the time of writing she was down to a lower weight than when she was just 12 years old – so it's not unlikely that she has regressed in sexual maturity, also.

Pop commentator Rick Sky has another theory about Geri's virtually non-existent love life. 'It is doubtful that she will ever find true love with a man because she seems pretty satisfied without it,' he says. 'She has fame instead. She may voice regrets about not being able to find "the one" but in truth she has made a conscious decision to replace love from one person for love from the masses – her fans.'

There was a short burst of activity in October 2001, when Geri fell for coffee tycoon Bobby Hashemi, who founded Coffee Republic and is now reputedly worth £45 million. The pair were spotted leaving London's famous Claridge's Hotel one morning, which alerted the world to the romance with Bobby, a polo-playing former New York investment banker. It was a happy few months: Geri was wined and dined at famous London restaurants such as San Lorenzo and The Ivy by the 37-year-old Hashemi – and often stayed at his luxury £3,000-a-week Claridge's suite.

The couple had been introduced by Bobby's sister, Sahar, who shared a yoga instructor with Geri, and for a short time it looked as if Bobby might be the one. Keen to adopt her new boyfriend's interests, Geri took polo lessons and went to watch him play with his team Java at Cowdray Park in Sussex. But again it was not to last, not least because Geri wanted the relationship to develop too quickly and wanted to move in with Bobby.

Of course, the opposite happened and within three months the relationship was over. Friends reported a series of heated rows, one friend confiding, 'Bobby liked the slow pace of the relationship and was horrified that Geri wanted to speed things up. Moving in together is a big step, especially when they've only been together three months. Bobby wants to see how things go before making a commitment. He's always been honest about these things and will continue to speak his mind.' For her part, Geri declared her shih-tzu, Harry, was 'more reliable than any man'.

She got over it. To cheer herself up, Geri went on holiday to Africa with Nina Campbell and Nina's daughter Alice, while a friend of Geri's said, 'It all finished over Christmas. The relationship just wasn't going anywhere, so Geri decided to end it. It was hard at first but Geri's over it now and they are still friends.'

By May 2002 Geri was at one of the most vulnerable points of her career, if not her entire life. She had completely pushed the other four Spices out of her life and managed to upset or infuriate many of her closest friends. Even her trusty personal assistant, Tor Williamson, had quit her job and waved goodbye to Geri's rollercoaster life in favour of settling down to start a family of her own.

With her eating disorder spiralling out of control, it wasn't long before a desperate Geri, who had been working on a variety of projects in Los Angeles, checked into the Cottonwood de Tucson clinic,

Arizona. It was nearing the end of April 2002 and George Michael had distanced himself from Geri, deeming her 'too interested' in garnering publicity. Almost on cue, Geri was to pick up a new soul mate. Step forth Damian Warner, playboy and fellow patient – in his case, for drug addiction.

Geri's love life may have long played second fiddle to her musical career, but now that her music career was beginning to lag she had all the time in the world to spend cavorting in the sunshine with the 26-year-old playboy. The pair met in the clinic where he was receiving counselling for drug problems. Geri supported him and when they eventually left the clinic, the pair spent three days at a nearby hotel where they were frequently spotted laughing and kissing.

Geri, if the pictures of her looking radiant revealed anything, was besotted with her new boyfriend. At the time of writing, the couple are still together and there are rumours that the relationship is becoming serious. There is a possibility they will live together although marriage is not yet on the cards.

And it is just possible that Damian really is the right man for Geri – as long as he can put his womanising past to one side. Like Geri, he's an addict, which means that he has at least a small chance of understanding her obsession with food. At the height of her friendship with Robbie Williams, Geri supported him in his battle with alcohol, because she, too, knew what it was like to be in thrall to an external force. Perhaps Damian can do the same for Geri and lead her to a love match, at last.

9

You Must Have Been a Beautiful Baby ...

Geraldine Estelle Halliwell was born on 6 August 1972 in Watford General Hospital. A self-proclaimed 'mongrel', Geri was the daughter of Laurence Francis Halliwell, a Liverpool-born car dealer who turned 50 just six days after Geri's birth, and Ana Maria Hidalgo, a Spanish-born nanny 23 years Laurence's junior. The marriage was to prove a tempestuous one: what started out as a passionate love affair turned into a series of rows, disillusionment and divorce. It was a difficult atmosphere in which to grow up – and it was this background which made Geri determined to escape and establish herself as a world-famous star.

Ana, too, had expected something more. Born in Huesca, northern Spain in 1948, Ana was one of seven children and left home at just 17 to work in a factory in Switzerland, before moving on to become an au pair. A very striking woman, she moved to London shortly afterwards with the intention of becoming a nanny, but met and married Laurence almost immediately, before giving birth to the couple's three children. It later emerged that she had not realised exactly what she was taking on when she came to tie the knot.

'My dad was a car dealer from Liverpool,' Geri later recalled. 'His mum had an affair with a Swede and my dad was born. But then she married a Mr Halliwell. My dad could have been a rich man. He was a bit of an entrepreneur but he was lazy. He met my mother when he was walking around in London and she'd just come over to be a nanny. She was 18 years old and she'd never even seen the sea. He'd been married before and divorced. He already had two children but he chatted her up in the street. He made out to her that he was something he wasn't: some rich guy. Her eyes lit up and she thought, Yeah.

They only knew each other for three months before they got married. He was 23 years older than her but he lied about that as well and she didn't find out his real age until they got to the registry office.'

Laurence was not an obvious choice as husband for a naïve young girl from Spain. He'd been born in Liverpool in 1922, before moving to London with his family when he was still a young child. He left school early and went on to become an engineer at RAF Northolt at the beginning of World War II, later setting up his own car dealership in Watford. As Geri said, he'd been married once before meeting Ana, producing two half-siblings for Geri: Paul and Karen Halliwell, who were both in their late twenties when Geri was born. Geri became close to Karen and it was her much older sister that she turned to when her eating disorder first manifested itself in 1994. And it was Karen who persuaded her to check in to Watford General's psychiatric ward. She also rented a room in Karen's house for some time in her turbulent teenage years as Karen tried to help her wrestle the demons that blighted her life even as a child.

Geri is the youngest of three children from her father's second marriage. Her eldest full sibling is Max Halliwell, who was born in 1967, five years before Geri. The only member of the family to attend university, Max married Susan in 1991 – Geri flew over from Majorca to be a bridesmaid – and lives with her in Berkhamstead, Hertfordshire. Natalie Halliwell came along two years later: she married in 1990 and has a son called Alastair, who was born in 1995. Geri describes herself as a true mix of both parents, with her mousy brown hair flecked with red, whereas Max is blond, like his late father, and Natalie is dark like Ana. She was tiny as a child, nicknamed 'la enana' – the dwarf by her Spanish aunts. In fact, Geri is still tiny: even at her most voluptuous it was her personality, rather than her physique, that could easily fill a large room.

Like so many people who become famous and successful in later life, Geri did not have a happy childhood. Apart from the rows between her parents – Geri once described cups of tea and plates of spaghetti flying across the room – there was little money around and her mother was finally forced to go to work as a cleaner when Geri was six. 'It was tough on her because my father was not a reliable character,' said Geri. 'She was going out to work every day and trying to control us three kids. She was quite temperamental and domineering. If I did something wrong, I knew I'd be in big trouble when I got home.

'My sister and brother and I were left to our own

devices. We'd fight but if any one of us grassed to my mother we got hit. I used to fend for myself, make my own peanut-butter sandwiches. I'd put my own bunches in my hair and get myself ready for school. I'd go home and nobody would be there and I'd make my own dinner. So I've always had to provide for myself. It had a massive effect. I was a latchkey kid but I don't say that in a self-pitying way.'

Food played a role in Geri's life right from the start. Apart from making those peanut-butter sandwiches, as a child she loathed vegetables, but was forced to eat them by her mother: she would spit them out, be forced to eat them again and have her jaw held shut by her mother as she chomped. For a woman who grew to have such a difficult relationship with food, this was not the most auspicious of beginnings.

Ana was born a Catholic, but when Geri was still young she became a Jehovah's Witness, a conversion that still echoes in Geri's life. And no matter how reasonably she talks about it today, as a child it must have been extremely difficult for young Geri. Children want to fit in with everyone around them and to be accepted as normal: any perceived eccentricity can cause agonies for even the toughest of children. 'My mother joined the Jehovah's Witnesses for a while and they don't celebrate birthdays or Christmas,' Geri said much later on.

'It was a bit embarrassing as a little kid because things like that really matter, don't they? Kids can be cruel. When everyone else said, "Look what I got for Christmas," I kept quiet. Christmas was an ordinary day for us, nothing happened.

'We didn't get any presents and we didn't have birthday parties. Now I find birthdays a great pressure. Isn't that ironic? I don't like them and I don't like everybody looking at me and all the fuss. I never want to be enslaved by materialism. I think that's the trap so many people are in. Money doesn't make you happy. It can set you free and pay all the medical bills. It gets you from one place to another in better style, but it's all relative. If I see greed in someone, it makes me feel sick.'

The experience was difficult for Geri in very many ways. 'Mum used to take me from door to door saying, "The end is near",' she once said. 'It was a bit embarrassing. We also had to sit quietly during hours of preaching sessions at Kingdom Hall and that was murderous. I didn't start getting presents until I was about 14, when Mum left the church.'

Ana, meanwhile, felt thoroughly disillusioned by the whole experience. 'My expectations were too high,' she explained. 'They were a bunch of hypocrites who were just as materialistic and greedy as the rest of us.'

Even so, Geri knew from early on that she wanted to escape Jubilee Road, Watford and the two-up, two-down house in which she spent her entire childhood. Right from the beginning she displayed the exhibitionist tendencies which were to lead her to become one of the most vociferous members of the most successful girl band in the world – and had her father had her way, Geri might have become a star when she was just a child. Given that Geri has her fair share of psychological problems as it is, however, and taken with the fact that many erstwhile child stars suffer as adults, it is probably fortunate for Geri that her mother took a dim view of the matter. 'I never went to stage school but I was an attention grabber,' said Geri.

'My mother used to clean at Watford College. She had to polish all the floors. There's a huge library, with big tables and mirrors. She'd be working away at one end of the library and I'd get on top of the table and sing in front of the mirror. I was always a daddy's girl and, because he could see talent in me, he took me to an agent who said she'd get me work. But my mother was strict – she wouldn't let me do it and that was that. But it drove me on. I believe in Oscar Wilde's philosophy that the only way to cure temptation is to yield to it. The more you suppress something, the more you want to do it. I'm living proof that it's the truth, really.'

Geri's mother was certainly not happy about her daughter's desire for the limelight. 'I never pushed the children to become famous. That has come from her,' she said in Molly Dineen's documentary. 'I used to tell her to stop it. I used reverse psychology. I hated it because her father, without my permission, took her to an agency – you know, one of those talented children's agencies. She was eight years old. I went crazy. Actually, I freaked out. I went for his head.

'You know, some parents are very pushy because they see money there, an investment. I see a child. You need to be a child first. If you see talent, it can wait – it will catch up later. So always with Geri I tried to stop it. I said, "When you're older you can do what you want." And she did. She was like a volcano ready to explode!'

She certainly was. Geri once said, 'I don't know what I'm doing, but I'm damn well going to do it!' – something that would appear to have been her philosophy right from the word go.

Her brother Max confirmed as much. 'As a toddler she wasn't that much different to the rest of us, but eventually it became clear that Geri would be well suited to show business,' he said. 'At school she was quiet and got on with her work but at home she would always be singing at the top of her voice and

192

dancing. She had one favourite song which ran, "I wannabe a night club queen, the most exciting you've ever seen".' So there you have it. A wannabe right from the start …

In fact, it was from her father that Geri initially got both her love of music and the drive to see it through. 'Dad adored jazz and female voices,' said Max. 'The house would always be full of Shirley Bassey, the Three Degrees and The Supremes. Geri loved it all. When she was at Watford Girls' Grammar and aged about 11 she did a one-off show there, a kind of school production. Afterwards, some of the girls had a go at her. They said, "Who do you think you are?"

'She came home very upset but Dad calmed her down. He told her she could do whatever she wanted, that she could achieve anything if she wanted it enough. He didn't care what anyone thought about him and Geri came to take on the same philosophy. I think things really sparked for them when Geri began performing naturally. Deep down, he shared a great deal with Geri. And they were both chancers. That came naturally to both of them.'

It was not all bad: the family would occasionally make trips to English seaside resorts and during the summer Ana would take the three children to visit their Spanish relatives, while Laurence stayed at home. Geri has always been aware of both sides of her parentage – hence later songs such as 'Mi Chico Latino' – as her mother was always determined to teach her children that they were as much Spanish as they were English. On another occasion Geri went on a school trip to Ibiza and Laurence came along to help the teachers: one later remarked that Laurence and Geri needed more looking after than everyone else put together. Whatever his other faults, Laurence certainly doted on Geri: despite the lack of money he would buy her the odd present and once even built her a doll's house. Geri has been obsessed by toys since then: they remind her both of what she lacked in childhood and what her father would strive to give her.

In the Dineen documentary, Geri is pictured in the toy section of an American department store. 'We all want to be a fairy, don't we?' she says, pointing to a little girl's fairy outfit. 'What are we doing here?' asks an understandably confused Molly. 'I love toys. I love it,' Geri replied. 'I know why it is, I've looked into it psychologically. It's because, when I was a little kid I didn't have too many. I had a doll's house my dad made me, but we didn't have Christmas or birthdays when I was a child because Mum was a Jehovah's Witness for a couple of years and also we were so poor we just went to jumble sales.'

Poor Geri. All things considered, it's a wonder she turned out as normal as she did. Her entire adult life has been about escaping the unhappiness of her childhood: the lack of money, the lack of presents and – ironically – the lack of normality. Geri was marked out to stand aside from the crowd from the start – her mixed heritage, her mother's religion and the fact that her parents could not maintain a happy relationship all meant that Geri was never going to be like the majority of little girls. Above all, though, what Geri wanted to escape was the tedium of her existence: the boring little two-up two-down in a rather bland town north of London. Geri did not want to live the life she was born to: she was prepared to go all-out to be a star.

That was in the future, though. Home life was tough and it became more so when Geri's parents separated. She was only nine. Ana had pretty much taken on all responsibility for the family right from the moment she married Laurence and now there was to be no pretence at all that Geri's feckless father was able to look after his clan.

'We stayed with my mum while Dad lived in a flat nearby,' Geri recalled – Laurence had moved into a council flat in Garston. 'He had a bad hip and didn't work from the day I was born. Right from the beginning my mother just got on with it, basically. She's a resilient woman. I was very needy, always wanting confirmation that I was loved. I was that insecure.

'He'd tell me marvellous stories about how in Liverpool during the war they sold bikes to the Americans because there was petrol rationing. And he talked to me about all his female conquests. He was a total rogue, a ladykiller. He could always get women. But it kind of made him more endearing. He always had lady friends and he still had his testosterone going when he was elderly. Actually, my father was very liberated before his time.'

Laurence adored his lively youngest child, but he was also something of an eccentric, who ended up in a high-rise flat that overlooked the M1. 'He was divorced and lived alone,' recalled Doreen Andrews, a former neighbour. 'He was a bit weird. We could see his kitchen from our flat and I would often say to my husband, "Look. There's Laurie walking around with nothing on again."'

As for Geri, despite the disruption in her life, she was sympathetic to her parents' plight. Indeed, she understood it – particularly that of her mother. Like Geri, her parents wanted to achieve something with their lives, but unlike Geri, they were not able to do so. 'Both my parents seemed to be full of disappointment,' she said. 'I think Dad did truly love

her, but she lost respect for him. The bitterness
started and they began draining each other's energy.'
It was a difficult situation for the adults, but even
more so for the children, who were to learn early on
that it is only too easy to end up dissatisfied with life.

Geri was very attached to both parents, and this
comes through in the Dineen documentary, in which
she is seen fussing over her mother. 'I would hate my
mother to get famous,' she said. 'Like one of those
celebrity mums. I want my mother to remain my
mother. She sees my restlessness. My mother can
spot that. She came to me the other morning and
said, "Wake up, Geri." I thought, I really do love you
actually. Then I had this horrible horror, because I
had just begun to love my father and then he died. I
thought, Oh my God, one day my mother's going to
die. That is quite scary, realising that eventually
you're going to be alone.'

She might not have turned out to be overtly
academic as an adult but Geri was a bright child:
after attending Callowland Infant School from 1977
to 1980 and Walter de Merton junior school from
1980 to 1985, she passed the 11-plus, which led her
to a place in Watford Girls' Grammar School from
1985 to 1988, while Max and Natalie both attended
Leggatts, a mixed local comprehensive school. She
had only been allowed to try for Watford Grammar

by dint of much pleading with her mother, but Geri was not really happy. She felt she fitted in neither at school nor at home. 'As a child, sometimes I was sure I was adopted and my real mother was a princess who would come and get me one day,' she said. 'Once I saw a picture of a model in C&A and thought, Yes, that's my real mother. I thought everyone was better off than me. I imagined they were all living a fantasy life with a perfect family.'

Fantasy played a big part in Geri's childhood and continued to do so when she became an adult. In her autobiography, she admits inventing tales to make herself sound more interesting.

These habits persisted in later years. When the Spice Girls first became famous, rumours circulated to the effect that Geri was descended from the Spanish aristocracy. 'That was one of my little white lies to make myself sound more glamorous,' Geri admitted later on. 'It was the same with the *Halliwell's Film Guide*. When I went for interviews for stage jobs I used to say the chap who wrote it was my great-uncle. All my survival instincts are products of my environment. I'm nothing special. I perceive myself as just a reflection of society. There is no such thing as a two point two children household with a washing machine and Labrador. There are so many kids out there exactly the same as me.' Geri was being disingenuous. It is true to say there really is only one Geri Halliwell.

When Geri was in her mid-teens, her world changed dramatically for one very good reason: she discovered music and particularly Madonna, who – appropriately enough – became Geri's idol. Madonna was another woman of limited musical ability who was determined, come what may, to escape a difficult background. Like Geri she lost a parent early on – although in Madonna's case it was very early on, as her mother died when she was only six – and like Geri she wasn't too fussy about what she had to do to get noticed. Both started out doing nude modelling and both were to experiment with many changes of image throughout their careers. Funnily enough, they are even physically quite similar: both are tiny, both have naturally mousy brown hair and both are obsessed with their bodies.

And, above all, both found an escape from their background through music. 'When she discovered her love of music, she didn't really look back,' said Geri's brother Max. 'And by the time she hit 16, her world changed completely. Virtually overnight, she began revelling in dance and club scenes. It was an instant transformation. It was like a switch had been pulled. Geri went absolutely wild. The world suddenly opened up for her and she didn't look back.' Indeed it did. Geri attended the first ever illegal rave to be held in this country in a field near Elstree, Hertfordshire, after which she spent a blissful summer partying at raves all across the country. It was a world away from her repressed home life, from the tedium of a small-town existence and from the rows that marred her parents' marriage. It was Geri's first taste of freedom and she loved every minute of it.

That summer marked a turning point in a number of ways. Just before her rave-driven existence began, to her mother's delight Geri got a job as a receptionist in the Olympia Hilton Hotel in west London. This was real respectability. Geri did not enjoy it, though, and quit soon afterwards. Ana was livid when she found out that Geri had left what she considered to be a prestigious job and the two had a fierce row: Geri eventually walked out of the house and went to live with her father. This in turn lasted only a short time: Geri took Laurence's car out without permission and scraped it. The resulting row ended with Geri going to rent a room from her half-sister Karen in a house that Karen owned on Queen's Road, Watford.

'It was all pretty quiet until she hit 16 and then she blossomed,' said Max. 'She hared around the place and for six months, when she was around 17, she went to live with Dad. Dad hardly knew what she would be getting up to next. Once she came back home in the early hours after a party with a friend and they decided to go on to a rave in London. They couldn't afford a taxi fare so they "borrowed" Dad's car and raced off. The next morning he saw the car had gone. So he called the police. Just as they were leaving the house, Geri and her friend arrived back, minus a headlamp. She saw the police and asked what was going on and Dad told her he was reporting her. She was worried sick. But he made her sweat for about a week before letting her off the hook. I think she paid for a new headlamp, though.'

On another occasion, Geri came up with the bright idea of painting everything in her father's flat black. 'Dad exploded,' said Max. 'He couldn't believe his eyes. Everything was dripping with black paint. Geri simply said that black was more fashionable. Eventually he became resigned to the new colour scheme. Typically, she got away with it.'

By this time Geri had left school with eight 'O'-levels and had started a two-year course at Cassio College, Watford in travel, tourism and finance. She was not really sure what she wanted to do, though, and quit after just one year, but this was not her last shot at further education: in 1991–92 Geri took a beginners' ballet class for men and women one evening a week at Cassio and also embarked on a three-night-a-week 'A'-level Drama course. She later transferred to an 'Introduction to Psychology' one-year course. Then in 1993 Geri began an intensive one-year 'A'-level English Literature and Language course. It was a three-hour lesson, one day a week at Cassio College, Watford. Shirley Russel, who is now retired and still lives in Watford, taught her.

'I was genuinely shocked when I first spotted Geri in the papers,' she says, and her description of the young Geri goes a long way towards explaining the woman Geri is today. 'She was a bright, caring girl with plenty of vitality and enthusiasm, but her academic skills weren't up to much. I never expected her to go so far. I'm extremely surprised she got where she is because to me she's just an ordinary kid. I suppose it's all the marketing people they took on.

'She never came across as materialistic and I'm sure she was never in it for the loot because money didn't appear to bother her. What surprised me more than anything was seeing her as a Spice Girl, because in class she always looked so natural, with barely any make-up and fairly average dress sense.

'The only thing that distinguished her was the fact that her phone was always going off. Few people carried mobile phones in those days, but Geri insisted on keeping hers on in class. I'd say, "Geri, for goodness sake, turn that phone off." But somehow you couldn't be too annoyed with her, she was very disarming. In retrospect, I can see that it was probably because she was waiting for her agent to call or something, but at the time I had absolutely no idea she was trying to break into show business. I later learned she was working as a Turkish game show hostess at the time, but you simply would never have known.

'It was a part-time course, three hours a week. Geri wasn't at all disruptive in class; in fact, she was much more idealistic and more serious-minded than most of the other students. She would speak at length if you let her about world problems and was really very earnest. She is intelligent, I'm sure – nobody can take such a wide interest in world issues as she did without a degree of intelligence – but she simply wasn't academic.

'I think she was extremely bright and she clearly cared about people a lot. It came as no surprise to me that she became a UN ambassador, because, to me, that is the ideal job for her. It suited her, because even in class she used to preach. She didn't know an awful lot about world issues but she was keen to learn about them. Any chance she got, she would extend a topic of discussion to somebody in the Third World or people in poverty – and sometimes

I'd have to tell her off for veering off the subject. But, generally, it was difficult to get cross with her.

'I always smile when I see photographs of her because I think, I know she's a really nice kid, whatever anyone says about her. She deserves to be respected I think and it's a shame that she's not. A lot of people snipe at her but you've got to admire her enthusiasm. She usually got her homework in on time, but she was better at personal relations than college work. She got an E, which is the lowest pass rate, and her grammar and spelling were a little weak. It was obvious she'd never get an A or a B.'

It could almost be the Geri of today: eager to learn, eager to preach, eager for self-improvement but with an occasional shaky grasp of the actual facts and figures. Then again, Geri's extra-curricular activities were beginning to take up a lot of her time by that point, which may well be one reason she didn't excel academically. She was having too much fun.

Geri's sister Natalie also testified that her younger sister could be a handful when she was a teenager, to the extent that the two sisters would actually fight one another physically when arguments broke out. When the official history of the Spice Girls, *Real Life, Real Spice*, came out in 1997, Natalie wrote, 'When she was 15 or 16, Geri was a bit of a wild child – a bit uncontrollable. The worst fight we ever had was in

Spain when the two of us went to a bar where she fancied the barman. The only way she could get his attention was by ordering drinks. We had about six beers lined up in front of us. She couldn't drink them but she kept ordering more. She kept telling him how much she fancied him, but he wasn't interested.

'I dragged her out and told her to stop, because she was acting like an idiot. She swore at me and stormed off back to my auntie's flat down the street. I walked home about 200 yards behind her and when we got there we had this massive fight which Geri started. She waited until I was taking my jeans off and they were around my ankles, so I couldn't move very well. Then she pounced on me and started hitting me. I hit her back and soon we were rolling around on the floor. She bit my calf really hard and drew blood and we tried to strangle each other. When our brother Max came in, we were both lying on the floor exhausted. He said, "Oh my God, what the hell's going on?" We were black and blue.'

In many ways, this actually foreshadows the rows Geri was to go on to have with Mel B when the two fought each other for dominance within the Spice Girls – although they never quite managed to beat one another black and blue.

When not attempting to murder one another, the sisters were actually very close. Natalie stuck up for young Geri when she was showing off and shared her initiation in the art of kissing. 'I gave her advice about boys and stuff,' she wrote. 'The first time I kissed a boy I came straight home and ran up the stairs and said to Geri, "Guess what? I've kissed a boy!" She said, "Really? What was it like?" And I said, "Oh, it's a bit slobbery, actually. I had to wipe my mouth with the back of my hand afterwards."

'We've been lucky to be able to share all our secrets with each other. We even went out with the same guy – at different times, though. When we see him now, we still laugh. We both left home as soon as we could at 16. I went to work in Ibiza as a kiddie club rep and Geri rented a room in Watford from our older half-sister, Karen. Once Geri threw a party. You've never seen anything like it. It was just a little end-of-terrace house, but she had 150 to 200 people there, squashed into all the rooms. There were police circling the road and the house was a wreck. It was a really wild party.'

And Geri really had entered a wild phase. She was out on her own now, an independent woman who had broken away from Watford and her mother and who was out to experience life in the raw. Geri was still very young, it was the end of the 1980s – and for all her Labour Party endorsements, Geri adored Margaret Thatcher – and there was everything to play for. The only trouble was that Geri was not entirely sure what she wanted to do. She was interested in music, yes, but was not the most talented singer in the world. Those ballet classes apart, she'd had no training as a dancer. She was thinking about breaking into television but was not sure if that was the right move forward – what was a girl to do? The answer, when it came, was quite simple. Geri would do everything – and then some.

10

Wild
Child

By 1989, with the Spice Girls still just a gleam in the eyes of the marketing men, Geri was desperate to get noticed and she didn't care how she went about it. And so she embarked upon a series of career choices that were to come back to haunt her once she made it to the big time – although, typically for Geri, she was able to laugh them off. Many a star would have been devastated by a series of topless photos coming to light once they were internationally famous, but Geri was blasé and matter-of-fact about it all.

It was when Geri was in the middle of her tourism

course that she really decided that life had to hold something more. 'I thought, Hold on a minute, you only have one life. You've got to get out there to fulfil your dreams, she said. So she did. 'I'm like Dick Whittington – I get a vision and that's it.'

Geri was a striking girl even then, and it was her looks that began to get her noticed. She got a job at Video Collection, a Watford-based company that checked the classification of videos, by day but by night she was frequently to be seen at the Game Bird pub in Bushey, and at London clubs including the Crazy Club, Café de Paris, the Wag and the Ministry of Sound. In fact, by now she was clubbing regularly and opportunities began to present themselves. 'People started saying, "Do you want to be in this video and do you want to come to dance?" They were paying me £40 to dance every Saturday night at London's Astoria. It was just spontaneous, club freestyle dancing.'

In May 1990, Laurence had a mild stroke but by then he was devoting himself to Geri, as it became increasingly obvious quite how much the two had in common. 'Geri once had an audition near Heathrow and told Dad one hour before she was due on stage that she needed a lift,' Max recalled. 'They found themselves in a massive motorway jam and Geri was bouncing around saying she was going to be late. So she told Dad to drive all the way up the hard shoulder to get to the place on time and insisted that if they were stopped, she'd sort it out. Inevitably, they came screeching up to a police car. Without hesitating, she told Dad to take frequent pulls on his asthma inhaler. The police took one look at the scene and waved them on. Geri and Dad both thought the whole thing was hilarious. Of course, she got to the audition on time.'

Geri and Laurence were becoming closer and closer as time went on. 'The two shared something special, she was the youngest and he pretty much devoted his retirement years to helping her attain her ambitions,' said Max. 'That's not to say she couldn't have done it on her own, or that he did not show equal affection to us all. But as her brother, I can see the similarities between the two. His personality explains a lot about who Geri is and what she wants from her own life.'

Geri was getting wilder. She was a squatter now: her boyfriend Niam's sister Mary had helped Geri to smash a window in a granny cottage on the South Oxhey council estate and Geri had moved in, fixing the curtains and cleaning the bathroom, before being summoned to court and then evicted. She continued to try for everything she could: she was by now working for a promotion agency in Watford that provided staff for exhibitions and conferences and it was at this time she was first asked to pose topless. Geri had been to a photographer to get pictures to go with her CV and he suggested the pose – Geri declined. But the idea had been planted in her head.

Geri was still partying her way around England and that, combined with her non-stop self-promotion, was beginning to take its toll. She was stealing food to survive and ended up in trouble when she was arrested with a chequebook and cards on London's Shaftesbury Avenue on 15 October 1990. She appeared at London's Bow Street magistrates on 21 November 1990 and was sentenced on five theft and fraud charges.

Found guilty, she got a two-year conditional discharge and was ordered to pay £360 in compensation. She seemed at this point to be getting nowhere. In her autobiography Geri recalls a miserable 18th birthday, spent alone in her squat with a bottle of rum – tears rolling down her cheeks, she wondered if she would drown in the bath if she drank the whole bottle.

It was about to get worse. Geri found a lump in her breast and, after visiting the doctor, had to undergo an operation to have it removed. She then had to endure a three-day wait to discover whether it was cancerous or benign and, although it proved to be the latter, it was a terrifying experience for Geri. 'It was an absolutely hideous time,' she said. 'I thought, Oh my God. I've got cancer.

'I feared I might lose one of my boobs. The idea was absolutely hideous. I hadn't been checking my breasts or examining them in any regular routine – you don't think you need to at that age. But one day I noticed this lump protruding from my right breast and, when I felt it, it was about the size of a Smartie. I was so scared.

'I was well aware of the possibilities, I thought I had cancer. I went straight to the doctor to get it checked out. There is no history of breast cancer in my family and no one expects it will happen to them at such a young age. But there is every chance it could. My doctor sent me to hospital right away to have the lump removed and examined. It was explained to me that if it was cancer, I would have to have a mastectomy. I was so shocked I didn't really know how to react. It's an awful thing to happen to a young girl because it changes the whole way you see yourself and your self-esteem.'

The three-day wait was dreadful for Geri, who was unable to concentrate on anything until she knew exactly what was wrong. 'I was in such shock that I didn't really know what to do with myself,' she said. 'I wasn't actually in hospital for very long but the wait for the results seemed to be forever. I didn't really burst into tears because I didn't know how to express my feelings. It was a tough time, absolutely hideous, indescribably awful. My family were brilliant in supporting me. I remember my mum gave me £30 so I could have a day off from my dancing. But I had to go straight back to work when I came out of hospital because I needed the money – I had to get on with life. I also thought about how some people don't discover a lump until the cancer is so widespread that there's nothing they can do about it. The thought did cross my mind about that. If it was breast cancer, it could have spread right through my body.'

Even when she found out that the lump was not, in fact, malignant, it took Geri some time to get over the experience. 'I was tremendously relieved,' she said. 'But it also made me realise quite how precious life is. You can't take anything for granted and it's made me look at things from a different perspective. I still have a scar on my breast from the operation and it will act as a constant reminder to me. It will stay with me always. That experience still haunts me – the little feeling that one day, next time, it could be a different story. Now I'm even more aware and make sure to examine myself properly. There's always the chance that another lump could come back that could be malignant.'

Since then Geri has done some work for breast cancer awareness – indeed, it was this very issue that led to her final row with the other Spice Girls.

With her health scare behind her, next stop was Magaluf in Majorca, where Geri ended up dancing at BCM, Europe's biggest night club. Here she went a step further: she danced in a cage suspended 10 feet above the dance floor and already she was enjoying showing off her body. 'It was erotic and a bit seedy as well,' said one of her fellow dancers a year after Geri became famous. 'But Geri certainly didn't seem to mind. She wasn't one of the best dancers but made up for it because she loved to show off her body, even though she wasn't in as good shape as she is now [this was when Geri was Ginger Spice]. When Geri arrived, she first of all did the usual dancing on stage in saucy gear. But you could earn a lot more money if you went in the cage almost naked. It was the erotic part of the dancing. Geri opted to do that to earn extra cash. The cage girls would dance in a G-string and tassles only, leaving very little to the imagination.'

Geri lived with friends in a flat on the outskirts of the resort, nestling in the hills above the city. One friend recalled how Geri, then a blonde, was not put off by the work. 'We all felt pretty cheap doing it, but we needed the money. Actually, Geri didn't seem to mind it too much. She loved being the centre of attention and seemed to enjoy men looking at her. She had grown up pretty quick and was mature for her age. She seemed like a tough cookie, but I never got to know her that well because she was quite guarded.'

Another friend at the time was Kelly Smith, who recalled that this was Geri's first experience of what was to come. 'She really enjoyed her time in Spain,' she said. 'She was a star out there. She was a wild party animal and didn't mind showing herself off. She always wanted to make something of herself. Geri kept saying she was going to sing and become a star. She was a real wannabe. We thought she was funny when she went on and on about becoming a big star. But now we all realise she has had the last laugh.'

It was also at this point that Geri got into topless modelling. 'I lived with a tall, gorgeous girl and she had some topless pictures done,' Geri recalled soon after the Spice Girls had become famous. This time she was not so coy. 'I said to the photographer, "Oh, can you do some of me, please?" He did and they were great. I showed them to my flatmate and she said, "You can be a glamour model." I was pleased because I'd thought I was too short. OK, maybe it was topless modelling, but I don't regret it. Obviously, since the Spice Girls started, those pictures have been exploited, but the money's in somebody else's pocket.'

Many understood Geri's decision to do the

pictures, not least her father. 'Dad was very proud of the photos,' said Max. 'He thought she looked beautiful in them. He certainly had no problem with the photos. Besides, he knew they were no more than a stepping stone to bigger and better things.'

Ana was not so happy, but had plenty more to occupy her. For a start Max was getting married to Susan – Geri, as mentioned earlier, came back to be a bridesmaid – and then Ana was to meet her own future husband, Steve Parkinson. Geri also had a worrying first brush with bulimia, but for now, at least, was unaware of the problems it would bring.

After her stint in Majorca, Geri came back to Britain and signed up with a modelling agency. 'It was probably the strangest agency you can imagine,' she said. 'But funnily enough, I did actually get some good jobs through it. I did a Katherine Hamnett jeans advert and they were looking for a fifties-looking girl who was prepared to go topless. I was. And I did the odd bum and boob shot. I did some really tacky stuff, actually, but I'm glad I never did the full monty.'

The agency was MOT, which is well known for its 'glamour' shots. Geri's modelling card showed her propensity for being economical with the truth: it read 'Height 5ft 5, Bust 34C, Waist 24, Hips 34, Dress 10, Shoes 3–4, Hair red-auburn, Eyes blue.' Geri also later posed for Beverly Goodway photographic agency for a Page Three special for the *Sun*. In later years she was able to laugh about the pictures – 'To be honest, it was boring,' she told Michael Parkinson when she appeared on his show, shortly after leaving the girls. 'I found it very, very dull in the end. Standing there with the window open to keep your nipples firm was not good.'

Geri did some more topless work but this time she was not quite so sanguine when the story came to light: a four-minute film shot in Oxford which showed her strutting around first in tight trousers and top and then completely topless. This film – like the other nude pictures – surfaced once the Spice Girls were famous and there were real fears it could damage their clean-living image. 'There's talk of Geri calling in the lawyers,' said one group insider. 'She's not at all happy.' That was not at all surprising – the film was a lot more sleazy than Geri's still pictures – but she soon forgot about it.

And still at the time Geri was not sure where her future lay. She was rushing around all over the place, spreading her net as wide as possible, casting about for what would be her future career. After doing a course at Reuters in presenting, Geri hardly had a moment to call her own. 'I had six jobs a week,' she said. 'I was teaching aerobics, working behind a bar and cleaning a woman's house. I was doing everything so I could pay my rent and save £300 to make a demo record. I auditioned for a part in a West End political comedy but failed to get it. I really wanted to do it. The director said to me, "Geri what's the last thing you've read? I bet it was *Cosmopolitan*." And he was bloody well right. I thought, I can either just plod on or I can do something about this. So I decided to go back to college. I started doing English literature and it really caught my attention. I felt passionate about it.'

Before starting her English literature course, Geri did begin to make some headway, even if it was not quite what she had been expecting to do. She had left the squat, moved into a series of bedsits and, briefly, into the home of her boyfriend Sean Green's parents. Finally, by Christmas 1991, she had had enough of England, men and failing to get anywhere. She flew out to Turkey, of all unlikely destinations, where she finally got on television in a Turkish version of *The Price Is Right* called *Seebakalim*. Geri made her name in Turkey – which, incidentally, was to be the location of the Spice Girls' first live concert – by modelling beds, exercise bikes and washing machines. The compere was a middle-aged, handsome Turk named Erhan Yazioglu, who was a big star in Turkey and with whom Geri had a brief fling – in fact the two were briefly reunited when the girls visited Turkey some years later.

The programme was made by London-based Fremantle, the independent production company that was behind *The Price Is Right*, as well as other game shows such as *Every Second Counts* and *Bob's Full House*. It also had the rights to an American game show called *Lets Make A Deal*. Fremantle sold the franchise for *Let's Make A Deal* to a Turkish channel, Kanal 6, and Geri was one of three girls chosen to be 'hostesses' – glamorous girls who smile a lot and wear tight black outfits and high heels. It was filmed in Istanbul in the weeks leading up to Christmas 1992. A three-week, all-expenses-paid shoot meant enough pre-recorded shows to last until the following summer.

If the show proved popular, TV bosses planned to make more. The boss, Howard, worked from the company's Camden office. He was in his forties and, according to Geri's autobiography, pretty sleazy. The two other girls were called Cheryl and Sarah – both blonde and both from the north.

Television was still a novelty in Turkey and this show was the channel's flagship programme. The girls were put up in a plush hotel in the heart of Istanbul. After the show, Geri was always besieged by middle-aged men and young boys wanting her autograph outside the studio. But, because she didn't speak the language, her minor celebrity status didn't mean much to her. She went back to London and kept searching for her big break. The show was re-commissioned but Geri never made any more programmes.

Back in England, Geri was trying as hard as ever to get noticed. She became 'Miss Motivator', a part-time gym instructor, auditioned and failed to present the *Disney Club*, a Saturday-morning children's television show, and then sent in an audition tape to the *Big Breakfast*. Chris Evans, no less, ever the soul of generosity, featured the tape live on air and poked fun at it into the bargain. Geri battled on. By now she had left Sean and was living on her own, continuing to teach aerobics and working at a barbers' shop at the weekend.

Outwardly she was as cheerful as ever, but the stress was taking its toll. Geri began to avoid eating with her family and on her own would eat only fat-free food. No one yet realised she had a problem, though, and there it might have ended were it not for an event that was to prove more devastating than anything that has happened in Geri's life before or since – the death of her father.

Laurence Frances Halliwell was and always will be the most important man in Geri's life and his death at the age of 71, when his beautiful young daughter was just 21, was a dreadful trauma. Laurence had both asthma and a weak heart, and it was a combination of the two conditions that was to kill him – he had a heart attack from which he never recovered. One of the first indications that something was wrong came when Laurence missed an appointment: a friend alerted Max and Karen. The two drove to Laurence's flat where they found him on the floor and were faced with the grim task of telling their three siblings the bad news. Geri took it especially badly and was inconsolable when she attended the funeral.

'We drove there together, Natalie, Geri and myself, and Geri cried all the way there and all the way back again,' said Max. 'Of course, we were all shattered by his loss, but it took Geri months to get over it – longer, I think, than the rest of us. As they say, you don't know what you've got till it's gone, and that hit home for Geri.'

One of the dreadful ironies about it was that, after all the years of trying, fame and success were finally just around the corner. Geri was soon to audition for the Spice Girls and there was no one who would have been prouder to see her than Laurence. Max was well aware of that. 'When people ask what makes Geri tick, I point to my father and his influence,' he said.

'We all miss him terribly and we all know how much it would have meant to him to see Geri on top of the world. Nowadays we still talk about him and it's clear Geri still mourns him. We have the odd giggle about him, his passion for car boot sales and collecting junk. But there is always this sadness that he's not around now. After Dad died, Geri missed him more than she thought she would; she realised just how much support he gave her. I know he would have been puffed with pride to see where Geri has got to. Geri is definitely her father's daughter.'

Geri's grief did not go away. Her weight began to plummet, ending up at about six stone. By her own admission, she was living on a diet of 'coffee, crushed ice and apples'. Nothing could lessen the pain. 'I was devastated, I was gutted,' she said in 1997. 'I was distraught. I felt that he'd been snatched away from me. I went and saw his body at the hospital. He looked grey, dreadful, old. It was awful. And for a while I was in denial. I didn't want to deal with it. I still haven't come to terms with it. If anyone tells me someone close to them has just died, I feel compelled to talk to them and say, "Share the pain with me." I think, God, if you feel like I felt, you need someone.

'I'm very saddened because my dad died before I became famous. He never saw any of it. Out of all my family, he would have been the most enthralled by it. He'd have been such a proud father. I'd have taken him absolutely everywhere with me. He'd have loved it. I take after my dad a lot. He was like the Artful

Dodger, living off his wits, but he was a wise guy. I do feel his presence around me. I believe in spirituality and the afterlife. I have to – otherwise there's too much hurt.'

Geri also spoke about her feelings in Molly Dineen's documentary. 'My life has been like a lifetime speeded up into a chunk,' she tells Molly. 'I've had bulimia, anorexia … When my father died, I went completely anorexic.'

'How did he die?' Molly asks.

'Of a heart attack. It was horrible, because it was my [half] sister Karen's birthday. There had been a big party and I think I was away in Turkey doing a game show so I couldn't go. Everyone else turned up but my dad wasn't there and they all thought he'd just forgotten. So they went round on Monday morning looking for him and knocked on the flat door. His flat is a pigsty, like off *Steptoe and Son*, he used to go to jumble sales. Anyway they found him naked with a present next to him, dead. It was the most horrible thing. He wasn't completely lovely, but he was sweet in his old age.'

But still – rightly – Geri's search for fame went on. At the beginning of 1994 she put together a demo tape at a recording studio near Watford Junction, before going to an audition for a film called *Tank Girl*, where she made the acquaintance of one Victoria

Ginger shenanigans. *Top*: The stuff boys' dreams are made of – Geri and Kylie kiss on *TFI Friday*.

Bottom: It was a much-publicised but brief affair: Geri and Chris Evans relax in the sunshine.

Raining men? Geri larks around with Robbie in happier days.

Watching the celebrities.

Top left: Geri and George Michael dine with David and Victoria Beckham in St Tropez, shortly after Geri left the band.

Top right: Geri with pooch Harry.

Bottom left: With Kenny Goss, George Michael's partner.

Bottom right: George and Geri: their friendship has become strained due to Geri's thirst for publicity.

Going solo. The covers from Geri's first solo hit, 'Look at Me'.

eri's lean figure makes a splash.

op left: Entertaining the Royal Marines in Oman and, *top right*, having
n with the troops.

ottom: Geri revs her engine at the Party in the Park in 2001.

Top: A far cry from Geri's childhood home. Her house in Langley.

Bottom left: Geri attracts the attention of the press by plucking a fan from the crowd to accompany her to an awards ceremony.

Bottom right: Geri is famous for her dedication to yoga.

p: Geri smiles bravely, despite having just been banned
m driving.

ttom: Two women who have worked tirelessly to achieve their shared
als of fame and fortune.

Geri proudly wears the ring given to her by her beau, Damian Warne

Adams. Nothing came through. Geri became increasingly depressed and increasingly doubtful about her future until one day, lying in bed, she noticed an old advertisement she'd cut out from *The Stage*. She took it up to examine more closely and felt a certain frisson as she read the following words:

'R U 18–23 with the ability to sing/dance? R U streetwise, ambitious, outgoing and determined?'

11

When Geri Met Mel B

(and Emma and Victoria and Mel C)

Much has been made of the Spice Girls' slogan 'girl power', but if truth be told, the Spice Girls came into being entirely as a result of the ideas of a group of men. The first two of these men, and the two who originally came up with the idea of an all-girl band, were Bob Herbert, a show business actuary from Lightwater, Surrey, who tragically died in a car crash in 1999, and his son Chris.

The two had form. Herbert's daughter Nicky had, some years previously, dated Luke Goss, one of the twins who made up the group Bros. Realising the boys had some talent, Bob Herbert had allowed the boys to rehearse in his house and even got his aunt Ethel, herself a musician, to help them along. It worked: Bros were a huge hit – but by that time had left the Herberts, who did not benefit from their success.

The experience, however, left the Herberts keen to try again. The early 1990s were a great time for boy bands, with the likes of Take That and New Kids On The Block dominating the charts, and so father and son saw an opening in the market: for another five-piece band, but this one made up entirely of girls. Received wisdom was that such a band would not automatically be a success – teenage girls like to have crushes on their singing stars while teenage boys are more concerned with sporting heroes – but the Herberts correctly sensed that received wisdom was wrong. They thus linked up with Chic Murphy, a second-hand-car salesman who had once managed the Three Degrees – and late in 1993 put an advertisement in *The Stage* that was to shake the world of music.

Geri saw the advertisement but did not respond straight away – she cut it out, put it to one side and forgot about it, and as she continued to pursue a career in modelling the first auditions were held. On

4 March 1994, 400 girls turned up to a studio in south London: each was given 30 seconds to sing and were given marks out of ten for singing, dancing, looks and personality. A shortlist of 11 was drawn up.

At about this time, Geri suddenly came across the advertisement again and decided to follow it up. She rang Chris Herbert and begged to be allowed to attend the final audition: curious about the eager-sounding wannabe at the other end of the telephone, he said yes. Ian Lee, who ran the Trinity Studios in Woking, Surrey, helped train them. He recalled what happened when Geri arrived. 'When she walked in, everyone could see she was a bit older than the rest of the girls, so Chris asked her how old she was,' Ian said. 'She said, "I'm as old or as young as you want me to be. I can be a 10 year old with big tits if you want." She got the job.'

But not before she auditioned for it. The 12 girls – Mel C was also a newcomer, as she'd missed the first auditions due to tonsillitis – were divided into two groups and given half an hour to work out a dance routine to go with 'Just A Step From Heaven' by Eternal. Everyone was pretty dreadful, but the numbers were finally whittled down to five: Geri, Victoria Adams, Melanie Chisholm, Melanie Brown and Michelle Stephenson.

They were called back for a further audition and

finally sent to live together in a guest house for a week to see if they got on. They did. 'On June 7, the girls came to the studio to work together,' Ian recalled. 'Chris had put them all up in a local B&B and for a week they got to sing and dance together. They sounded absolutely awful. Geri had problems singing in tune and none of them could move together. After a few days you could see something gelling but it was no overnight miracle. It was bloody hard work.'

The girls and the Herberts were all prepared to give it a go, though, and so the real work began. The girls were put up in a three-bedroom semi on Boyne Hill Road in Maidenhead belonging to Chic Murphy. Victoria and Michelle took one room, the two Melanies the second and Geri got one all to herself. They received £60 a week on top of their social security money and Ian was paid £100 to let them use the studio. 'Each of the girls had something to offer but none of them had any really outstanding talent,' said Ian. 'Geri was well endowed with a feisty character, but could not sing. I remember being there with the girls and saying to her, "Geri, you're out of tune." She would then go off to the toilet and we could hear her practising in there.'

At first, the girls came across as rather shy, but as their confidence increased, so their behaviour became more boisterous. 'I was standing in the studio one day,' said Ian. 'The next thing I knew, my trousers were around my ankles. The girls were just standing there laughing their socks off.'

Originally, the girls were called something quite different and the name of the group was actually thought up by Tim Hawes, a songwriter based at Trinity. 'The girls were originally called Touch,' said Tim. 'The idea was that you could look, but you couldn't touch. But Tim wrote a song with the girls called "Sugar and Spice" and after that their name was changed.'

And as they learned their trade, the girls would put on shows at Knaphill Studios to an audience that included borough council officers, who clearly didn't know what had hit them. 'You would see a group of these middle-aged council chaps standing there dribbling with their tongues hanging out,' said Ian.

Another person who was closely involved with the girls in the early days was Pepi Lemer, a voice trainer hired to get the girls into shape. Initially she was brought in for a lengthy once-a-week session at £20 an hour, but the girls were so bad this was swiftly increased to two four-hour sessions a week. It was not easy going. 'The first time I saw them was in a dance studio,' said Pepi. 'They'd had to learn this song called "Take Me Away". I remember them being quite attractive in their different ways, but terribly nervous. They were shaking and, when they sang, their voices were wobbling. It has to be said they weren't very good. My first impression was, "There's a lot of work to be done here."'

Geri in particular needed help with her voice. 'They were really starting from scratch, the only one who could sing was Emma. The others had to be trained,' Pepi said. Geri, on the other hand, burst into tears when she was told she was singing out of tune. 'I told her, "If you take it personally, you can't be in this business. You have to be tough." They were pretty rough. Geri's voice didn't lend itself to melody very easily.' But Geri toughened up and Pepi grew to respect her sheer grit and determination. 'If we had to practise more, some of the girls might moan and say, "Can't we do something more interesting than scales and breathing?" And she'd turn around and say, "That's going to get us really far."'

There were other problems, as well. Two months on it was becoming obvious that Michelle Stephenson was not working as well with the other girls as they had initially hoped, and it was decided she would have to go. The Herberts had to tell her she was no longer wanted. 'She wasn't like the rest of the girls,' said Ian. 'She was quite reserved and pensive and wouldn't always agree to do the things the rest of them wanted. The girls used to moan about her and it was obvious that something was going to have to be done. Then her mum got cancer and she was offered a place at university, so she quit the band.'

Michelle has always been extremely generous about the girls and looks back on her time with them with affection. 'It was nothing like as luxurious as the one in *Popstars*,' she said of the house in Maidenhead in an interview in 2001. 'It was more like university digs. And we were only given £60 a week to live on. There was one single room, a room with twin beds and a room with a double bed. Geri got the single because she was the oldest – no discussion. Victoria and I were first up the stairs so we grabbed the twin beds and the two Mels shared the double bed. It was very confusing initially because at school and college my friends called me Mel. So whenever someone in the house called out "Mel" I'd be answering. I had to keep reminding myself that my name was Michelle. Can you imagine it? Mel C, Mel B and Mel S – it was just getting ridiculous.

'But I got on very well with all of them – it was a case of having to, because we all spent so much time together. Mel B was really cool because she was very down to earth – she still comes across as exactly like that. I really liked her because she always said what she thought. There was no messing around. I really like people like that, who are straight to the point. Geri was the bubbly one, full of life. She would get us all up in the morning to go running. You didn't have to go, but you felt that because everyone else was, you had to make the effort.

'There were tensions. When you all live in a house, there will be problems. Something as simple as queuing for the bathroom in the morning caused the biggest arguments. It wasn't like in *Popstars* where they all have luxury bathrooms. We had one bath and we didn't even have a proper shower. We had to fix the shower-head on to the taps. And we were all girls, not a mixture of girls and boys. Boys are generally quicker in the bathroom, but we all took ages. Mel B took a bit longer than the rest of us because she had to control her hair. But, on the other hand, we didn't have the same pressures as the Popstars. We weren't being followed by cameras every step of the way – so we didn't feel we had to put on loads of make-up all the time. We could sunbathe in the front garden and chat to the neighbours. There was no secrecy surrounding us. We were in the studio every day. We were different, because there weren't all that many all-girl groups around at the time. That was part of the Spice Girls' success – there was very little competition for their kind of set-up. The main competition as we saw it would have been Eternal – that was it.'

Michelle is also very telling when it comes to the more mundane details of life in the house, not least the little eating idiosyncrasies that were growing even back then. 'We all cooked but everyone had different tastes – Geri was really into bean sprouts,' she said. 'Victoria was addicted to cornflakes with honey – she'd eat them at any time of the day. She got me hooked on them, too. At other times we would eat out at Pizza Hut or at some place cheap. Geri had a little car and we'd all climb in when we were going out. She was a good driver, but was notorious at roundabouts. She could never decide which exit she needed to take and the rest of us used to joke about how many times we'd go round before we got on our way. Every time I've seen her on TV or in the papers since then I've thought of her driving!

'When we stayed in, we'd often rehearse for the next day. We weren't the Spice Girls in those days. We were called Touch. Our bosses said it had to be something with five letters so that a letter would stand for each of us. None of the songs we recorded were released by the Spice Girls. The music was nothing like they are doing now. It was pretty awful. The lyrics to one song went, "Where do you come from, falling from the sky, you're someone very special, I'm flying, I feel so high." It was very, very young pop. I was more of an indie chick – I liked Oasis and the Prodigy. The others were into Take That.'

But Michelle was not much longer to be part of the Spice story. Her ambitions actually lay in the field of acting rather than singing and after her mother became ill she decided that life was too short not to do what she really wanted to do. The Herberts – relieved – agreed, and so she left. After leaving the group, Michelle travelled in Europe and then returned to Goldsmith's College in London. She has since recorded backing vocals for singers such as Ricky Martin and Julio Iglesias and has also been a reporter for Carlton TV's *Wired* series as well as presenting a six-part reality TV series for ITV called *Wild Weekends*.

'I'm very happy with what I'm doing and don't regret a thing,' she says. 'It [working with the girls] was only six months of my life.'

Of course, there was initial panic that five had become four, but then Pepi remembered a talented singer she had come across some years earlier, Abigail Kas. Abigail auditioned and went down well with the Herberts, but there were some fears she didn't have the right mindset to join the group. 'I took her to the audition and she sang nicely,' said Pepi. 'Chic was there and he said to Abigail, "Look 'ere, gal, if you've got a boyfriend you better give 'im the elbow, we want total commitment."'

Abigail turned down her chance to join the band and became an aerobics teacher. 'Every time I see them, I think, It could have been me,' she once said.

Fortunately Pepi had yet another ace up her sleeve: Emma Bunton, who was picked despite Chic worrying about whether her legs were too big (sometimes you can see why all the girls were so obsessed with food, with the one exception of Mel B). The Spice Girls were born. 'Chris held a panic audition and Emma was picked,' said Ian. 'She was far more suited to the rest of the girls, although she would go on about how she missed her mum. She and Victoria were real family girls and always went home at weekends. Melanie Chisholm, the real talent in the band, would spend all her spare time watching football.'

When the Spice Girls first became famous a couple of years later, the story that originally did the rounds was that they were just five girls who kept bumping into one another at auditions, until they finally decided to give it a whirl together and, hey presto, the show was on the road. That version of events is a great irritation to Ian. 'I couldn't believe it when all these stories came out about how the girls did everything themselves,' he said.

'They were a put-together band. They'd never met

until they were picked from 400 others and Emma Bunton and Geri Halliwell weren't even considered for the original line-up. They couldn't sing and they weren't the greatest dancers but they had one thing in common and that was blind ambition. They spent a year working like slaves to get things right and once they got things sorted, they dropped everyone and took themselves off.'

When the Spice Girls finally burst on to the scene in 1996 they were indeed a completely polished and professional product. It had taken very hard work behind the scenes, though, and their lifestyle was a far cry from the glitz to which they were going to become accustomed. 'They lived quite simply,' said Ian. 'They'd eat lunch at the local teashop or bring in sandwiches. They usually wore the same clothes every day. Geri and Melanie Brown were instantly singled out as the leaders. They always had an opinion and they both wanted to be in the driving seat. They used to fight like cat and dog. Geri would stand there with her arms by her sides and her fists clenched as Mel would have a go at her for singing out of tune. Mel Chisholm would always act the peacemaker and the other girls would just watch in stunned silence.

'Geri would freely admit she wasn't a great singer or a dancer, but she was a damned hard worker. She'd spend hours on her own perfecting her singing or working on her dance steps. She was determined to succeed. She kept saying, "Time's running out. This is my last chance and I'm going to make it." She was a tough nut. She always had a vivid imagination and she'd expect people to believe her whatever.' Indeed, in her time at Trinity Studios, Geri penned a song called 'Release'. The chorus ran, 'Babe, I'm gonna make it, Boy I'm going to take it, If I haven't got it, Then I'm gonna fake it.'

In fact, despite the rows and the rivalry, Geri and Mel became very close friends for a time, not least because of a similarity in backgrounds. 'Melanie Brown and Geri were the ones who'd do all the partying,' said Ian. 'And even though they'd do most of the fighting, they were the ones who'd go off together. They had quite similar backgrounds and neither would ever talk about their families. It was like they had a special bond. Mel would come in on a Monday morning and discuss all the men she'd been with. She loved sex and she loved talking about it.

'Geri never did. We all used to tease her, then on Christmas Eve, we were sitting in the Garibaldi pub across the road and she said she hadn't had sex for two years and that she was a born-again virgin. Everyone fell about laughing, but she was serious.'

It was, however, Geri who realised the importance

of making contacts in the industry. She was constantly networking and constantly seeking out the right people to meet. 'She was the one with the clearest vision,' said Ian, 'the one who knew exactly what she wanted for the band. If she saw an opening, she'd go for it.'

The chaotic life led by the girls was actually captured on film in the documentary *Raw Spice*, made by Neil Davies and the late Matthew Bowers. Matthew was actually an acquaintance of Geri's and so it was due to her that the duo met the other girls. 'We met the girls and they were dying to do it,' says Neil. 'I wanted to make a series and follow the girls, see how far they'd go and how far the pop world would manipulate them. Mel C was always in tracksuits and raving about football. She'd always try to be nice to everybody. Mel B was great – like a tomboy. She was just having a laugh, getting up to antics. Geri was desperate to make it, she was pushing all the time. Her hunger spread among the rest of them. Emma was lost, tearful and missed her mum tremendously. Mel B kind of looked after her. Victoria was shy and retiring. She was worried about her weight.'

The film provides an insight into the less than glamorous world the girls came from – and the fact that, right from the start, Geri knew where she felt her place was to be in the band, namely, as its leader. 'I'm the brains behind the group,' she claims. 'Without me, they are nothing. I'm quite a motivated person. I just want to get there. I'm hungry for fame and I want my ego fed. Mel B and I are the most dominant people in the group. We have a love-hate relationship.'

'Geri's a bossy boots sometimes and I get a bit annoyed with her,' chips in Emma.

'We've got two strong characters in the group, me and Geri,' says Mel B in her own contribution to the debate. 'We do have really bad arguments, with swearing and things flying. It can get really nasty, sometimes.' And indeed, the film shows the two girls having an argument because, natch, Geri messed up a harmony line.

All of this was a first for Geri. Accustomed to fighting life's battles on her own, she now had four friends, colleagues and soul mates to fight with her. 'I feel like I've adopted you as my new family,' she tells the girls. That did not, however, extend to sharing bedrooms. 'No one can live with me,' she says. 'I need my space.' Typically of Geri, who, despite everything, is perfectly upfront about her failings, she also talks about the fact that it can be hard to keep up with the others. 'I'm not a trained dancer, so learning choreographed routines is a nightmare,' she confesses. 'I have to do it ten times over but everyone else gets it in one.' Geri was also already planning how she would spend her hard-earned cash, once she got round to earning it. 'I'm going to have a castle with a swimming pool and an island in the middle and lots of drug-oriented parties.'

Geri was keeping her options open, though. At this stage there was no guarantee the girls were going to make it out of Maidenhead and into music history, and so Geri was still keeping her eyes open for other opportunities. One of these was a job as a £15,000-a-year presenter on L!VE TV, which Geri auditioned for on a day off. Luckily for her, she didn't get it.

'If we'd offered her the job, she would have definitely taken it over the band,' said Nick Ferrari, who was head of programmes at L!VE TV. 'She would have been in straight away. No question about it.' As it happens, it was yoof TV guru Janet Street-Porter, then a senior figure at the station, who turned Geri down. 'You have to know Janet to appreciate her genius,' said Ferrari cattily. 'To turn down one of the all-time icons of pop music and advise her to become a traffic reporter on BBC Radio Plymouth shows the kind of judgement which has put her where she is today.

'Geri was very upset when she got turned down. In the end, of course, she was very fortunate that she didn't get it. Look where she is now. She was committed to the band but she was 100 per cent committed to this as well. She was experienced enough to say that not all bands make it. The music industry is precarious and she'd have been mad not to explore other options.' This was not, incidentally, Geri's only attempt to get on British television: in 1993 she also appeared in a pilot for a show called *The Fashion Police* in which she was called upon to run around the streets in a military-style blue hat bellowing, 'This is the Fashion Police and, baby, you're busted.' Very fortunately for Geri, nothing came of that one, either.

As Geri explored her options, the rehearsals were continuing, the girls were practising and slowly – very slowly – the Spice Girls as we know them were coming into shape. By 1995, the transformation was almost complete. 'By that time they'd become really good,' Ian said. 'Chris was a great artistic director and he'd got them all working so that their weaknesses were hidden. The way they look, sing and dance together today is exactly the way he got them to, even down to the way they stand. He was the one who got Mel Chisholm to do her acrobatics as part of the act. He wanted them to be sexy and sassy, which they were. You could see that they were going to make it. And they started to act like real popstars.'

That they most certainly did. Real popstars have

a tendency to get their own way, no matter how many people's feelings they have to trample on in the process, and Geri and the girls were now ready to take charge of their own destiny – or, at least, to hand it to someone else. The Herberts had made the girls ready to take on the world: the girls were now ready to take on the Herberts. Put simply, they wanted someone else to manage them and if truth be told the Herberts, along with Chic Murphy, were beginning to feel the same. And like the divas they were shortly to become, the girls managed it with maximum aplomb. 'The bloke wanted us to sing someone else's songs about love and that's shit,' explained Mel C afterwards. 'We just weren't having it.'

The line peddled afterwards was that up until this point the girls had not signed a contract and that the Herberts now demanded one, with 25 per cent of profits going to them. The girls were not happy with that arrangement and walked out. Another rumour is that the Herberts sold the girls as a group to the man who became their manager, Simon Fuller, for £50,000, and this is the story that would appear to be closest to the truth. 'The girls said they'd pay back what they owed and sort it out amicably,' said a source. 'Then they went to see Fuller and he became their manager.'

The Herberts themselves have always remained quiet on the subject of the deal. 'We settled with the girls last year,' Chris said in 1996. 'That's the end of the story for us.'

Whatever really happened, they put on a show – perhaps their very first show as the Spice Girls – by having a very public argument.

'The last time I saw them, they were working in the studio, when suddenly there was this massive row between the girls,' said Ian Lee shortly after the girls first became famous. 'The whole building could hear them screaming and shouting at each other and then they all burst out of the room and stormed off. Afterwards I even wondered whether the whole thing was staged. Perhaps they wanted us to tell the Herberts that they'd split. Still, they disappeared and the next thing was that we read they'd been signed up by Annie Lennox's management, Simon Fuller, and had done a deal with Virgin.

'I was really pleased when they got to number one and I tried to contact them to do something for Trinity and support the charity organisation which is here to help young artists get on their feet. But I was blanked by their management. All Emma wanted was to be on the cover of *Smash Hits* and the rest of them wanted to be on *Top Of The Pops*. They've done all that now and good on them. They worked hard and they deserve it. It just seems that in a few short months the business has made them hard enough to brush aside their past and make out that none of us ever existed. Considering all we went through together, that is such a shame.'

Indeed, the girls were not generous about crediting their former mentors with their success. Another person who found herself left out in the cold was Pepi Lemer, who merited no mention in the official story of how the girls got to the top. 'When the girls moved on, they sent me a card saying, "Thank you for everything, we could not have done it without you,"' she once said. 'So why won't they now give credit where it's due?'

12

Successful Spice

Stage one of the process – getting the girls into shape – was complete. Now it was time for stage two: to find a record company to sign them up. The Spice Girls were ready to take over the world and Simon Fuller was exactly the right man to help them do it. A veteran of the pop music industry, Simon entered the business in 1983 as a publishing scout at Chrysalis Records. He struck gold almost instantly. 'I remember Simon bringing in Madonna's "Holiday",' said Terri Hall, who worked with him for five years. 'And this was when she was completely unknown. Simon had been offered the song and the artist for

$10,000 and he was pushing very hard for Chrysalis Music to take it. Chrysalis said, "Pick the song up but don't bother with her, she ain't going nowhere."'

Two years later Simon struck out on his own, taking Terri with him. Again, he lucked out almost immediately. The newly founded management company had two acts on its books: a rock band called The Adventures and a solo artist called Paul Hardcastle. Hardcastle had up his sleeve an anti-Vietnam song called '19' which was released a few weeks later. Within no time at all, it was selling 65,000 copies a day. 'It was mental,' said Hall. 'We were in the office every night till eleven, exhausted, but even then Simon would be saying, "In five years I see us more of an umbrella company with a publishing arm and we'll do films and manage bands and do our own merchandising." It wasn't because he had a huge ego and wanted to build an empire, it was just what he was going to do. I've never met someone with so much drive and vision. He always said, "Ambition is not a virtue," but he ate, slept and breathed his work.'

The success of '19' set Simon Fuller on the way to making an even greater fortune than that of many of the people he was to represent. He acknowledged that immediately: he named his company '19' by way of thanks and all his ventures since have had the number

19 on them. He also set about finding new artists and the next one up was Cathy Dennis. She had a string of Top 40 singles in Britain, a brief spell in the US and, more recently, co-wrote 'Can't Get You Out Of My Head' for Kylie Minogue.

Simon's next really big move came in 1990. The Eurythmics had just split up and Annie Lennox was about to strike out on her own. Simon lost no time: he approached her with an offer to make her an international solo star. She accepted. 'Although the track record for artists leaving dissolved bands and going on to become solo stars wasn't that great, he couldn't see how Annie could fail,' said a business associate. He was right and Annie Lennox is now one of Britain's richest female solo artists. More recently, Simon has been behind the success of S Club 7 and *Pop Idol*.

One of Simon's great strengths is that he's an easy man to work for. The music industry is full of prima donnas: Simon is not amongst them. 'Simon is extremely light-hearted,' says Terri. 'He's about as far from that "banging his fists on the table" type manager as you can get. He's very polite, he won't shout and scream but he gets what he wants by being thoughtful and studied. If there's a problem, he goes away and thinks about it and comes back with a solution. He's also very playful, always joking. There'd be times when you'd think, Can't he just be serious for a moment? That sounds contradictory for someone who has achieved so much, but that's exactly what he's like.'

That said, Simon also has an extremely hard-nosed side. 'The first thing you have to realise about him is that he's utterly brilliant – and utterly ruthless,' says one business associate. 'He oozes a rather nervous charm until you disagree with him – then you see a different side.'

The side that the girls first saw was charm personified and, as with much of the murky early days of Spice history, there are conflicting accounts as to how they really met, not least because, for a time, the girls became extremely sensitive to the charge of being a manufactured band. In fact, they quite often denied it outright, leading to a good deal of confusion about how they came into being; it was only in later years that the role of the Herberts and Chic Murphy was fully appreciated. 'We've had so many people try to say they've managed us, but we've all been in the music industry for years and we've done it ourselves,' said Mel B in 1996. 'We do everything ourselves, we're completely into girl power and there's nothing us lot can't handle.'

In her autobiography Geri says that the girls first heard of Simon from friends of theirs, the people who ran the production company Absolute, and that these men thought the two parties might be able to do business. So they passed on a demo tape that the girls had made to Simon, who soon after got in touch.

Another version is that the girls performed a showcase in November 1994 and were bombarded with offers from a dozen managers. Simon got them because, 'so many others were saying, "Dress like this, sing that song," and he was cool and understood we wanted a say in our careers,' said Mel B.

Yet another version – and this is the one music industry insiders go for – is that the girls placed an advertisement for a manager. Simon, who also realised the potential of an all-girl band, called and that was it.

'I thought, Shit, I know there's something here, I know I can get them good songwriters and good songs,' he says. 'But how the hell do you market a girl group? And I consciously, methodically, did my homework for weeks. I thought, OK, girls buy girl magazines, they go and see girl movies, they hang out together. But with music they buy boys. I worked out that girl groups had invariably been sexy and that this threatened girls with the thought that they might take away their boyfriends. So the Spice Girls had to be different. Girls have got to identify with them, so they can't be threatening. And everything they do has got to be marketed on those lines.'

Certainly it was Simon who got in touch first, a decision that none of the parties involved were going to regret. 'They went to Simon because they respected Annie [Lennox] and he was simply bowled over by their music,' said Muff Fitzgerald, their spokesman at Virgin Records (somewhat disingenuously). 'The whole thing about being put together by someone is just a myth perpetuated by the music press. They are pulling the strings here and that makes some people uncomfortable.'

When the girls walked into Simon's office in Rampton's Dock, Fulham, it would appear to have been love at first sight. That charm did its work. Geri recalls him saying, 'I think you're fabulous. With or without me, you girls are going to make it. But if you tell me where you want to go, I will try to take you there. You tell me to stop and I'll stop.' Take us there, said the girls. I will, said Simon. He did. And the first thing he did was sort out the name of the band. Until then it had been merely Spice. Simon turned that into the Spice Girls and they were off.

And so, having sorted out their manager, the girls needed to find a record label. This was not as difficult as it might have been a few years previously, not least because the girls were beginning to create a stir in the industry. People were becoming curious and wanting to know who they were. 'No one really knows for sure how they came together, but they were pushing themselves for a long time,' said Selina Webb, managing editor of *Music Week* shortly after 'Wannabe' was released. 'They would keep appearing at industry parties and people kept saying, "Who are those girls?" They seem to be controlling their own destinies and don't appear to have been manufactured. Their personalities are simply too strong. Perhaps there was someone in the beginning who brought them together but they are definitely calling the shots now.'

They were also in the right place at the right time. The girls and Simon were not the only people who could see the potential of an all-girl band: the whole of the music industry was beginning to wake up to its possibilities, too. 'We could tell a movement away from male-dominated pop was coming, and was that's true right across the board, from indie and dance to pop,' said Ashley Newton, deputy managing director at Virgin shortly after the girls signed. 'There's a gender shift happening and they're exactly right for now.' He was impressed by them, as well. 'When we saw them singing in our office, we realised they weren't some pieced-together vision by some male svengali. They have their own agenda.' They were also pure pop. 'At the beginning of last year, we saw that we had nothing that was out-and-out contemporary pop,' he said. 'We were offered a tremendous amount of music but they were all basically copy-cat acts.'

Simon took the girls on a tour of the major record labels: they performed either by singing a cappella or with a backing tape. Interest from a variety of labels was immediate and strong, as Simon narrowed the choice down to RCA (Annie Lennox's label) and Virgin. 'It was very exciting and very competitive,' said Ashley Newton. '[The Spice Girls] brought something fresh and we had a fresh perspective on pop music, as we don't have a history of it.'

And it was with Virgin that the girls duly signed. The deal was worth a total of £500,000: on the day, each girl was presented with a cheque for £10,000. 'Suddenly we had record companies and publishers queuing to sign us,' recalls Geri. The day we signed with Virgin I wanted to stand at the top of Big Ben and shout, "We're going to be famous, did you hear that, FLIPPIN' FAMOUS!" We signed the contracts and, as the champagne corks popped, we were each handed a cheque for £10,000.'

The girls started out as they meant to go on: on the day the deal was signed, 13 July 1995, they were very late for the celebration. Eventually a stretch limo drew up alongside the waiting executives, the door was opened – and five inflatable dolls popped out, each dressed up to look exactly like each girl. The bemused record executives took a moment to realise it was a joke: the girls themselves arrived a few minutes later, full of *joie de vivre*.

The fivesome then went off with Simon Fuller to

celebrate. He took them to dinner in an elegant restaurant in west London called Kensington Place, which had once been a favourite of Princess Diana. The evening was riotous: Victoria, unused to drinking very much, was rendered practically incapable after a couple of glasses of champagne. The girls had to prop her up until they got her into a cab, where they managed to get her knickers off. Geri promptly threw the prize out of the window, to the chagrin of the cab driver and the hilarity of everyone else.

They had only just begun. Two weeks after signing with Virgin the Spice Girls were jetted out to Los Angeles to meet with TV and film executives to promote the idea of a Nineties-style *A Hard Day's Night*. They stayed at the Four Seasons Hotel and were well placed to meet people in the industry: Simon had ties in the US with the William Morris Agency, who also represented Annie Lennox. Jeff Frasco, a US agent, arranged a string of meetings with Hollywood film producers and TV executives.

The girls met people from Fox Studios, Dreamworks, Disney, NBC, CBS, Fox TV, singing 'Wannabe' a cappella-style and giving them the full Spice treatment. It worked. And Geri was on typical form: when she found out that Courtney Love was staying in the Four Seasons she rang up, pretending to be a friend of Amanda de Cadenet's. Along with Mel, Geri was invited up to her room for a cup of tea and spent an hour talking to her about rock music. After six days in LA, the girls felt they needed a holiday and flew to Hawaii for a week's holiday on the island of Maui. They stayed at the Kea Lani Hotel on Polo Beach. The good life had begun.

And then, publicly at least, there was a period of calm. Virgin had invested a lot of money in the girls and it was essential that the label – and the girls – got everything exactly right. Back in London they enlisted the services of Absolute, made up of Paul Wilson and Andy Watkins, as the production team, while Matt & Biff – Matt Rowe and Richard Stannard – helped write the songs. The girls divided their time between recording studios in Hammersmith, Richmond and Old Street. By this time Geri was living with Karen in Chorleywood and the two Mels had moved into a house opposite Geri's childhood home in Jubilee Road, Watford. It had been owned by Geri's Auntie Doreen and when she died Ana and Steve Parkinson had bought it, done it up and let it out.

It was in spring 1996, when the girls were recording in Sheffield, that Geri had a brilliant idea. She slipped out of the studios and raced to a nearby jewellery shop to buy five identical gold rings. She had them each engraved with 'Spice' and presented them to the girls as 'anniversary' presents. 'We're each one of five. Together we can do anything,' she said.

Outwardly, though, the girls were still hidden from the world. 'It was our belief that we should nail the album before releasing the first single,' said Newton. 'Then we're not going back to the studio to record tracks once the promotional work has begun.' It was a very clever strategy. The girls began to get a taste of what was to come as they were marched first into the studio and then around the world to make first the album and then the accompanying videos.

On Monday, 19 April the video for 'Wannabe' was filmed. It was shot in an empty building next to St Pancras station, decorated to look like a classy old manor house. The idea was to portray the girls in the act of bombarding record company offices and causing havoc and mayhem wherever they went. The video appeared to be shot as one continuous take from beginning to end, but was in fact two separate takes, seamlessly synchronised. Each girl got to show off her image in the video, with Mel C doing backflips along a grand oak dining table and Emma blowing kisses and fluttering her eyelashes to all the old men dressed as aristocrats and their butlers. The *Big Breakfast* sent a crew to do a story on the shoot and the Spice Girls did their first ever official interview.

In an early shot, Geri can be spotted glancing down to make sure her feet are in the right place – even after all the months of practice she was not as sure of the dance routines as the other girls, and it still showed. As she herself admitted, dancing in a cage in Majorca is no substitute for stage school.

And then, the album *Spice* in the bag, it was time for the girls to show exactly what they were made of. The music industry knew of their existence, but that's pretty much all it knew. It had yet to be introduced to the girls individually.

The first major introduction came in February 1996. Virgin had booked several tables at the Brit Awards and were determined to show off their new stars. Geri wore bright-green lurex trousers that flared at the knee and a vest top. She'd bought the material at Berwick Street market and had made the outfit herself with the help of her half-sister Karen.

The girls found themselves in extremely lofty company. They shared a table with Lenny Kravitz, Vanessa Paradis and husband-and-wife Ken and Nancy Berry, who headed Virgin and EMI records. To her delight, Geri was introduced to Take That by their PR woman Nikki Chapman. It was an eventful night – the year that Michael Jackson performed and Jarvis Cocker ran on stage to steal the limelight. Geri even confronted Tony Blair that night, with: 'Mr Blair, I'm Geri and I'm in an all-girl band. We're going to be huge. We're about to make our first video, would you be interested in appearing in it?'

Tony declined, saying he was too busy – although the greater probability is that he remembered Neil Kinnock being the subject of ridicule when he appeared in Tracey Ullman's video for 'They Don't Know About Us'.

In March, as part of an early publicity boost, Simon set up a meeting with the assistant producer of *TFI Friday*, Suzie Aplin, who was then Chris Evans's girlfriend. The girls met Suzie at the Radio 1 studios and staged an impromptu performance of 'Wannabe'. At the end of the song, Geri spotted Chris Evans looking through the glass doors. He mouthed, 'Why don't you just go back to *Live and Kicking*?'

But the girls were to get their revenge. Back at Geri's house she and Mel B decided to send a fax to the ginger tycoon. It read:

Dear Chris (ginger bollocks!),

Hi, this is the Spice Girls (Melanie and Geri).

Don't judge this book by its cover, mate. There's more to us than that!

We are sure you appreciate balls and honesty. We are the same breed.

Spice Girls.

The girls had made quite a splash at the Brits, with everyone wondering about the new band on the scene, and they followed this up with a further bravura performance. Virgin Records took them to the races – Kempton Park racecourse to be exact – where, along with other Virgin signings, they were housed in the company's hospitality tent. The other signings contented themselves with performing a few numbers to their captive audience but the girls felt they could do better than that. For a start they dragged one of the producers of *Live and Kicking* into the ladies loos and sang an a cappella version of the song to him. And then came the real publicity blitz.

At a sign from one of them, all five rushed outside and clambered on to a bronze statue of Red Rum, before launching into a rendition of 'Wannabe' – the first ever public performance of their first hit. As soon as they realised what was happening, the stewards manhandled them down to the ground, but the girls had made their mark. They were euphoric. 'I spooked out three blokes who tried to pick me up. It was cool,' said one, unnamed, member of the band.

'Yeah, and two of those were big, butch security guards,' said another.

It was a spectacular publicity coup and it was witnessed by one Vincent Monsey, chief executive of music channel The Box. The girls could not have picked a better audience. 'When I saw the Spice Girls on top of Red Rum, their personalities came right through and I knew they would do something big,' said Monsey. 'They had self-propelling talent.' He wasted no time and, six weeks before its release, set out to acquire a video of

'Wannabe', which The Box ran 70 times a week – an honour usually accorded only to number ones.

The channel was ideal for the girls. At that stage The Box had a higher audience share than MTV Europe and was viewed by 25 per cent of 25 to 34 year olds in the cable television audience, which at that point was about 400,000. 'The Box has definitely played a part in the Spice Girls' success,' said Ray Cooper of Virgin Records. 'The fact is, The Box has exactly the right demographic when you're breaking a new young act.'

The support from The Box was all the more invaluable because some aspects of the music industry had still to be convinced that an all-girl band could work. Teen magazines, in particular, held on to the idea that girls do not like girl bands. 'Our female readers have always hated all-girl bands,' said one magazine editor. 'They fear they will steal their boy idols.'

'At first the music press blanked them, particularly the teen press such as *Top Of The Pops* magazine,' said Robert Sandall of Virgin. 'They did not think that people would go for them. As soon as the record started happening, then they were on top of them.'

What everyone was slower to realise was that this was one girl band that was singing out in favour of female friendship. After all, their first and, to this day, most famous song, 'Wannabe', contains the lines 'If you wanna be my lover, you gotta get with my friends/Friendship

lasts forever, friendship never ends …' As Geri herself
was later to put it, if only.

It was Geri, though, who realised immediately that if
they were to get anywhere, they had to appeal to young
girls. 'We don't want to alienate the girlies,' she said.
'We're not too pretty so that we offend them, we're just
like them, we want them to join our club.' It did the
trick. Girl power was born.

And as interest grew in the band as a whole, so the
individual girls began to attract attention and little
potted biographies were distributed to tell the world
who they were. Mel B is 'a bit mad, a bit spontaneous
and easily bored'. She is of mixed race and brutally
honest. Emma is from the south of England and the
baby of the group. 'She's a Top Shop girl with her
blonde hair and pink clothes. She drives a Jeep and
looks like Barbie.' Mel C from Liverpool is a tomboy.
She wears tracksuits, talks about football, has a tattoo
and drinks a lot. Oh, and she doesn't like men much.
(It might be that last slightly unfortunate attribute
that later gave rise to the totally false rumours that
Mel is a lesbian.) Victoria is a lady. She wears
designer clothes and dark glasses and won't be seen
in public without make-up. And Geri? She's 'lived on
the edge'. She's wild and wacky, is half Spanish and is
interested in star signs.

And finally the girls began to win round the teen

mags. 'We still need popstars,' said Kate Thornton of *Smash Hits* magazine, shortly after the girls became famous. 'Until six months ago, we had a real problem finding acts for the cover. Now we're spoiled for choice. People have this thing about being credible. Supergrass were trying to walk away from what they had done because it was popular. But that's exactly what pop should be about – popularity. They're [the Spice Girls] not ashamed of what they stand for, so they have credibility. They're as credible as Oasis in their own field. I call them "Oasis with a wonderbra".'

Later in the year Kate put the girls on the cover. 'We're glad to have them around,' she said. 'Otherwise the cover would have gone to a safe bet such as Boyzone. Loads of bands come into the office, we get about three a week, but [the Spice Girls] were different. They went to great lengths to explain that they had a lot to say for themselves. What's great about the girls is that they're new. I think they appeal to girls more than boys. Every girl has a dream and they've made it happen. For me, "Wannabe" is the best pop record of 1996.'

Oliver Smallman, managing director of the 1st Avenue label and management company, saw them as someone else. 'Spice Girls is a replacement for Bananarama,' he said. 'They do their job and we need them.'

What has not been widely appreciated, however, is that by the time they'd started doing that job in the UK, they'd already been having trial runs elsewhere. Before 'Wannabe' was released in their home market, they had been performing in Japan and South East Asia. 'People [in the UK] think they're an overnight success, but a lot of planning went into the timing of the releases,' said Lorraine Barry of Virgin.

The girls were also keen not to confine themselves to this sceptre'd isle. 'We wanted to be an international act, not just big in the UK,' said Mel C. 'For me, the clincher with Virgin was that international was a priority from day one,' said Simon Fuller. 'We thought this was something we could give to Japan and Asia first and still not let the other territories suffer,' added Lorraine Barry of Virgin. Their first single went on to sell 100,000 copies in Japan.

And then came the greatest publicity coup of all – and for once, it wasn't stage managed by the girls, Simon Fuller or Virgin. A reporter for *Top Of The Pops* magazine came to interview them, and it was he who came up with the idea of giving them nicknames. It was a brilliant idea and it stuck. Victoria became Posh Spice (a soubriquet she had later to live down when it emerged she was nothing of the sort), Mel B was Scary, Mel C was Sporty, Emma was Baby and Geri, then a voluptuous redhead, became Ginger. As a marketing ploy it could not possibly have been bettered.

Finally, in July 1996, 'Wannabe' was released in

England. It went straight to number one, knocking ex-Take That singer Gary Barlow off the top slot after just one week. Everyone was euphoric, as well they might have been, and comparisons with another five-piece teen band were numerous. 'Going to number one hasn't sunk in for us yet,' said Mel C. 'We've been working so hard for the past two years. It's a great compliment to be compared to Take That, because they were so successful for such a long time. But we are different. They were controlled by a management team. We are on our own. At the end of the day, we all write our own stuff. We are not Take That, we are the Spice Girls.' On another occasion they were happier to accept the comparison. 'We're Take That with tits!' they cried.

They certainly started playing up to their image with a vengeance. Out came all the stories about living in Maidenhead, except they chose to emphasise the good living rather than hard work aspect of their existence. 'When we shared a house in Maidenhead for nine months, it was like girls behaving really badly,' said Victoria (of all people). 'We'd have parties and invite all these boys around and make them strip off. We'd be shouting and whistling at them – then we'd sling all their clothes out of the window and laugh as they ran around naked. Our parties were the talk of the town.'

The country reeled. More – much more – was to come. 'In Japan they were singing things such as

"Get your tits out for the lads",' giggled Victoria. 'What a laugh!'

'We've got about a fiver between us,' snapped Geri, practical as always. 'Everyone thinks if you have a number one you're immediately rich – but we've not seen any of the money yet. We can't wait to go out and buy some new clothes.'

'I'll chase a bloke I like, but it makes men nervous,' boomed Mel B.

Geri was thinking about men, too, but in her case it was boy bands that were taking up her thoughts. Life had been too easy for them. 'They just have to get their abdomens out and target the teen market – good for them but not us,' she declared.

Mel C wanted to be a footballer and played as a midfielder for Rickmansworth Ladies team. 'But it has been difficult recently because of our number one,' she confided.

Geri was thinking about men again. 'I am mentally single,' she remarked. 'Although it is nice to have someone around for a good old snog!'

Emma was thinking about being a baby. 'They mother me and it's nice because I get spoiled,' she said coyly. 'Girl power is important. We've got a growing army of girl fans who know where we're coming from.'

Geri's mind was by this time also on more serious matters. 'My tummy button's pierced,' she squeaked. 'I met the Backstreet Boys recently and I told them I had a W tattooed on each of my bum cheeks so that it spells WOW. They believed me!'

And so it went on, but behind all the posturing the girls were making musical history. 'Wannabe' entered the *Guinness Book of Records* when it became the first debut single by an all-girl band to go straight into the charts at number one. Not only did it knock Gary Barlow from the top slot but – ironically – it also held back a cover version of George Michael's 'Freedom' by Robbie Williams. It stayed at number one for seven weeks, reached the number one slot in 21 other countries and sold 2.7 million copies in total. Girl power was set to take over the world.

13

Faster
Spice Girls!
Kill! Kill!

The world had never seen anything like it. The Spice Girls seemed to have appeared out of nowhere and, practically from the moment they were unveiled by their record company, they created an absolute sensation. One newspaper remarked, 'Although Spice's puppyish line-up have been together since 1993, and with Virgin Records for the last year, they've never played live or undergone the other usual initiations. They simply emerged,

Wonderbra-ed and oven-ready and became number one.' The world watched open mouthed. Just who were these girls – and where had they come from?

The girls rose to the occasion magnificently. 'We're just five girlies who have touched down on the planet,' cooed Geri. Everyone chose their favourite Spice Girl and was immediately introduced to the concept of girl power: 'It's not like the old feminism where you had to burn your bra,' explained Mel B. 'You can wear your bra and your mascara but do it for you, not for the lads.'

Girl power was also pretty scary: at the Birmingham Radio 1 Roadshow in the summer the girls terrified members of Let Loose and East 17 – both boy bands – by mooning at them and threatening to trash their dressing rooms. The poor lambs were given security guards to protect them from this new breed of Amazon.

And then the inevitable happened: the kiss-and-tells began. Geri was the subject of one almost immediately, but this was a kiss-and-tell with a difference. The lucky man, cameraman James Dutton, was only too keen to tell – but it emerged they'd never even kissed. Some years earlier, he and the then 17-year-old Geri had become friends when he was in the middle of a temporary separation from his wife, and he had found himself in her bedroom, with Geri in the bed and James sitting on it. 'She looked pretty ordinary with no make-up,' he said.

'I was sitting on her bed with black satin sheets and I wondered if they were a gift from a sugar daddy. She said, "I've got to get dressed now" and I said I would leave. She said, "No, just turn around," and I was aware that there was this very sexy girl there. When I did look round it was peculiar. She was all made up and I knew I couldn't just be friends with her. She was my mate and I knew it was going to be really difficult. But I couldn't take my eyes off her. I think she realised that and she was flirting. She looked like a movie star and I thought, There's no way I can just be a mate with this girl.'

But that's all he ever was. The two had met at a rave near Watford and, having swapped phone numbers, they became friends. But it was Geri who held back from a romantic encounter and even encouraged James to patch up the relationship with his wife. He did. James in turn listened to Geri as she confided her ambitions to be a star. 'It was all about her struggles,' he said. 'She didn't have any money. I think she came from a reasonably poor background but she had this amazing energy. I felt slightly sorry for her. There was this girl that looked great and had a lovely personality, although she didn't have a huge amount of ability, but who wanted to be a singer.

She said she had a terrible voice but she used to sing to me down the phone. She was one of those kids living in a bedsit, struggling to make ends meet.'

Two things stand out from the interview. One is Geri's fear of not making it and the other is the fact that, as throughout so much of her life, she seemed not to have many friends. This is one of the strangest aspects of Geri's personality: despite the fact that she is lively and outgoing, she seems to find it almost impossible to maintain any long-term friendships, possibly because of a certain amount of self-obsession.

'I'd be sympathising with her and her battle in life to get on and how nothing was happening,' James said. 'She used to get quite down about where she was going. I just thought, This girl has quite a strong personality but I knew there was this vulnerable side and I thought she would just get used and tossed to one side. She had the enthusiasm but didn't seem to have the contacts.' She also seemed lonely, with few friends and no boyfriend. 'I think that was why she was phoning me – she actually appreciated the fact I wasn't trying to get into her knickers,' said James. 'I wasn't trying to come on to her all the time whereas I think a lot of the guys she knew were. I think it was because I wasn't a flash git with his arm hanging out of a Porsche that we became friends.'

And now, all these years later, Geri was still single: in fact, she admitted in her first ever solo interview that she hadn't had sex for nearly a year … 'I've just been walking around the park on my own,' she said wistfully. 'I want that companionship, someone to be affectionate with and have sex with. I have a great life, some real laughs with the girls. But it would be nice to go home and have someone just for me, someone who is going to tell me everything is all right.'

Geri was also feeling broody. 'I've thought about adopting a baby,' she said. 'And I would be willing to bring up that child on my own. I remember seeing a documentary a few years ago about the Dying Rooms in China, full of abandoned baby girls. It really upset me and I could see myself adopting a child like that. I've got enormous respect for any single parent or mother and not having a man wouldn't stop me from having a family. I want to be a mother but I know I would hate to lose myself completely in motherhood. I can see myself in five years' time living in a big house in the country with a husband, a brood of children and a dog.'

She got the big house and the dog, but the husband and children are still in the future – although at the time of writing Damian Warner looks as if he might fit the bill. No matter. Back then the girls were in an absolute whirl and coping well. Almost inevitably, the nude pictures surfaced: Geri's response was, so what? And then, in September, their second number one was released, 'Say You'll Be There'. Just like the first, it went straight to number one.

And just like the first, it had an absolutely sensational video to back it up. This lot had the girls dressed in black PVC, starring in a slightly incomprehensible film which would appear to involve saving the world, although the video doesn't bear too close an examination. It is, however, enormously entertaining to watch. The video was loosely based on the movie *Faster Pussycat! Kill! Kill!* Geri dreamed up the girls' B-movie style names. She was Trixie Firecracker; Victoria became Midnight Suki; Mel C was Katrina High Kick; Emma Kung Fu Candy and Mel B Blazing Bad Zulu. Filming took place in the Mojave Desert, California, and pre-sale figures for the single were the highest Virgin had ever taken. Just before its UK release, the girls did a whistlestop tour of the Far East that included Japan, Hong Kong, Thailand and Korea. Once out, the song was selling 100,000 copies a day.

The world really was waking up to what a sensational act the Spice Girls had become. 'We haven't seen a pop act sell this fast since Take That split up,' said a spokesman for HMV. Virgin was even happier. 'Girl power is seeing off the boy bands. The attraction for boys is obvious because they are five very pretty girls with a lot to say for themselves,' said a clearly delighted spokesman. 'But a lot of young girls bought the last single as well, because at last they have role models who aren't middle-aged and singing about love – they are just out to have a good time.'

And, of course, to sell a lot of records, too. By October, all eyes were already on a Christmas number one, with odds being slashed from 25/1, where they had been just two months previously, to just 6/1. 'We're quietly cocky,' said Robert Sandall of Virgin. 'For the Spice Girls, it will be the icing on the cake.'

The girls, meanwhile, were busy appealing to every section of the record-buying public they could think of and next on the list was the lesbian community. Mel B started it, by having her tongue pierced and then (she claimed) getting all the other girls to snog her so they knew how it felt. Then it was Geri's turn. What did she think of pop singer Louise? She has 'lovely breasts', the fiery one replied. And what did she think about the group having lesbian fans? 'We want girls screaming at us, not just boys,' Geri replied. Girl power really was for all the girls.

Next stop on the Spicerama was turning on the Oxford Street Christmas lights. This was an honour more often accorded to bands (or people) who had been famous for slightly more than four months, but the Spice Girls were breaking all the rules, so why not this one too? No less than 5,000 screaming fans gathered in the freezing November cold to see them switch on the display. It was the moment, Geri later said, when she really realised they'd made it.

The girls could do no wrong. They seemed almost incapable of opening their mouths without providing a sound bite and Geri was the most articulate of the lot. 'We can strike a chord, give feminism a kick up the arse. Women can be so powerful when they show solidarity,' she said in an interview with *The Face*. On another occasion she announced, 'There are always preconceptions that you are some sort of bimbo or, if you've got something to say, you're a bitch with attitude. You can't win. So I'm saying, don't take me for granted. If a macho guy thinks I'm a bimbo or easy, I'm not. I've got brains and intelligence.'

That was not enough to stop the publication of more nude pictures, however. The magazine *New Talent* (and its talent does not refer to musical ability) managed to get yet more pictures of Geri in the raw. This time round she tried to stop publication, but couldn't when it was discovered that copyright belonged to the photographer. 'Many girls appear here because they want to get noticed and become famous,' said a spokesman. 'People do tend to get a bit shy about these things when they become famous, but we think she has a beautiful body.'

But Geri wanted to be accepted for her mind as well, and she managed it in a spectacular fashion when the Spices were interviewed for *The Spectator* magazine – a sort of house magazine for the Conservative Party. Simon Sebag Montefiore interviewed the girls and discovered, to everyone's shock, that they were as political as they were musical. 'We Spice Girls are true Thatcherites,' declared Geri, who Simon described as resembling 'nothing less than a leggy, pouting, pneumatically Eurosceptic John Redwood'. And Geri had more to say. 'Thatcher was the first Spice Girl, the pioneer of our ideology – girl power,' she proclaimed. 'But for now we are desperately worried about the slide to a single currency. Britain was the first to break away from the Roman Empire. When push comes to shove, the pounds, the dollars and deutschmarks can't be equal. They can't all be the same standard.'

It emerged that Geri had views on just about everything, starting with the monarchy (this was before the girls started hobnobbing with Prince Charles). 'The royals are the best soap opera in the world,' declared Ginger. 'But also, if you look at our British constitution as a big football match, they are like the most objective referees. Prince Charles talks about faith and the environment, yet the media blames him for his divorce in a nation of divorcees. Well, the Spice Girls don't think he's done anything wrong. It's unfair what they say about him. He's a tolerant humanitarian. But best of all, he is a true eccentric. In the future, over time, we'll appreciate that. The media's wrong about him!' All told, it is not surprising that Charles got on with the girls so well.

Tony Blair, however, did not rank so highly in the girls' estimation. 'His hair's all right but we don't agree with his tax policies,' said Geri. 'He's just not a safe pair of hands for the economy. But the real problem with Blair is that he's never had a real job. In the olden days a politician could be a coal miner who came to power with ideals. Not Blair. He's just a marketing man. No ideals!'

The world then learned that not only was Geri's hero a Conservative politician – Sir Winston Churchill – but that she was thinking about standing as a Tory MP herself. 'Our V is for Victory and my smoking cigars are Churchillian,' Geri informed

278

Simon, while drawing on what he referred to as a 'thoroughly unChurchillian cigarillo' and throwing him a V sign. 'We need more women MPs. That's why we're considering politics,' she went on, in reference to the soon-to-be-vacant Kensington and Chelsea seat (in the event it went first to Alan Clarke and then to Michael Portillo). 'I'm considering whether to throw my Spice into the ring and stand. If the people want me, I could not refuse. I'd be like Glenda Jackson.'

Tony Blair put a brave face on it. 'Tony will not stop listening to the Spice Girls just because they like Mrs Thatcher,' said a tactful aide.

The interview made headlines across the board – even the *Financial Times* carried the story – and left Simon Sebag Montefiore, amongst others, very impressed with the new generation of popstars. 'It was light-hearted, but there was a serious side,' he said. 'The Spice Girls are influencing a whole generation of youngsters and no one really knows how that generation thinks. It was a very pleasant interview. These are no bimbos. I expected them to espouse typical left-wing popstar politics, with a few pathetic ideas on the legalisation of heroin and some fuzzy thoughts on individuality and community policies, but I found them bright, articulate and with a full grasp of the great issues of the day.'

They also had a full grasp of what made brilliant publicity and that was it. Their first album, *Spice*, was now out, as was their third single, '2 Become 1'. Both made it to number one, the single topping the Christmas chart. There was a brief moment of embarrassment when it turned out that four of the girls had been lying about their age – 24-year-old Geri was pretending to be 22, 22-year-old Mel C was laying claim to 20, 20-year-old Emma was hanging on to 18 and 22-year-old Victoria was really 21 – but otherwise, world domination was going pretty much according to plan. The next hapless victim was Eamonn Holmes when he invited the girls on to the breakfast show at GMTV: what was their Christmas wish? he asked. 'I want to have your babies, Eamonn!' cried Geri, before all the girls crowded in on him asking for a kiss.

The show's insiders loved it. 'They were a real hit with all the blokes backstage,' said one. 'They were dashing around and flirting like mad with all the crew on the set. They were like a whirlwind, charming the pants off everyone. If that's girl power, they can come back here any time. We couldn't have asked for a better Christmas bonus than a visit from the Spice Girls.'

But the girls were too busy to go back. They rushed off to present the special Christmas edition of *Top Of The Pops*, where they met the children of Dunblane, who had recorded an anti-gun song, 'Knocking On Heaven's Door'. The girls were more than magnanimous, especially as the children's song was a rival to their own number, '2 Become 1'. 'The kids were wonderful and everyone had a fabulous time,' the girls cried. 'We won't mind if Dunblane is number one. It's a great cause and one we believe in.'

The children themselves were thrilled to meet the girls. 'The Spice Girls spent an endless amount of time with the children,' said Ted Christopher, the man behind the Dunblane single. 'They helped them have an extra-special day.'

'The Spice Girls are lovely lasses,' said Dunblane bassist Tommy Millar. 'They hung around with us all day during filming. Geri wanted a big cuddle from my wee son David and the other Spice Girls were egging him on to give her a kiss.'

Keyboard player Jon Young agreed. 'It was all giggles and cuddles and getting to know the children,' he said. 'On the way home they were all so excited they were singing Spice Girls songs for most of the journey. It was great to see how much the kids enjoyed the whole trip.'

There was a very brief pause for Christmas, but the girls were soon back on the road again. First

there was a short scoot around the US when
'Wannabe' was released across the pond – it made its
debut at number 11 and, almost inevitably by this
time, went to number one – to say nothing of
keeping the rest of Europe happy. The Spice Girls
were a hit just about everywhere, with boys and girls
alike. 'They're sexy, they're fresh, they're
revolutionary and they're really cool,' said Sabine
Wanninger of German teen magazine *Bravo*. 'That's
something the boys out there have long been waiting
for. Female aggressiveness-cum-eroticism knocks
them over.'

And then, in February 1997, came another
triumph: the Brit Awards. The previous year the
girls had attended as real-life wannabes: now they
were probably the most famous people there. And
Geri, in particular, stood out: she was wearing a
tight, thigh-skimming Union Jack dress that she
twice burst out of. 'If you wear a tight dress like
this, you've got to expect it,' she said brightly.
'Everyone has seen them before, so I don't give a
damn. This is the best night of our lives ever, so I
don't care what happens.'

It certainly was a night to remember. The girls
were nominated for five awards and won two: Best
British Single for 'Wannabe' and Best British Video
for 'Say You'll Be There'. They performed their

latest number, 'Who Do You Think You Are?', and Geri seized the moment to stand up for Britain. 'We owe all our success to Britain and we're proud to be ambassadors of pop for our country,' she said. 'Everyone has been amazed how fast we've hit America, especially us. We've done it even faster than the Beatles. Now everyone is expecting us to up sticks and move over there for good, but we'd never do it – we love Britain too much and we're dead proud to be British.'

Their one detractor was Liam Gallagher, who stayed away because he said he'd be too tempted to punch one of the girls. This, of course, merely provided the opportunity for yet more publicity. 'Come and have a go if you think you're hard enough,' sneered Mel C as she went up to collect an award. The audience – and the world – loved it.

The girls were revelling in their celebrity and whooping it up wherever they went. Geri and Mel C attended a Blur concert at the London Astoria and clambered up on stage. They danced halfway across until dragged back by a bouncer who clearly didn't realise who they were. 'Blur's security thought they were fans,' said an insider. 'He didn't have a clue they were from the Spice Girls. But when he realised who they were, they were given VIP treatment backstage.'

'We've been having a bit of fun and enjoying our girl power,' giggled Geri.

They were also enjoying their spending power. None of the girls has ever gone completely over the top with their finances but, with the exception of Victoria, the girls did not come from moneyed backgrounds and were set to enjoy their new wealth. 'We've all done quite nice things for our families,' explained Mel C. 'A few houses bought, a few new cars and stuff. We're just sorting out our families really. [But] most of it is in the bank because you never know what's going to happen tomorrow.' A few treats were in order, though: Geri splashed out on an Aston Martin DB6.

The girls also brought out a book detailing their thoughts about the world, but still Geri was having to battle with her racy past. Yet more photos emerged and this time round Athena was the one to upset her – the store giant was selling posters and cards of a near-naked Geri. 'They may not be the image the Spice Girls want now,' said managing director Kishan Shah, 'but we've had no complaints.'

In May the girls all cheered up again when they performed in front of Prince Charles for a Prince's Trust performance in Manchester which, yet again, made headlines. They sang three numbers for his royal Spiceness, but the highlight of the show came when Geri sang 'Do you wannabe my lover', pointing straight at the blushing prince, before blowing so many kisses she had to be dragged off the stage by Emma. The audience (and Prince Charles) loved it. Nor were the girls any less boisterous when they were introduced after the show. 'I think you are very sexy,' beamed Geri, who was almost bursting out of a blue and white ra ra outfit. 'We could spice up your life.' The other girls then proceeded to cover him with kisses, while Geri patted him on the bottom. Prince Charles looked quite overcome.

With that it was off to Cannes, where the girls managed the joint feat of launching *SpiceWorld: The Movie* and upstaging President Jacques Chirac. The film will be 'fun, adventure, romantic, saucy and naughty,' said Geri. 'It's a parody of ourselves. We are basically taking the mickey out of ourselves.'

They weren't the only ones. Geri received the dubious compliment of featuring in *The Archers*, when the then 14-year-old William Grundy named a prize Jersey heifer after her. 'It's great that the Spice Girls have filtered through to all walks of life – even the farmers in Ambridge,' said a Spice Girls spokeswoman.

Meanwhile, it was back to making the film, and the finished product, although critically panned at the time, stands up to scrutiny. The girls had been at the top for a full year and had sold 14.3 million albums and 8 million singles. Their earnings were estimated at £55 million and their first album had gone triple platinum. But the work was beginning to take its toll. Pictures taken on the set of the film show the girls looking exhausted, as indeed they were. 'People in the industry are saying good luck to them,' said a music industry insider, 'but how long can the girls keep up with the frantic pace? It's tough work and can be very stressful. They've just begun, but already they've made huge amounts due to clever management. They've got everything sewn up and it seems there's still lots more to be made as the girls all want long careers in pop.'

In retrospect, it is clear this was the beginning of the end. It was the girls' manager, Simon Fuller, who had established such a heavy workload for them, not least because he was determined to, quite literally, cash in as long as the girls were still hot. And it wasn't just the incessant country-hopping that was bringing in the money – Fuller was also arranging a series of extremely lucrative sponsorship deals that would make the girls even wealthier.

But the strain was taking its toll. All were shattered and Geri, the ebullient, desperate-for-fame Geri, was overheard screaming in the street at a photographer who would not leave her alone. She gave an interview saying she hadn't had sex for nine months, so nervous was she of men kissing and telling, and it then emerged that she had moved into an extremely isolated barn in Hertfordshire in order to get a bit of privacy. The Spice bandwagon was to roll on for a while yet, shedding the odd member and manager along the way, but this was the point at which disillusionment began to set in. And for all of the girls, in their different ways, there was no turning back.

14

The Beginning of the End

The girls might have begun to feel the downside of fame, but there was still some way to go before the cracks really began to show. For a start, there was a live tour to embark on. The band had been criticised from a fair few quarters about the fact that they had never done a tour – Noel Gallagher was one of their most vociferous critics – and now it was time to show what they were made of. Ironically, given the fact that it was she who walked out before the tour was over, Geri was the one who boasted most about what the girls were going to do. 'We'll show the world we can cut it as a live act,' she

boomed. 'To all the men coming along to the show –
we're gonna tour the pants off ya.'

And mixed in with all of this was the promotional
work they were doing. Knowing they wouldn't be on top
for ever (or even very long) Simon Fuller had signed
them up to promote just about everything you could
think of, which left them in severe danger of over-
exposure. Just one year earlier, the girls had seemed to
jump out of nowhere. Now they were everywhere,
including the cover of a lollipop. It might have brought
them in a good deal of cash, but it didn't do much for
their credibility.

The most innovative deal they did was with Pepsi, of
which more later. Apart from that, they really were
everywhere, starting with Walkers' Crisps. They did a
two-tier advertising campaign: first they launched a new
Cheese & Chives range with a limited edition featuring
pictures of the girls on the packets, and for the second
campaign the girls were featured across the whole range
of Walkers' Crisps and Doritos, with the chance to win
£100,000 and a range of Spice memorabilia, including
jackets, CDs and lapel badges. Both campaigns featured
advertisements with Gary Lineker and the girls, and they
certainly deserved the £1 million they were paid – the
Cheese & Chives range lifted Walkers' share of the crisp
market up 6 per cent, while overall their sales rose by
14.5 per cent. Geri's take on the whole thing was

typically succinct: 'There's nothing negative about crisps, know what I mean?'

Next up was Asda. The girls were signed to promote more than 40 products in the run-up to Christmas, ranging from cakes to a 'Spicey' pizza. There were no television ads, but the girls featured on billboards and packaging. It was reportedly a further £1 million in the can. Polaroid then got them at a bargain price: a mere £750,000, including £1 per camera sold. They featured in advertisements on MTV to promote the Spice Camera and different types of film. Impulse fared better still: it snapped them up for £500,000 to make advertisements to be shown on television and the cinema for a special body spray called Impulse Spice.

Chupa Chups then paid them £250,000 to promote a range of products including a ball containing 48 lollipops. Sony PlayStation coughed up £1 million for a SpiceWorld PlayStation game including five songs and video clips and Channel Five got them to support its launch for – nothing. It had signed up the girls before they hit the big time and so they sang a reworked version of '5, 4, 3, 2, 1' as '1, 2, 3, 4, 5'. They also shot a promotional video for the station and turned on the switch at Marble Arch. It might not have made them money but it created a lot of publicity.

And then there was the £1 million deal with Pepsi – a deal intimately wrapped up with the forthcoming tour.

It went like this. The girls signed up for a three-tier deal with Pepsi, the first ever of its kind. First they filmed a 30-second commercial, initially meant only for the UK, but which became so successful it was shown worldwide, and secondly made an 'on-can' promotion with pictures of the girls on the products. Pepsi drinkers could then send in 20 ring pulls for a Spice Girls CD which featured four previously unreleased songs. Given that cans of Pepsi cost 35p, £7 might have seemed a bit steep for a single, but Pepsi pointed out that the fans got 20 cans of soft drinks thrown in as well. And finally, the third tier concerned the girls' first ever live concert, which was to be held on 12 October 1997. Everyone who sent in for a CD was automatically entered into a ballot: 20,000 lucky winners were given tickets to the concert. As a way of weeding out unsympathetic reviewers, it was a masterstroke.

Pausing only to temporarily relocate to France for tax reasons, the girls headed off to Istanbul to give their first proper live concert. It was a massive success. In Istanbul's Abdi Ipecki Arena lights dimmed, smoke burst from the stage, fireworks banged and the band began. The lights went up to reveal a rollercoaster set with a gold Mini perched on it and then the girls came on: Geri first in a red spangly top, black mini shorts and a crown in her hair. The others followed and off they went, launching into a rendition of 'If You Can't Dance', which was followed by 'Who Do You Think You Are?'. They performed for 80 minutes in all, complete with four costume changes, two encores – the second was 'Wannabe' – and if it was Mel C doing most of the singing, backed up by Mel B and Emma, with Geri and Victoria hardly singing at all, no one carped. In fact, everyone loved it. The Spice Girls had finally proved themselves as a live act and the fans were overjoyed. 'I think they are cool,' said Didem Ozucler, a fan. 'They dance well and their singing is OK.'

'They were brilliant,' added her friend Elgin Demiray.

Even the critics liked it: 'The girls passed the test and proved their critics wrong,' wrote one.

And so it was off around the world on tour, starting in Europe, with *SpiceWorld: The Movie* due to come out on Boxing Day. It was at that point, with spectacularly bad timing, that the girls started to believe their own publicity and decided they could go it alone. All were exhausted from a frantic couple of years and they began to blame their manager, Simon Fuller, for piling up a workload which was simply too much for them to get through. And so, in an act of brutality that stunned many, they sacked him when he was on holiday in Italy recovering from a back operation.

It had been on the cards for some time. Just a couple of weeks previously Geri had been cornered by a journalist: what do the Spice Girls and their manager have planned next? she was asked. Geri was uncharacteristically evasive. 'Well, I've got loads of plans up my sleeve. But they are my plans – and no one else's. There are things about the Spice Girls that no one has any idea about. We are always honest, but we have our secrets, too.'

The sacking came as a complete surprise to absolutely everyone, not least Simon himself. And in retrospect it was perhaps not the girls' brightest move, for together he had made them superstars, and apart all of them have struggled to find a way forward. Had they remained under his wing, they might have been able to create solo careers, which is certainly what Simon had been expecting at the time. 'There's absolutely no reason the girls can't have solo careers while keeping the Spice Girls alive,' he'd said just a couple of weeks previously, at the launch of their second album. 'Our plan is for them all to follow their own paths but with the support of each other. I think Geri and Victoria could be actresses. Mel C is the new Annie Lennox. Emma has an amazing pop voice and Mel B is a real soul diva. I'm very excited about the future for all of them. We talk about everything together and no decision is made by one person alone. We work as a family unit.'

A very dysfunctional family unit, as it was to turn out, and Simon was reportedly extremely shocked when he discovered what the girls had done. And they had been planning it for weeks, with Geri as the instigator behind the move. She clearly wanted to manage the group – she and Mel B had been competing to be the *de facto* leader practically from the moment the girls met, and it was reported that either she went or he did. The girls chose Geri, which goes a long way towards explaining why they feel the way they do about her today.

At the time, everyone was anxious to paper over the cracks. Simon issued a very gracious statement, alluding to a 'parting of the ways' and continuing, 'It has been great for us to be part of the success of the group over the last two years.' The girls were slightly less generous: they were 'hugely grateful' to their management team but 'We feel in our hearts that this is the right decision for us. We would like our fans to know that we are excited about the future.'

Behind the scenes it was a different story. 'Privately, Simon is raging at their behaviour,' said a friend. 'He thinks they are ungrateful. He thinks they have stabbed him in the back and is really shattered. He saw the girls as friends, not just a group he managed. Simon's reaction is one of complete shock. It all happened very quickly. The girls decided to do it and they did it.'

And it began to emerge quite how carefully the girls had planned their move. In August, each one had set up her own company – Geri's was called Firecracker Productions. In September, they had demanded to be made directors of Spice Girls Limited, the company Simon had set up to manage their global affairs – and, that done, they were in a position to take charge.

Geri moved fast. She had wanted to be their manager and so she began behaving as such. 'Last week they were holding talks with a video production company about a possible deal and Geri was doing all the talking,' said a Spice Girls insider. 'She seems to have learned the business very fast, she's become very shrewd. I've seen Geri telling the other girls what to do and say when they meet people. She is the boss.'

Certainly Simon had been working the girls very hard, aware that their shelf life might turn out to be short. 'Simon's view is to maximise the girls' earnings while he can as it will soon come to an end,' said the insider. 'He knows he's overworking them but he feels he's got to do that to make as much money as possible. The girls believe they can pull back from the spotlight and continue their success for another couple of years.'

Everyone knew the girls were worn out but whether they had acted wisely was another matter. 'They are exhausted and don't see why they have to keep piling on the work,' said a friend. 'They don't think they are going to fade away and feel there is plenty of time to make more money.' And, after all, they'd done it before – when they walked out on the Herberts. The only difference was that this time the stakes were a lot higher.

Others were a lot more cautious. 'I think there are two possible reasons why the Spice Girls have decided to sack Simon,' pop commentator Rick Sky said at the time. 'The first is that they are working too hard and want to take life a bit easier. In my experience money is behind these kind of break-ups. I think the girls have been foolish. They have not only bitten the hand that fed them, they have chewed it up and spat it out.'

'Geri made it clear that she and the others were not happy with the amount of control Simon had. She also talked about how they felt they were being worked too hard and he was making too much from them.'

Bizarrely, it appeared that none other than Nelson Mandela was behind the girls' action – and it was Geri in particular who drew inspiration from the charismatic leader. 'Meeting Mr Mandela had a profound effect on Geri,' said a member of 19 Management. 'She told me, "I can't believe we've met a national hero. I can't believe we've become this big."' And so, her attitude changed. 'It was gradual, but up until that point she, like the rest of the girls, believed the band would only be around for a couple of years. But after the meeting it was obvious she began really believing the hype. Before, Geri was getting increasingly wound up by the way the band was going. She felt that they were being over-exposed by Fuller, who did not have a long-term plan for the band. In many ways, the Mandela meeting was the final push for Geri.

She said meeting him made her feel empowered to sack Fuller. Geri has no idea what she's taking on. Fuller may have made a lot of money from the band but at the same time he ran a very slick operation.'

Seasoned industry observers thought the girls were mad. 'There is a part in every artist's career when they start to believe their own publicity,' said Pete Waterman, the man who made popstars of Kylie Minogue and Jason Donovan and who, funnily enough, was one of Geri's co-judges in 2002's *Popstars* series. 'This is when the danger signs start and the red light has just come on.' He, of all people, should have known – but still the girls paid no heed.

One of Simon's tactics had been to keep the record label, Virgin, at arm's length while he ran the girls' careers. Virgin was thus not too sorry to say goodbye to him, not least because they thought that, through their promotional work, the girls were becoming massively over-exposed. 'The general feeling is that the Spice Girls have been marketed successfully to the detriment of the music,' said one Virgin insider. 'And that's down to Simon. Where is the music in all this work for Walkers' Crisps and whatever else?'

There was also some disquiet because the second album had not been selling as successfully as the label had hoped. It went to the number one slot with sales of 191,000 but, although that was respectable, it was nothing like the first week sales of *Be Here Now* by Oasis, which reached 750,000.

Geri, however, was determined to prove herself. 'She has an awareness of the industry and the media,' said a band insider. 'She knows how and when to do things to get on the front pages, like kissing [Prince] Charles. The others are happy to let her be the spokesman. Most of the time, they follow her lead.'

They spoke too soon. Simon negotiated an estimated £15 million payoff and left. Geri was all set to take control, with just one problem – the other girls didn't want her to. They had always been a unit, each equal to the other, and so they wanted it to stay, with the result that no new manager was appointed and they all took on various areas of responsibility themselves. It was an unusual – and some would say rash – way to run a pop group. 'There are definitely no plans for Geri to take over,' said Sharon Hanley, their spokesperson. 'We really don't know what is going to happen, it is too early to tell.'

Matters were made worse over the following days when the girls were booed at the end of a concert in Spain and then virtually ignored when they went to Rome to record a Saturday-night television show. No fans were waiting at the airport, reportedly forcing the producers of the programme to hire a dozen children to make a fuss. In fact, press coverage became so negative

that the girls issued a statement: 'We're not splitting up!
We're not fighting! Girl power!'

The signs were already there, though. After
performing with the other girls in a Royal Variety
Performance, during which she almost burst out of her
dress (again), Geri and the other Spices made a quick
trip to Los Angeles. There Geri met Brad Pitt – and
bombarded him with questions about how to become
an actress. 'Geri sees Brad as a friend and adviser and
someone who knows the industry well,' revealed a
friend. 'She is fascinated by Hollywood and was quizzing
Brad about acting classes and the type of role she should
go for. She is determined to make the transition from
pop star to actress – just like her idol, Madonna.'

Back in England, the girls filmed *An Audience With
The Spice Girls* and set about publicising their film
SpiceWorld: The Movie, which was set to be released on
Boxing Day. Various interviewers were given access to
them in the run-up to the big day. Geri was asked if she'd
pushed the girls into sacking Simon in order to take over
herself. 'That's an insult to the other girls,' she snapped.
'The four of them have got just as much intelligence and
will of their own, I'm not that domineering. Bottom line,
every decision we take has got to be all five of us agreed
and all five of us took a decision to sack our
management.' So were they believing their own
publicity? 'No, what we've shown is actual girl power in

action. We've shown we do take our business seriously
and we take our destinies into our own hands. We've
always took [sic] responsibility for everything we've
done – it's just easier for the world to digest if it's not five
girls doing it, if there's a man behind it.'

Somehow the show staggered on. *SpiceWorld: The
Movie* came out and received decidedly lukewarm
reviews, although, in retrospect, it's a good deal more
amusing than anyone admitted at the time. (One of its
writers, incidentally, was Kim Fuller, Simon's brother, and
one of the characters in the film, the girls' manager,
played by Richard E. Grant, utters the following line:
'You haven't got a life! You've got a schedule.' Make
what you will of that.) And finally, in February 1998, the
girls embarked on their world tour.

15

Epilogue – Spice Alone

The tour was in full swing: the girls were in the middle of taking over Europe, with the United States charted in for later in the year. Geri was rich beyond her wildest dreams, with a fortune estimated at about £19 million. She had a glorious house – even if she came to want to sell it – a handsome boyfriend – Christian Horsfall, from whom she was also soon to part – and everything in the world to look forward to. Contrary to all expectations, the group had survived the sacking of Simon Fuller, were wowing audiences across the world and Geri was a woman with a mission. 'We're five girls who each has a brain,' she declared. 'Mine is ticking along all the time. Sometimes I tell myself, "Just take each day as it comes." But I can't help thinking the future is out there and before you know it, it'll be yesterday, so you have to think ahead sometimes.'

Never a truer word was spoken. Having failed in her ambition to manage the Spice Girls and finding life on the road a lot less fun than expected, Geri was having serious doubts about her future with the girls. She was fed up with having to share the limelight and annoyed that they had not given her time off to give an interview about her breast cancer scare. And so the inevitable began. The atmosphere was tense. The world's most famous pop group were gathering for an appearance on the National Lottery show in May 1998, but one of their number was missing. 'Where is she?' hissed the organisers to the girls.

'Where is she?' hissed the girls to one another.

No one knew the answer, but one thing was for sure: Geraldine Estelle Halliwell, aka Geri, aka Ginger Spice, was missing. And nobody knew where she was …

Samantha Al⋯⋯⋯ lives in Lincolnshire with a variety of animals and a schedule almost as busy and exciting as her plots! She writes a number of columns for newspapers and magazines, is a teen-age agony aunt for Radio Leeds and in her spare time she regularly competes in show-jumping, dressage and eventing.

Other Books in the
Hollywell Stables series

HOLLYWELL STABLES

Revenge
3

Samantha Alexander

To Koris,

Enjoy your holiday!

lou

13/5/95

X

MACMILLAN
CHILDREN'S BOOKS

First published 1995 by Macmillan Children's Books

a division of Macmillan Publishers Limited
Cavaye Place London SW10 9PG
and Basingstoke

Associated companies throughout the world

ISBN 0 330 338579

Copyright © Samantha Alexander

The right of Samantha Alexander to be identified as the
author of this work has been asserted by her in accordance
with the Copyright, Designs and Patents Act 1988.

1 3 5 7 9 8 6 4 2

A CIP catalogue record for this book is available from
the British Library

Phototypeset by Intype, London
Printed by Cox & Wyman

Chapter One

"They're coming this way!" my little sister Katie shrieked from the top of the muck heap.

"Mel, quick, help me!" my brother Ross shouted from across the yard, where Dancer was kicking at her stable door in a frenzy of excitement. Dancer was a beautiful racehorse we had saved from pneumonia, but she was very highly strung.

"What's going on?" Sarah, our stepmother, came running out of the house with her red hair flying all over the place and still wearing her carpet slippers.

"It's the hunt!" I shouted. "It's the Burlington Hunt. They're in our wood!"

No sooner were the words out of my mouth than the hounds were in full cry.

"They're in our field," Katie yelled, sliding down the muck heap and racing across to us. "They're heading straight for us!"

And there was no mistaking the sound of galloping hooves. It was like a stampede. A hunting horn filled the air, sending a cold shiver of dread up my spine – somewhere a fox was running for its life.

1

"How dare they come on our land?" Sarah fumed, bracing herself for a real fight.

None of us supported fox-hunting. We were a sanctuary for horses and ponies; we believed in saving lives, not killing in the name of sport.

"Mel, help me with Dancer's top door," Ross shouted, pushing Dancer's nose back into the stable. She was working herself up into a lather. "If we don't shut her in, she's going to jump out!"

Luckily, all the other horses were still in their stables, and although they were listening with their ears pricked forward, they weren't going crazy.

I could hardly believe what I saw next.

"There!" I pointed in the direction of our barn.

Crouched by the open door was a beautiful red fox. For a split second it stared at us with huge frightened eyes. Its whole body was trembling and one of its hindlegs dangled helplessly, caught in what looked like a strand of barbed wire. It was the first fox I'd seen close to. It hovered uncertainly and then half dragged, half flung itself through the open door.

"Quick!" Sarah yelled, running over the gravel towards the barn.

"Sarah!" I screamed, as the first hound leapt over the field gate, hot on the fox's scent.

2

"Oh, my God!" Ross murmured, and charged after her.

Sarah was desperately trying to unhook the barn door.

"Hurry!" I shouted, as more hounds leapt the fence in a great wave of yelping bodies.

Sarah flung shut the massive arched door just as the first hound dived at the paintwork.

"Sarah!"

Suddenly she was pinned up against the door by a flood of hounds, all going wild with frustration.

"Where's the huntmaster?" I shouted to Ross, but he couldn't hear me. Sarah must have been on the verge of fainting with fear.

"Oh, no!" I had suddenly noticed our two cats, Oswald and Matilda, running out of one of the stables, their fur standing on end. "Oswald, come here!" I managed to scoop up Oswald, but Matilda dived between my legs and ran into a rosebush.

I'll never forget what happened next. I know now that there was nothing I could do, but if only I hadn't picked up Oswald . . .

He was ripped from my hands by two hounds and tossed into the air like a helpless ball of wool.

"Oswald," I screamed. "Oswald!"

"Melanie!" Sarah shouted, fighting her way across to me and whipping me round so I couldn't see what was happening.

3

But I didn't have to see. I knew.

Katie couldn't stop sobbing. I was just numb all over. Ross looked as if every drop of blood had drained out of him.

The huntmaster arrived on the scene within seconds, but it was too late. Oswald was dead.

"I'm terribly sorry," the huntmaster said, looking down at us from a huge black horse.

The huntsman was rounding up the hounds and the rest of the riders were huddled in a corner of our field, looking subdued.

"I'm sorry," the huntmaster repeated. "What more can I say? It was an accident."

"How dare you?" screamed Sarah. "You've come on to our property without permission and you've killed an innocent animal. You're barbaric, the lot of you . . ." She paused for a moment, then, "I think you'd better leave," she said, jerking her head up and glaring at the man in the scarlet coat. "And don't think you've heard the last of this, because you haven't – not by a long chalk."

We spent the rest of the day in shock. Hollywell Stables had never been so quiet. Matilda, our other black and white cat, couldn't understand what was going on. Oswald had been there from the moment she'd been born and now he had disappeared. She kept popping in and out of the cat flap, looking for him, and she refused to touch any of her food.

4

Sarah rang up the news desk of the local paper and was furious when they showed little interest in what had happened to poor Oswald. They said they had done too much on fox-hunting already, which I thought was totally unfair. They were supposed to be there to report news, not ignore it.

We had gone to check on the fox immediately after the hunt left and had found it lying dead in a pool of blood. Its hindleg had been deeply gashed by the barbed wire. Sarah said it must have got caught up in a fence during the chase. When James, our vet and a good family friend, called round later, he said the fox was an old vixen and had most likely died of a massive heart attack. The chase had all been too much for it.

"Don't get involved, Sarah," James warned. "Just leave it alone. The hunt is part of country life, and, believe me, there are worse ways for a fox to die."

It was about three o'clock in the afternoon when the telephone rang. Sarah was in two minds whether to answer it. The last thing we wanted was any visitors; we were all still far too upset.

The caller didn't stay on the phone for long. Sarah listened intently without speaking, then slammed the phone down so hard the ornaments shook on the table.

"Who was that?" I asked, feeling worried.

Sarah was leaning against the banister and her hands were shaking.

"What day is it?" she asked in a hollow voice.

"Wednesday," I answered.

"The date, Mel!"

"It's 17 February, but why do you—" And then it suddenly dawned on me.

"It was Bazz, wasn't it?" Ross had just come up behind me. His words hung in the air and my stomach curled up into a tight knot of dread. If I closed my eyes, I could still picture Bazz's cruel, pulpy face leering at me. He was the person who had deliberately set fire to our stables and had neglected Queenie so badly that she had nearly died.

Today was 17 February – the day of his trial. With all the upset over Oswald we had completely forgotten.

"He's got off," Sarah said, hugging her body with her arms. "There wasn't enough evidence."

"The inspector did warn us," Ross said, keeping calm.

"He's got off and he is going to cause trouble."

"You don't know that for certain," Ross stated.

"Don't I?" Sarah flared up, anger burning in her eyes now.

The night of the fire was something none of us would ever forget. If Sarah hadn't come home early, all the horses would have been burnt alive.

"He's dangerous, Ross, he'll do anything."

Sarah explained that Bazz's brother Revhead had been sent down for handling stolen goods and that Bazz blamed us.

"He can't touch us," Ross said. "He's got to behave or he'll be sent to prison for sure."

"He threatened me," Sarah said.

"What do you mean?" Ross asked.

"Isn't it obvious?" Sarah snapped, looking really unnerved. "*He wants revenge!*"

Chapter Two

"It's crazy!" Ross stormed up and down the kitchen floor, running his hand through his jet-black hair in exasperation. "The man must be out of his mind."

We were talking about Charles Stonehouse, the master of the Burlington Hunt, the man responsible for Oswald's death.

James had just reported to us that he'd been called out to the hunt stables in the middle of the night. One of the hunt horses, the black one we had seen yesterday, had gone down with colic. It was serious and James had feared for the horse's life. It wasn't actually colic but a condition called choke which James said had been caused by feeding him dried sugar beet. I thought everyone knew that sugar beet had to be soaked for twelve hours before feeding, but James said it was one of the farmhands standing in for the groom who had made the mistake.

"There's nothing I can do," James said. "I can't dictate to owners how to look after their horses.

8

All I can do is advise. Unless it's a case of out-and-out cruelty, my hands are tied."

Charles Stonehouse had every intention of hunting Big Boris, as the horse was called, the day after next. It was totally against James's better judgement and that, in my book, was cruelty.

"You've said yourself he needs to be retired," Ross fumed.

"He's sixteen years old," James said. "He's been hunted into the ground. His legs have had it. But there's no way Stonehouse will retire him."

"Well, I think it stinks," Sarah said, speaking up for the first time. "And I can promise you this: there's no way we're going to sit back and let something happen to Boris!"

"Where *is* she?" Katie moaned for the hundredth time from the next-door stable, where she was grooming Bluey, our little roan pony with the wall-eye. I was tackling Queenie, whose mane looked like a bird's nest; her forelock had been stuck up in spikes ever since Katie accidentally lopped it off with the scissors a few weeks ago.

"Where has she got to?" I mumbled out loud, looking impatiently at my watch.

We were waiting for Sarah, who had set off two hours earlier to collect some Hollywell Stables

9

mugs which had a picture of Queenie on the front. We'd already had tea-towels and Christmas cards printed up, and special Hollywell sweatshirts, which were selling like hot cakes.

It had been Mrs Mac's idea to have proper merchandise made up to sell to the public. She was our one and only fund-raiser and her boundless enthusiasm kept us going in moments of despair. She was in the kitchen at the moment, baking two enormous apple pies, and Danny, who had come to stay with us for half-term, was helping her. Danny was nine years old and Katie's best friend. Since we'd first met him, last summer, he'd taken to horses and to Hollywell like a duck to water.

"Coeee! I'm just putting the kettle on," Mrs Mac shouted from the back door, where she stood, covered in flour. "Where's Ross?" She looked flushed in the face.

Ross had last been seen trying to find Jigsaw, our golden Labrador, who kept disappearing and nobody knew where. Mrs Mac thought he'd fallen in love with the spaniel down the road, but Ross wasn't convinced. Love was a very sore subject with Ross at the moment, because Mrs Mac kept teasing him about all the Valentine's Day cards he had received. Ross was annoyingly good-looking, but he hated anyone to mention it.

"Who's this?" Katie said, coming out of Bluey's

10

stable and across to mine with more horse hairs on her face and jumper than on the whole of Bluey and Queenie put together. She was looking at a little red Mini that was chugging up our drive.

"Beats me," I said, straining to get a glimpse of the driver. As a sanctuary, we were open to visitors every day of the week, but usually they rang beforehand and arranged a time to arrive.

Probably the tallest and gangliest man I'd ever seen clambered out of the driving seat, looking totally embarrassed. Katie and I stood staring in wonder as he rearranged his suit and flowery tie and picked up a notepad and tape-recorder.

He loped across to us on legs like stilts and held out his hand. "Roddy Fitzgerald," he said. "How do you do? I'm from the *Weekly Herald*."

Katie's lower jaw dropped to her knees and I had to nudge her in the ribs to bring her back to her senses.

He was just asking if I was Sarah Foster when Jigsaw came bounding into the yard from the field and made a beeline for Mr Fitzgerald.

"Stop him!" Ross panted from some distance behind, looking as if he'd just completed the London marathon.

"Oh, no," I murmured, as I noticed Jigsaw's nose and front paws plastered in thick, black mud

11

– and he was heading for Mr Fitzgerald's immaculate suit!

Before I could even try to stop him, Jigsaw launched himself into the air and planted both his front paws on Mr Fitzgerald's trousers – even Jigsaw couldn't reach as high as his jacket. Two ugly great marks were left behind and Mr Fitzgerald looked horrified.

"Oh, Mr Fitzgerald, I'm so sorry," I said, wondering how much the cleaning bill would be and whether we would have to pay it.

"Please," Mr Fitzgerald said, delicately brushing at his trousers and looking at his dirty hands in a state of shock. "Call me Roddy."

Ross led him off to the house to clean up, while Katie and I gave Bluey and Queenie some extra hay. Then we saw Sarah turn up the drive in our old Volvo.

"That man is impossible!" she protested, dragging out a huge cardboard box from the boot of the car. She went on to explain why she had been away so long: she'd been to the hunt stables to see Charles Stonehouse!

"I had to," she said. "I had to try to talk some sense into him about Boris. But do you know what he called me? An interfering do-gooder, just out to cause trouble. Can you believe that?"

She was fuming and I thought it best to try and distract her.

"Well, let's get this box into the house," I said. "There's somebody who wants to meet you."

We were just approaching the back door when someone inside started screaming their head off, and it sounded very much like Mrs Mac.

Filled with panic, we flung open the door, not knowing what to expect, and there she was, perilously balanced on the kitchen table, waving her rolling pin in the air and shrieking, "Mouse! Mouse!"

Danny was scrabbling around on his hands and knees under a chair and Ross was leaning against the wall, doubled up with hysterics.

"Sarah, do something!" Mrs Mac screamed in desperation.

But Sarah was too busy looking agog at Roddy Fitzgerald, who was perched next to Mrs Mac on top of the table, clutching his tape-recorder in both hands, as pale as the flour on the sideboard. His head was nearly touching the beams of the ceiling but, best of all, the trousers were gone and he was stood there, white-legged and knobbly-kneed, in his boxer shorts!

"Got him!" Danny shrieked, appearing from under the chair, holding what looked like a terrified white mouse, which immediately flipped out of his

13

hands and dived behind the washing machine.

It took ages to entice Roddy and Mrs Mac down from the table, especially as the mouse couldn't be found anywhere. Danny was starting to panic, because the mouse belonged to a school friend and he was supposed to be looking after it. He'd been hiding it in his pocket since he'd arrived, and apparently its name was Timmy and its favourite food was chocolate.

Roddy introduced himself to Sarah, who tried to take him seriously – which wasn't easy what with his polka-dot boxer shorts. Mrs Mac had whipped off his trousers to dry the muddy patch in front of the coal fire, but Roddy looked a whole lot happier once he had managed to pull them back on and started to ask Sarah questions about the hunt.

Ross went outside to fetch Dancer and Terence, our two racehorses, in from the field, and Katie and I listened to the interview with growing fascination. Roddy had just come out of journalism college and he was a junior on the weekly local paper. This was his first assignment, but he seemed to spend more time telling us about his own life than asking questions about the hunt.

Sarah gave him a Hollywell Stables mug to make up for his ruined trousers and he promised to come back soon with a photographer. Katie spent the rest of the afternoon insisting she was going to become a journalist and interviewing everybody with a hairbrush, which she pretended was a microphone.

"Come on, James, you've got to tell us," Sarah demanded later that evening, as James sat in our kitchen looking pensive.

We were trying to butter him up with custard creams and pots of tea, but it wasn't working. James and Sarah had been romantically attached for several months and James was like one of the family: we all thought the world of him. He would never replace our real dad, who had died three years ago, but he didn't even try to. He was more like a friend. Our real mother had deserted us when we were quite young and if it hadn't been for Sarah marrying our dad and taking us on as her own, we'd probably have been put in a home.

"James, are you going to tell us or not?" Sarah said, beginning to lose patience.

We were trying to find out where the hunt was meeting the next morning. It was all kept under wraps until the last minute to outsmart the hunt saboteurs. Apparently the Burlington Hunt had been plagued by a group from the university led by someone called Zac, who had been stirring up trouble, even going so far as to break the law.

The only people who knew where the meet was being held were the hunt members, and they would never tell us, not in a million years. The location was usually advertised in *Horse and Hound*, but the hunt had deliberately asked for the information to be taken out, in order to make it harder for Zac and his mates to follow them. But many of James's clients were local farmers and they would tell him without a second thought.

"This is serious," James said eventually. "It's not a little game that you're playing. There'll most likely be police there and you could get hurt."

"James, just tell us!"

"I'm warning you, Sarah, be careful. You don't know anything about hunting . . ."

"It's not the hunt we're bothered about," Sarah snapped. "It's Boris. It's our job to save horses, just in case you've forgotten."

James sat and thought for a minute. "You've got to keep me out of this. If the hunt find out I told you, I won't be very popular!"

"James!"

"Okay, it's at eleven o'clock tomorrow morning at the pub in the next village. And for heaven's sake, stay out of trouble!"

Chapter Three

We arrived at the hunt meet in plenty of time. There were horseboxes and trailers parked everywhere, all along the grass verges and crammed into the pub car-park.

Beautiful horses in gleaming double bridles and polished saddles were leaping around, stamping and snorting. Even a hairy cob, usually docile, thundered along the road at a fast trot with a red-faced girl bouncing up and down in the saddle.

"Hey, look at this," Ross whispered in my ear, as a lady on a lovely chestnut waltzed up the road riding side-saddle, complete with long skirt, hat and veil. An old man was riding alongside, wearing a black top hat, but neither of them acknowledged us.

Outside the pub more horses were standing around in groups, mostly held by grooms – huge, strapping hunters with feet as big as soup plates. But there was no sign of Boris.

Everybody was giving us frosty looks and Sarah said they probably thought we were saboteurs.

"Talk about being given the cold shoulder," Ross said. "This is like being sent to the North Pole."

A tiny toddler on a Shetland pony started shrieking his head off when he got towed into a tree, and then another horse wearing a red ribbon on its tail started lashing out with both hindlegs at a pretty palomino.

"Look!" Katie pointed to where a cattle wagon had just pulled up and hounds were being let down the ramp.

At the same moment Charles Stonehouse stomped out of the pub.

"Look over there, behind that lorry," Ross whispered excitedly. "It's Boris!"

Sure enough, a girl groom was leading a massive black horse out into the pub forecourt, where Stonehouse was waiting. I instantly recognized him as the horse we had seen at Hollywell, because of his huge Roman nose and great loping ears. He must have been all of seventeen hands.

"He looks well enough," Ross said.

"Why have they kept him hidden?" I asked. "Why have they only just brought him out?"

"I'll tell you why," Sarah said, looking critically at Boris's action. "Because he's not a sound horse!"

Stonehouse lurched into the saddle and clattered off up the road without saying a single word, not even a civil good-morning. All the other riders fell in behind like a cavalcade and we dashed back to our old Volvo to follow them. If something happened to Boris, we wanted to be there to save him.

The hounds had already covered quite a distance. Sarah didn't hang about. She pushed the Volvo into gear and cranked off up the road before anybody had fastened their seat belts.

As soon as we caught up with the hunt, something completely bizarre happened. Hurtling along the road from the opposite direction was a blue Transit van. It was heading straight for the hounds and it didn't look as if it was going to stop.

"What's happening?" someone shouted from the roadside, genuine fear bristling in their voice.

The van skidded across the road at the very last minute, causing three of the leading horses to rear up. The back doors burst open and at least a dozen people leapt out, wearing balaclavas and holding aerosol cans. Before anybody could do anything, they started spraying into the hounds' faces, right into their eyes and noses.

I remembered Sarah telling me that this was what saboteurs did. The spray was called Anti-Mate. It had a lemony smell and totally confused the hounds. For a short while they wouldn't be able to smell anything at all, not even a fox.

But before they could do serious damage, Charles Stonehouse spurred Boris straight into their midst. The horse blundered forward on wooden legs and then lurched sideways as two of the saboteurs tried to spray their aerosols into his face.

"Do something," Sarah yelled, leaning out of the window and trying to attract the attention of a man with a walking stick.

"We're too far away," Ross said, frantically winding back the rusty sun roof on our Volvo and sticking his head and shoulders out into the fresh air for a better view.

The fieldmaster quickly led the riders into a nearby field so they were off the road and the huntsman was desperately trying to get the hounds under control.

Sarah slammed her foot on the accelerator and wheeled up the grass verge, past two cars and right into the midst of the action.

"How dare you?" she yelled, leaping out of the car and grabbing the nearest saboteur by the collar of his coat and shaking him.

Boris was rearing up in blind panic, pawing at the air with his forelegs and shaking his head from side to side. Stonehouse sat tight and, as soon as Boris came back down on all fours, wheeled him round in a circle. The poor horse didn't know what was going on. Stonehouse grasped both reins in one hand, yanking Boris in the mouth, and then lifted up his hunting crop, complete with leather thong, and brought it cracking down on the arm of one of the saboteurs, sending the spray canister flying out of his hand.

Within seconds the saboteur, the only one without a balaclava, grabbed hold of the end of the crop and wrenched it out of Stonehouse's hand.

"You maniac!" he screamed, looking murderous, clutching his injured arm. "You've had this coming, Stonehouse . . . I've waited a long time for this!"

And then he wielded the hunting crop high in the air and brought it slashing down across Stonehouse's thigh. Everybody gasped with horror.

"You filth," Stonehouse grated between clenched teeth, his body set rigid with pain and anger. "You miserable excuse for a human being . . ."

"Get him, Zac, get him," one of the saboteurs shouted.

Zac leered up at Stonehouse, his thin ratty face the picture of smugness. Stonehouse dug his spurs into Boris's sides and rode straight at him. Zac leapt to one side just as Boris's shoulder nearly powered into him.

"You're mad," Zac yelled. "You're off yer flaming rocker."

Stonehouse yanked Boris round and came at Zac again.

"Stop 'im," Zac shouted to the rest of his gang. "Ger 'im off me!"

But they stood motionless in their balaclavas, shrinking back towards the van, nervous and unsure.

Charles Stonehouse looked ready to commit murder. His face was set in stone and he never took his eyes off Zac. Boris stumbled and nearly fell, but Stonehouse lurched him up and drove him on.

"The poor horse can't see," I said, as Boris kept shaking his head, looking totally disorientated. Red marks showed on his sides from where the spurs had dug in.

Zac set off, running down the road, but Stonehouse was after him.

A police siren wailed further up the road. The saboteurs dashed for the van and screeched off in the opposite direction.

"Quick!" Sarah yelled. "Into the car!"

We dived into our seats, with Ross hanging out of the sun roof, and shot off up the road after Boris.

"He's running for that field," Ross yelled from above, losing his balance and nearly standing on Katie's head.

"Hold on," Sarah shouted, fighting with the gear stick and jerking the car forward.

"He's shot through a hedge," Ross said, and I could vaguely make out Zac running through a ploughed field like a hunted animal, with Boris plunging after him.

"Oh, my God," Ross yelled. "It's Stonehouse – he's riding Boris at the hedge!"

We stopped the car and ran like crazy towards them, but it was too late.

Stonehouse slammed his crop down on Boris's quarters and rode like a demon towards the hedge. It was madness. The hedge was at least five foot high with a huge drainage ditch at the front and he'd be jumping straight out of thick plough. It would be hard enough for a young, fit horse, never mind poor old Boris.

"Don't do it," Sarah screamed, but her voice was whisked away on the wind and Stonehouse kept on riding.

"He'll kill himself as well as Boris," I shouted, feeling totally helpless and sick inside. The huntsman came pounding up behind us, took one look at what was happening and spurred his horse forward.

"The stupid fool," he cursed. "He'll finish him off for good this time."

"He's not even given him a decent approach." Ross's voice wavered.

23

"He'll never be able to judge the take-off," I said.

"Boris – don't jump!" Katie screeched, digging her hand into mine.

One . . . two . . . three. Boris launched upwards. The mud sucked at his feet like quicksand and it was obvious he wasn't going to make the height. Stonehouse cracked him again with the crop and leaned forward. It was too late to turn back now: they were both airborne.

I wanted to close my eyes but I couldn't. All I could see was Boris reaching upwards, stretching, scraping his forelegs through the unrelenting thorns.

"He's over the ditch," Sarah shrieked, in a voice glimmering with hope.

"Go on, Boris," Ross yelled, raising his fist in the air.

Boris arched his back in a massive effort, folding up his forelegs as tight as he could.

"Come on, laddie, you can do it!"

He probably would have done, if it hadn't been for Stonehouse leaning too far back on the landing and jabbing him in the mouth.

Boris tried to stay upright. I could almost feel him struggling to keep his balance, grunting with the effort. But gravity was against him. His forelegs crumpled underneath, his nose hit the plough and he somersaulted right over.

We were running then, running towards the hedge; scrabbling down the drainage ditch; scratching for a hold at the hedge branches; trying to get to Boris as fast as possible.

Stonehouse had been thrown to one side and I could already see him getting to his feet. Boris was up too, but he wasn't moving.

"Mel, here!" Ross shoved me in the back towards a gap where he was holding up a strand of barbed wire. Sarah was pushing through a hole further along, with Katie behind her. The huntsman was galloping down the side of the field, looking for an easier place to jump.

We were through the hedge. Stonehouse was staggering towards us, clutching his arm.

"I've broken my collarbone," he gasped, looking winded and plastered in mud.

But it was Boris we were more interested in.

"Boris!"

The poor old horse stood very quietly, holding one foreleg in the air, gently pawing it back and forth. His eyes were blinking, running still from the spray. His whole body quivered like a terrified dog. The front of his legs were cut and bleeding from the thorns in the hedge and his lovely Roman nose was blackened with mud. He was trying to snort the dirt out of his nostrils.

"There's no name for people like you," Sarah flared up at Stonehouse, thorns tangled in her red hair and mascara running down her cheeks in black streams. "You're a monster, do you know that?" Her lips were trembling with white-hot anger.

"Oh, get off your silly high horse," Stonehouse barked back, spitting out some mud from his mouth and brushing down his ripped jacket. "The horse was on his way out anyway, we both know that. Your precious little vet told you, didn't he? That's why you're here today, looking to cause trouble. Well, it's not going to work. You try taking me on, lady, and I'll stamp all over you."

Sarah gasped in shock and Katie and I looked at each other in amazement. Ross was taking off Boris's saddle and trying to feel his leg.

"And you can leave him alone." Stonehouse turned to Ross. "He's broken down, any fool can see that. He's finished."

"You're a creep," Sarah screamed, "a bullying creep!" And then she picked up a handful of black soil and pelted it straight at Stonehouse.

"Now, now," he taunted, a thin smile etched around his lips. "Steady on, old girl."

"What's going on here, then?" a deep voice

boomed up behind us. I turned round and came face to face with two police officers.

"Gentlemen, not only is this lady trespassing, but she's disturbing the peace and she has also tried to assault me." Stonehouse was loving every minute of it. He even seemed to have forgotten about his broken collarbone.

In the distance Zac was being taken away by more policemen. He kept trying to sit down, but they frogmarched him back to the road.

"I'll get you for this, Stonehouse!" he kept yelling over and over again.

"Do your worst, creep," Stonehouse shouted back and then laughed out loud.

"What are we going to do about Boris?" The huntsman had finally arrived on the scene and was examining Boris's injured leg, while Ross held his horse. Sweat was running down Boris's neck in rivulets and it was obvious he was in agony. His leg was already swelling up like a balloon.

"You know what you've got to do," Stonehouse snapped, marching across to the saddle on the huntsman's horse and opening up a leather bag that was attached to the pommel. He pulled out something black and shiny and thrust it at the huntsman. "Now get on with it."

My breath caught in the back of my throat and Katie's fingers tightened around mine like a vice.

We were all staring at the black shiny object.

It was a revolver!

The huntsman reached out reluctantly to take the gun from Stonehouse, while Boris struggled backwards as if instinctively he knew what was about to happen. Stonehouse glared at us with pure loathing and then gave his order.

"Shoot him!"

Chapter Four

What happened next seemed to take place in slow motion.

"No!" Sarah dived forward, pushing Stonehouse back into the mud.

The police officers moved in on each side of her.

"You interfering fool," Stonehouse bawled. "You saw what happened, officer, it was assault!"

Katie flung herself in front of Boris. "I won't let you do it," she screamed. "I won't let you kill him. I won't, I won't." And then she burst into tears and started hugging Boris's chest.

Ross had his hands full trying to hold on to the huntsman's horse, which was pulling backwards, and the policemen were insisting Sarah go with them to the station.

"You can't take her away," I kept saying, feeling really frightened. "She's done nothing wrong."

But they wouldn't listen.

"Don't panic, Mel. I won't be long."

"You can't leave us," Katie screamed.

"Ross, you're in charge," Sarah said. "I'm relying on you."

Stonehouse stormed off in front of the policemen and Sarah, and I put my arm round Katie and tried to look brave, which wasn't easy when I was quaking inside.

"We're not going to let you shoot him," Ross said to the huntsman, who was still holding the gun and looking uncomfortable.

"The horse is in pain," he said in a limp voice.

"He's snapped a tendon," Ross said, "not broken a leg."

"He'll never work again."

"So we'll retire him. He'll have a happy life."

"I'll lose my job."

"Stonehouse doesn't have to know," I joined in. "We'll take him to Hollywell and he won't be any the wiser."

"The man's a psychopath," Ross said.

The huntsman looked down at the gun in his hand and ran his finger over the trigger.

"Please, sir," Katie said in a small voice.

It was Mrs Mac who brought our horsebox to fetch Boris. How she managed to drive it I'll never know, but when she jumped out of the cab she was bright red in the face and short of breath.

The horsebox was a present from a famous rock star who had become one of our closest friends. It was an old Vincent box and was our pride and joy.

"You take the reins," the huntsman said, as he went to lower the ramp. I stroked Boris's nose and promised him he'd soon feel better, but I think he was in too much pain to listen. It had been murder leading him back to the road and every step he took I could feel the pain shooting through him. His leg was now so swollen up, the skin was stretched taut and looked ready to burst.

Unfortunately, we hadn't yet been able to afford to have the horsebox ramp converted, which meant Boris somehow had to clamber up rather than be mechanically lifted in. The huntsman was fantastic and without him I don't think we'd ever have succeeded. It was obvious he had a special way with horses and we were all eternally grateful.

"About Stonehouse," he said, as we were about to leave. "I don't want you to think all huntmasters are like that."

He looked at us with soft, gentle eyes, a really sensitive man. But no matter how much I liked him, I still couldn't condone hunting.

"Mel, fetch me the Elastoplast! Katie, the scissors!"

James was in the stable with Boris, working

hard to bandage his leg. I couldn't believe the amount of gamgee he was wrapping round the tendon. It must have been a foot wide. Boris stood like an angel, somehow knowing we were trying to help him. James had already given him a painkiller, which seemed to be working, and Katie was feeding him a sliced apple to take his mind off his leg.

"There, all done," James said, standing back to admire his handiwork. The bandage was enormous. "He's got to stay in his stable," James continued. "He needs a low-protein diet and a course of powders. Mel, you're going to have to watch him. He's a fit horse, in a few days' time he'll be itching to get out of his stable."

Boris started nodding his head and then rested his chin on Katie's head as if in agreement.

"He's a gentle giant really," James said, scratching the horse's neck affectionately. "Just make sure he doesn't stand on your toes!"

Danny came out of the house, carrying mugs of tea which he was spilling all over the place and clutching a packet of Jammy Dodgers between his teeth. Danny had missed out on all the action, because he'd stayed at home with Mrs Mac. We had to have someone to guard the stables, just in case Bazz made an appearance. Sarah was still convinced he was up to no good.

"How long has Boris got to stay in?" Ross asked James.

"Six weeks."

"You're joking." I nearly choked. I didn't know a horse could be left in a stable for six weeks!

"Under no circumstances must he be let out," James insisted. "If that tendon is ever to heal properly, he's got to stay as quiet as possible."

"We'll look after you, Boris," Katie promised.

"Now, come on," James said. "Let's have a look at his eyes."

Luckily the saboteurs' spray hadn't done any serious damage. How could they call themselves animal lovers when they did things like this?

James soon had Boris patched up and by the time we left him with a feed in his manger, Mrs Mac had brought Sarah home from the police station. Danny was bursting to know whether she'd been put in a cell or if she'd met any criminals, but Sarah didn't want to talk about it.

James, however, had every intention of doing just that. He was furious with Sarah for getting arrested and he was going to tell her so.

"How could you be so irresponsible?" he started, as we all sat down in the kitchen, exhausted. Jigsaw sat beside James and put a muddy paw on his lap. "I told you to stay out of trouble and

33

what do you do? Get yourself carted off by the police."

"These things happen, James. Don't be so pompous."

"You're supposed to be running a sanctuary, not terrorizing the whole community."

"We did no such thing," Sarah stormed, throwing some teabags towards the teapot and missing completely.

"Oh, so pushing over the huntmaster and shouting at local coppers is normal behaviour?"

"Shut up, James. You're just upset in case you lose face with the hunt. Don't you realize we've saved Boris's life? But then, of course, you're too pro-hunting to care."

"That's not true Sarah and you know it."

"Do I?"

Ross and I looked at each other with growing alarm. This was developing into a major argument.

"Hunting is the best way to control the fox population," James stated. "If you'd stop being over-sentimental and think logically, you'd come to the same conclusion."

"Rubbish!" Sarah shouted. "Foxes are totally misunderstood creatures."

"You're talking nonsense," James warned.

"Hey, this is all getting a bit out of hand." Ross tried to lighten the atmosphere.

"Stay out of this, Ross," Sarah said. "James is just being stubborn."

"Oh, that's what you call it, is it? Have you ever seen a fox poisoned, gassed or snared? I'm telling you, Sarah, it's not a pretty sight."

"Why can't they just be left alone?" Sarah said. "Why do they have to be hounded into the ground?"

"So they can spread disease, rip lambs and poultry to pieces, and generally cause mayhem? They're not cuddly toys, you know."

"Oh, just go, James. I've had enough." Sarah's temper was reaching boiling point. "I simply cannot understand how you can support hunting, and quite frankly I'm not sure I want to know you any more."

The silence that followed was earth-shattering.

"If that's what you want, then it's fine by me," James finally said in a level voice. "But this isn't totally about hunting, is it, Sarah? It's about getting even with Charles Stonehouse. All revenge does is keep the wound open. It's not going to bring Oswald back!"

Sarah still had her back to James, so he walked over to the door, turned the handle and left, gently closing the door behind him.

"Well, congratulations," Ross said coldly when James had driven away. "You've just got rid of one of the nicest guys we've ever known."

"I'm not ringing him." Sarah was adamant. "If James wants to apologize, he knows where we live."

Instead, she locked herself in her study, determined to start her next novel. As well as running Hollywell Stables, Sarah was a romantic novelist. We all thought her stories were brilliant – and so did her publisher, which was lucky.

The next day Boris seemed much better and was already fiddling with the bolt on his door and trying to talk to Dancer, who was in the next stable. Katie had fallen in love with him, but we had to watch her carefully. We all agreed that when a new horse came into the stables, we had to be on our guard until we got to know them. Often badly treated horses lose their trust in human beings and retaliate by kicking and biting. Only a few weeks ago we had rescued Terence, whose nerves had been completely shattered. Boris, however, seemed to be amazingly friendly and made it quite clear from the start that he loved people and attention. Ross couldn't wait to measure him and he turned out to be seventeen hands high. He was the tallest horse we had ever rescued.

The bad news was that James didn't come to

check up on him. He sent his junior partner instead. Sarah was obviously upset, but she tried to disguise it. We all knew, though, when we found the sugar bowl in the refrigerator and the tea-cosy on the milk bottle, that she wasn't her usual self. It didn't help either when Jigsaw chewed up the rhododendron plant which James had given her for Valentine's Day. Sarah whisked it up with the dustpan and brush and chucked it out of the window. Ross said it was symbolic of their broken relationship.

Mrs Mac was bursting with plans for newsletters and open days for the sanctuary, but none of us had the enthusiasm to follow them through. No matter how many animals you have, it still doesn't lessen the pain of losing one. Matilda had been slightly better since we'd put a hot-water bottle under her blanket and she'd finally started eating.

But if the morning had begun relatively peacefully, by the afternoon it was complete chaos. Everything started to go wrong.

First, the police rang to say that Stonehouse was still planning to press charges and also that he claimed we'd kidnapped his horse.

Then Danny came back from the village shop in floods of tears. He was trembling like a leaf and I hadn't seen him like this since he'd first arrived on our doorstep.

"It's, it's B-Bazz!" he finally managed to get out. He hadn't stuttered for months, but now he was a nervous wreck.

My blood ran cold. This was the last thing I wanted to hear.

"He f-followed me, he n-nearly ran me off t-the road!" Danny's body was heaving in great gasps.

"Danny, listen to me. It's OK," I said. "You're safe. He's not here. He can't get you." I held on to his shoulders and tried to get through to him, but he was terrified.

"You d-don't understand. H-he said he was g-going to kill me!"

Danny collapsed on my knee, sobbing, and Sarah came running through from the study looking devastated. I could hear Mrs Mac telling her that someone had rung three times when we were out at the hunt and they'd put the phone down each time.

How could I have been so stupid! All the warning signs were there. Sarah said he was out for revenge and I'd ignored her. I didn't want to face the fact that Bazz was capable of doing anything. With Bazz on the warpath, we were all in danger.

"I knew it, I just knew it." Sarah cried, pacing up and down. "He's out there, biding his time, just waiting. He's got something planned, I know he has!"

"Well, then, we'll be ready for him," I said, feeling the strength rising up inside me. "There's a limit to what he can do."

"He's probably planning on striking at night," Sarah said.

"We can take it in turns to stay up," I said. "We can leave all the lights on. Nobody go anywhere alone if they can help it."

"We could rig up some string across the drive and the stable doors," Mrs Mac suggested. "Something to let us know if anyone's about."

"Maybe we ought to get a burglar alarm?" Sarah suggested.

"We can beat him," I said. "Knowing Bazz, he'll probably try to set fire to the stables again. He's not got much imagination."

Danny looked a little less frightened.

"Yes, that's what we'll do," Sarah said. "Where's Ross? We must tell him."

But Ross had something to tell us. He dived through the back door, looking ashen. "Sarah! Mel!"

His whole jaw seemed to be fixed rigid in shock. "I've just been in the field," he rasped. "*It's Bluey! He's gone!*"

Chapter Five

"Bluey!"

The field was empty.

"Mel, there's no point shouting for him. He's not here." Ross looked as shell-shocked as I felt. "Over there." Ross pointed to the furthest corner of the field. "You'll see what I mean."

"Has Sarah called the police?" I whispered, blundering towards the edge of the field. "How did he get out?"

Ross didn't have to explain; it was all so obvious. The post-and-rail fence we had spent a fortune erecting was broken – smashed to the ground. There were heavy tyre marks all over the place. It wasn't a case of Bluey simply escaping from the field. There was only one explanation: he'd been stolen. And we all knew who'd done it.

"I'll kill him," I yelled, furious at the thought of Bazz being anywhere near any of our ponies. "How could this happen in broad daylight?"

"We'll get him back, Mel. I promise you."

Then I had a sickening thought. Bluey wasn't

freeze-marked. We had always said that as soon as we had enough money, we'd have all our horses freeze-marked. That was a number painlessly branded on to their skin which could be used to trace them.

"They'll never find him," I said in a numb voice. "It's hopeless."

"Mel, don't wimp out on me. We've got to be strong."

Ross brushed at his face with the back of his hand, wiping away tears that he was determined not to show. Tears wouldn't bring Bluey back; only keeping a clear head would do that.

"You're right," I said, biting into my bottom lip and fighting back the emotion. "I don't care if we have to scour the length and breadth of the country, we're going to find him!"

"And that's it?" Sarah said in a voice ringing with disbelief. "That's all you can do?"

Two policemen were standing in our kitchen, looking very matter-of-fact. I passed them the photograph of Bluey and they finished taking their notes. Katie couldn't quite believe that they weren't making a clay cast of the tyre marks in the field. "They always do in *Sherlock Holmes*," she said.

Sarah couldn't understand why they wouldn't accept her story about Bazz.

"It's not that we don't believe you, Mrs Foster. It's just that there's no evidence to suggest it was him."

"Oh, no? He only threatened me on the phone and terrorized one of the kids! Nothing to speak of, not actually murder or anything."

"Well, as I said—" The older policeman looked uncomfortable. "We'll certainly be in touch with this Bazz character and I'm sure we'll get your pony back for you. You've just got to be patient."

"Be patient!" Sarah barked as soon as they'd stepped out of the door. "They haven't got a clue how quickly ponies can completely disappear. They're treating this like a missing wallet!"

Apart from asking a few questions and sending out a report on Bluey, there didn't seem much else the police intended to do. An overwhelming feeling of hopelessness descended on me. Ross looked equally subdued.

"Well, it's up to us then," Mrs Mac said grimly. "If the police can't do anything, then we'll have to use our own initiative." She paused and looked up for a moment. "And here's one person who might just be able to help."

Roddy Fitzgerald had pulled into the yard in

his ancient Mini. Looking as awkward as ever, he ambled over.

"You want me to do what?" he said.

We all agreed there was only one thing to do and that was to get as much publicity about Bluey as possible. The more people who knew about him, the more chance there was of someone coming forward with information, especially if we offered a reward.

"A thousand pounds!" Ross said.

"We can't afford it," Sarah answered. "But then, we don't have any choice."

Money was in short supply and we still needed more hay to see us through the winter. The money from the rock concert had nearly run out and we now had another horse to feed – Boris. At the moment he was eating us out of house and home. A thousand pounds was just about all we had left.

"We'll worry about money later," Ross said. "At the moment, getting Bluey back is all that matters."

Bluey was the first pony we'd ever rescued. He was a lovely little twelve-hand strawberry roan, about twenty years old, with a wall-eye and a temperament like a gentle old grandad. We had saved him from two girls who'd kept him locked in a garage with no food or water. They'd given him potato peelings and the odd drink from a seaside bucket when they remembered and they'd

43

dragged him up and down the road all day long with no shoes on until his hoofs were so sore he could only hobble. We had found him on the verge of collapse.

Bluey had been the inspiration for starting Hollywell Stables, but since then in some ways he'd been pushed into the shadow of the other horses we had rescued. He was the kind of pony any young child would adore. He held no grudges against humans and took everything in his stride. If we didn't find him soon, I thought that my heart would literally break in two.

"So what do you think?" Ross said, looking at Roddy.

Roddy was fantastic. As soon as he realized what had happened, he was completely supportive. He was the first to suggest that the *Weekly Herald* run a campaign to find Bluey. He was convinced his editor would go along with it, even though every story he'd written up to now had been rejected. At last there was a glimmer of hope.

And we weren't going to sit idly around until the paper came out. Sarah was drawing up a list of all the people she could ring: riding schools, riding clubs, blacksmiths, feed merchants, tack shops – anybody with anything to do with horses. Even vets.

"You've got to tell him," Ross urged, when

Sarah pointedly refused to add James's name to the list. "You can't not tell him. For goodness' sake, Sarah, he's too involved. He cares."

James had treated all of our ponies and horses for one thing or another and he was as much a part of Hollywell as any of us. Sarah owed it to him to tell him about Bluey.

"If you won't, I will," Ross threatened, reaching for the phone.

"Don't you dare," Sarah gasped, standing up and grabbing hold of his arm. "This is our problem. We'll deal with it our way . . . There's nothing James can do. I don't want him to come back because he feels he has to. I want him to come back because he wants to."

I still couldn't understand why adults never said what they really meant. Sarah was desperate for James to get in touch – anybody could see that – but she was too proud to make the first move.

"We'll question all of Bazz's neighbours," Sarah said, deftly changing the subject. "Someone's got to stay here all the time. If Bazz can steal one pony, he can steal another. Who knows what he might try next? But we'll wait until we hear from the police before we decide about the scrapyard."

The scrapyard was where Bazz and Revhead had hidden Queenie. There was every chance that's where he had taken Bluey.

"If the police don't come up with anything, then we'll plan our next move."

"And what's that?" I asked, even though deep down I already knew.

"We'll break in."

Roddy had left earlier to go back to the newspaper and Mrs Mac said she had some important charity work to tend to.

Ross went to groom Dancer, while I gave Boris his second feed of the day. He was positively devouring High Fibre nuts and sugar beet, and the night before we had had to leave him two haynets instead of one. He was now in a bad mood because his leg was itching under the bandage, and he kept shuffling round the stable with tufts of gamgee stuck in his front teeth from where he'd been pulling at it. He had a funny habit of clapping his lips together when he was bored and had even taken to chucking his bucket over the stable door.

"Where has that dog got to?" Ross moaned when Jigsaw hadn't been seen for nearly an hour. Timmy the mouse was still lost too, and Danny had taken to leaving lumps of chocolate all over the house in an effort to lure him out.

"Jigsaw!" I yelled, cursing under my breath and plodding up the field, wondering why all our animals were so unruly. Then I thought about Bazz and started to run in a panic. What if he'd taken Jigsaw?

"Jigsaw, where are you?"

I was at the bottom of the field now, near the edge of the wood where a stream ran in a dip. This was where we had led a horse called Colorado to safety last summer. We'd hidden him in an old cowshed in our field which we'd since converted into an isolation unit.

A movement in the undergrowth.

"Jigsaw! Where have you been?" He came splashing across the stream plastered in mud and looking sheepish. "You naughty boy," I scolded, grabbing hold of his collar and clipping on the leadrope I was carrying.

The wood looked dark and creepy. Nobody ever went in it and there was a huge sign up saying PRIVATE – KEEP OUT. It ran along the edge of our land and Katie always swore that it was full of ghosts.

"What was that?" I jumped, and Jigsaw pulled and strained on the leadrope as if in answer. It sounded like someone digging.

Jigsaw lurched forward, barking, and somehow the clip on the leadrope came undone. He bounded

47

back across the stream and disappeared into the wood. Suddenly the barking stopped.

"Jigsaw!" My voice echoed back among the trees and then there was nothing. Just a deathly silence. Well, there was only one thing for it – I was going in. I didn't believe for one minute about ghosts and goblins. But even so, as I paddled through the stream and entered the wood, the darkness seemed to close in around me. It took a few minutes to adjust my eyes to the dim light and a bramble whipped me across the face, which did nothing for my nerves.

I tripped on a twig and I could swear that I heard footsteps running in the opposite direction.

Just as fear prickled its way up my spine, Jigsaw barked close by. I stepped out into a clearing and there he was, wagging his tail and grinning at me. Thank goodness!

As I reattached his leadrope, something caught my attention – a spade hidden in the undergrowth. The handle was sticking out from some branches and when I pulled it free, the spade part was thick with black soil. The same black soil that was plastered to Jigsaw's feet . . .

And then I saw it. I didn't know whether it was a fox's earth or a badger's set, but it was one or the other and the holes had been blocked up. There were footprints and freshly disturbed soil all over.

I knew for a fact that the hunt blocked up earths before a meet to keep the foxes above ground. This was called earth-stopping and was legal, although we all thought it was horribly cruel. Imagine being hunted, finally getting back to your home and then finding the entrance blocked up. It was totally unfair.

But other thoughts were rattling around in my head – thoughts that could get Charles Stonehouse in serious trouble. What if this was a badger set? The holes certainly looked big enough. If that was the case, then the law *had* been broken. Often foxes would run into a badger set but hunts were forbidden to block them up. So what was going on here?

The hand on my shoulder made me scream out loud. I whipped round, ready to hit out with the spade, and then stopped in mid-swing. It was Ross.

"What do you think you're playing at? I could have killed you," I yelled, furious that he'd deliberately tried to scare me, and succeeded.

But Ross was already examining the blocked holes. "It's a badger's set," he said, standing up and running a hand through his thick black hair. "There's absolutely no doubt about it."

We had barely had enough time to tell Sarah when,

talk of the devil, Charles Stonehouse drove into the yard. He pulled up in a Range Rover and trailer, looking angry and ready to do battle.

"So I was right," he snarled, when Boris put his head over the stable door.

"Leave him alone," Sarah warned, as Stonehouse marched over.

"Hello there, old boy," said Stonehouse in a voice I didn't trust, rubbing Boris's big bony nose. Boris backed off, flattening his ears.

"Why don't you just put him out of his misery?" Stonehouse snapped, catching us off guard, his voice harsh and grating.

"Why don't you get off this property?" Sarah sniped back.

"Not without my horse, I won't."

"Well, then, you'll have a long wait," Sarah threatened, leaning on the yard brush, her red hair blowing across her face, which was set rigid and stubborn.

"You've made one too many enemies, lady," Stonehouse answered, pointing his finger in the air and narrowing his hard, flint-like eyes. "I'm not the kind of person you should cross."

Katie spoke up. "We're not frightened of you."

"I could have you closed down." Stonehouse ignored Katie. "I could finish you completely – I know the right people."

"Don't you threaten me!" Sarah held her ground. "I don't scare that easy."

"How long do you expect to keep this pathetic operation running? A month, a year? Do you really think people care about clapped-out horses? Do you honestly think they'll keep coughing up once the novelty has worn off? It's all a waste of time and money."

I knew that some people thought this way. We had received a letter once from a man telling us our work was meaningless and the money would be better used for other charities. But surely horses had a right to a happy life? They were just as helpless as children. Sarah had torn up the letter and thrown it on the fire.

"Get out," Sarah ordered, taking a step forward with Ross closing ranks beside her. "We'll be here long after your precious hunt has gone. I'm reporting you to the hunt authorities – for blocking up badger sets to start with."

Stonehouse looked temporarily shaken.

"I thought that would knock the wind out of your sails," Sarah said.

"You're mad, completely mad! You can't make up stories and expect them to stick . . . You don't know what you're talking about."

Stonehouse was going redder and redder in the face. Any minute now, I thought, he's going to attack us. But what did happen next was hard to believe. We'll never know whether it was just coincidence or intentional.

Boris had been pacing round and round his stable while all this was happening, getting more and more agitated. Suddenly, before any of us could stop him, he picked up his feed bucket in his teeth and flung it out over his stable door.

It hurtled through the air like a missile. Stonehouse turned round just a fraction too late; there was no time to side-step the blow. The bucket careered into the side of his head, knocking him back a couple of paces, and then bounced off the bonnet of the Range Rover.

We just stood there with our mouths open, gaping. Boris snorted and stamped in his stable and Stonehouse looked at us accusingly as if we had arranged the whole thing.

"You're crazy, the lot of you," he bellowed, dabbing at his head with a checked handkerchief and seeing blood. It was only a scratch but he was carrying on as if he needed intensive care. "I'm going to get you for this! You're finished!"

He was so angry he could barely get his words out properly.

"Don't think I'm dropping the assault charge," he threatened, looking pointedly at Sarah. "And there's something none of you have considered . . ."

He was picking at some dried bran which had settled on his jacket collar and a muscle was twitching frantically in his cheek.

"If you're going to keep this shoddy fiasco going, you'll need more land, lots more."

He paused to give full weight to his next sentence, but Sarah interrupted.

"If you're about to say you won't sell us any land, don't waste your breath. I've already checked it out – Pembroke Properties owns nearly everything within four miles of here."

"You silly little fool," Stonehouse sneered, throwing back his head and relishing the moment. "I *am* Pembroke Properties!"

Chapter Six

"So he owns all the land. So what? We'll cross that bridge when we come to it," Sarah fumed, dark smudges of exhaustion showing under both her eyes.

It had been a harrowing morning. We'd had a frantic telephone call from one of the local riding schools, saying they'd seen a strawberry roan pony in a field near a dual carriageway.

We'd dived into the car and headed off straight away but it hadn't been Bluey.

"So that's that then," said Ross, when a chunky fourteen-hand strawberry roan trotted up to the gate. Katie had started crying – she couldn't help herself – and disappointment dragged at my heart like a ten-ton weight. We had been so sure that this would be Bluey. We'd even taken along his special red headcollar and three packets of his favourite mints.

Sarah said nothing all the way home and Ross just sat like a zombie. We left a "Missing" poster in the village post office, but none of us held out much hope. Every hour that went by meant less and less chance of ever seeing Bluey again.

"We can't give up hope," Mrs Mac said, rallying round with mugs of tea as soon as we arrived back at Hollywell. "We've got to believe he's going to turn up. Without hope we've got nothing."

I knew she was right, but at that moment I couldn't lift my spirits.

"There is some good news," Mrs Mac went on. "Roddy phoned to say that the article on Bluey is going in the paper and it should make the front page. Also the riding club lecture is still on for tomorrow night."

"What?" Ross interrupted in a loud voice.

We'd completely forgotten about the talk on Hollywell Stables that Ross was supposed to be giving to the local riding club. Mrs Mac was doing the organizing and Ross had agreed to it months ago.

"How can you think about a silly lecture at a time like this?" Ross barked, pacing up and down like a maniac.

"Ross!" Sarah scolded.

Mrs Mac looked totally flustered. "I – I'm sorry."

"You don't have to be," Sarah said, putting an arm round Mrs Mac and guiding her into a chair. "Life has to carry on. We've got ponies to feed, a sanctuary to run. We can't just go to pieces."

"Sarah's right." I stood up, furious with Ross for his outburst, especially as he was the one who'd lectured me about staying strong. "You owe it to Mrs Mac. You've got to do it."

"How can you be so insensitive?" I grabbed hold of Ross as soon as we'd gone outside to bring in the horses. "After all she's done for us."

"OK, OK, I lost it for a while. I've said I'm sorry."

"And so you should be, carrying on—"

"Shush," Ross said abruptly, cutting me off mid-stream. "What was that?"

"What?"

"Listen! If you can't hear that you must be stone deaf."

It sounded like a tractor or a JCB, and it was coming from the direction of our field.

"Quick!" Ross shouted. "The horses!"

We dived over the five-barred gate with our hearts in our mouths and thoughts of Bazz doing his worst.

The horses were going wild. Sophie, our little yearling, nearly galloped straight at me. The poor thing looked terrified and I had to wave my arms in the air to stop us colliding.

It was soon clear what was happening. A JCB was ripping up the post-and-rail fence which ran between us and the wood. Half of it was already demolished.

"You catch the ponies, I'll stop the driver!" Ross yelled, racing on ahead of me.

Sparky and Queenie were gingerly testing the ground to see whether they could jump the stream and reach the spring grass on the other side. If the others followed, they could soon all be running loose and there was a main road on the other side of the wood.

"Queenie!" I shouted, setting off at a sprint. All I had in my hand was a frayed leadrope and half a carrot. I didn't even have a feed bucket. How was I going to catch them?

"Stop!" Ross stood in front of the JCB, waving his arms in the air. "Stop!"

I managed to shoo Queenie off and three of the others, but Sparky charged past me. Suddenly the JCB engine cut out and Sparky hesitated long enough for me to slip the leadrope quickly round his neck.

There were rails and broken posts strewn everywhere. It looked as if a herd of elephants had just charged through. But at least my worst fear proved unfounded. Whoever was driving the JCB, it wasn't Bazz.

"Hey, listen, I'm just doing my job." A huge man climbed out of the driver's seat, grunting in a deep voice. He looked strong enough to rip up the fencing with his bare hands.

"But you can't do this," Ross exclaimed.

"Look, I'm just doing what the boss tells me."

"But it's our field," I said, dragging Sparky forward. "It belongs to us."

"Who are you working for?" Ross persisted. "Surely you can tell us that."

"You've just pulled down our fencing!" I blurted out.

"Your fencing? No, luvvy, you've got it wrong there. This is Pembroke land. It's their boundary. If they want the fence down, then down it comes."

"So you work for Charles Stonehouse?" Ross sounded incredulous.

"That's about the sum of it."

"But you can't just leave us with no fencing!" I said.

"Well, that's your problem, lassie. And if you don't mind, I'd like to get back to work!"

There was nothing we could do. I felt so helpless. We brought all the horses into their stables and Sarah rang the police, but they only confirmed what the driver had told us. Nobody had broken any law. Stonehouse was perfectly within his rights to pull down his own fence.

"Of course, it's deliberate provocation." Sarah boiled over as we all sat down to discuss the matter rationally. "The man's a monster. And James thought *I* was out for revenge!"

"We've got to stay calm," I reasoned, trying to cool Sarah down, and Ross for that matter. Although how we were going to cope with no field to turn the horses out into, I really didn't know.

"He's crafty," Sarah said. "I'll give him that."

Pulling the fence down was obviously an act of spite. But I was seriously worried about how far Stonehouse would go to put us out of business.

"Maybe we ought to reconsider reporting him," I suggested.

"I'm not going to be intimidated," Sarah snapped. "I'm getting on to the hunt authorities this very minute."

But she didn't get the chance, because right on cue the telephone rang.

"I'll answer it," I said, moving towards the hallway. I picked up the receiver and said hello, but nobody answered. I was just about to put down the phone, thinking it was a wrong number, when someone started talking in a muffled, deep voice. It sounded as if they had something held over the phone – as if they didn't want me to work out

59

who it was. But I would have recognized that voice anywhere.

It was Bazz.

"What do you want?" I yelled. "What have you done with him?"

Ross and Sarah came running through from the kitchen.

"I don't believe you," I screamed down the receiver. "It's not true! It can't be!"

"What did he say?" Sarah asked as soon as I'd slammed down the phone.

My mouth felt so dry I had to swallow hard. There was no easy way to tell them so I just blurted it out.

"Bluey's dead. He said that he was dead!"

I couldn't stop crying all afternoon. I kept hearing Bazz's laugh over and over again – a deep, throaty cackle.

"He's bluffing." Sarah was adamant. "He's just saying that to upset us."

"Well, he's certainly succeeding," Ross said.

Katie and Danny were in the sitting room, doing a wall-to-wall search for Timmy. We hadn't told them about Bazz's phone call and we didn't intend to. They were both upset enough about Bluey.

Sarah had informed the police, but she was convinced they didn't believe her.

"At least it's settled one thing," she said. "We go to the scrapyard – tonight!"

Just the idea of it brought me out in a cold sweat. But I knew we had to go through with it. Bluey was relying on us. If he was still alive, we had to find him.

The scrapyard lay in total darkness.

Nothing seemed to have changed. The only difference was that the main gate swung open this time and there was no sign of the guard dog.

"Come on. We haven't got much time," Sarah hissed.

We crept through the open gate into the main yard. We'd already agreed to make straight for the old pumphouse, where Bazz had hidden Queenie. It was more than likely he would have taken Bluey to the same place.

My heart was hammering so hard I could hardly breathe.

There was no noise coming from the pumphouse – nothing which sounded remotely like a pony. We crept along the brick wall towards the door, which thankfully wasn't locked.

"Be careful," I murmured, convinced Bazz was waiting to leap on us.

Ross pushed the door open.

My nose immediately wrinkled up at the smell. It was damp and musty, but there was something else, something almost sickly.

Sarah made the first move. She lifted up her torch and angled the beam straight into the building. The spotlight fell on the far wall – cobwebs, bits of old piping. Further down to floor level – a rusted-up lawnmower, a milk churn, a pile of tangled wire . . . But no sign of Bluey.

"He's got to be here somewhere," Ross insisted, refusing to give up. "I just know Bazz would have brought him here."

We scoured the building but found nothing.

"You must face facts, Ross," Sarah said. "We've got it wrong."

"Not quite," I said, coming back from behind a wooden partition, clutching some black horse hairs which I'd found caught up on a protruding nail. Bluey had a black mane and tail.

"So we were right!" Ross shouted. "He has been here!"

"Yes," Sarah said, "but where is he now?"

Chapter Seven

The newspaper was our only hope.

"It's got to work!" Ross insisted as we set about cleaning up the tack room – anything to take our minds off what was happening.

The paper was out today. Anytime now and it would be entering thousands of homes.

"Someone must know something," said Katie, ever hopeful, keeping her fingers crossed on both hands – which was also a good excuse for getting out of work.

According to Roddy, there was a big picture of Bluey on the front page with Katie holding him and our telephone number was at the bottom of the article. It was sure to catch people's attention.

We had spent the morning exercising all the horses, who were having to stay in their stables because of the fencing, or rather the lack of it. Ross had lunged the fitter ones, while Katie, Danny and myself had walked out the others. It had taken for ever and Boris was furious that he'd been completely forgotten. How we were going to keep him shut in for six weeks, I really didn't know. He'd already kicked the stable walls to bits, knocking out lumps of plaster. At this rate there wouldn't be any stable left.

Sarah had been trying to contact Charles Stonehouse all morning. He was nowhere to be found. She'd been in touch with the police, who'd chased up a couple of leads about Bluey although they hadn't led anywhere. We couldn't tell them about our visit to the scrapyard because we might be charged with trespassing. Sarah finally got them to agree to question Bazz again, which at least was something.

The hunt authorities were far more interested in what Sarah had to say. They took a very dim view of any huntmaster giving the sport a bad name and promised to take appropriate action. Reading between the lines, Sarah thought they'd already had trouble with Stonehouse. He had only been master for two seasons and we'd heard on the grapevine that he wasn't very popular; in fact, subscriptions to the hunt had fallen away quite dramatically.

"With any luck they'll get rid of him for good," Sarah said.

We were keeping a close eye on the badger set. Someone had been back to collect their tools, but unfortunately we didn't see who it was. We had unblocked the set holes straight away, but we were all worried that the badgers might have suffocated. We agreed that on the night before the next hunt in our area, we would stake out in the wood and catch the culprit. It made my blood boil to think that anyone could be so cruel.

About eight o'clock that morning there had been a frantic rapping at the front door. We all thought somebody had had an accident, but it turned out to be Zac, the saboteur who had been arrested by the police along with Sarah. I recognized him straight away – it was hard not to, with his lanky ponytail and goatee beard. Carrying a huge pile of animal rights leaflets, he pushed his way through the door and immediately started rambling on about the importance of fighting for what you believe in and sticking together against the enemy. Katie and Danny were giving each other secret looks and tittering behind his back. Even I found it difficult to keep a straight face when he spotted the sausages sizzling on the stove and started lecturing Sarah about the horrors of eating meat.

It soon became obvious what he wanted. To recruit us – as saboteurs!

Nobody could be more keen on animal welfare than us, but Zac's group was not what we believed in. How could people calling themselves animal lovers behave the way they did? Look what they did to Boris, not to mention the foxhounds.

Admittedly, not all saboteurs went to such extremes. It was important that people campaigned for what they believed in, otherwise how would anything ever get changed? Mrs Mac told us that Zac had a personal vendetta against Charles Stonehouse, which explained why he was so obsessed with the Burlington Hunt.

"There's something a bit fishy about him," Ross insisted, "and I can't quite put my finger on it."

"It's in!" Katie came shrieking out of the house, waving a newspaper in the air. "I'm on the front page!"

Danny charged after her, with Jigsaw bounding up and down trying to catch the paper, thinking it was all a big game.

But it was serious. Bluey's face stared out at us from the paper and I think we all felt a sense of loss and despair. The headline over the picture read: HOLLYWELL HEARTBREAK – HAVE YOU SEEN THIS PONY?

"It should be all over town by now," Ross commented, reading the article for the third time and pointing out the byline, which read "Roddy Fitzgerald". It was his first big story, or "scoop", as Roddy preferred to call it.

"That's somebody now!" Katie yelled as the telephone rang.

We ran into the house as fast as possible and arrived in the hallway just as Sarah was replacing the receiver.

"Some ignorant buffoon," she bellowed, looking shattered with disappointment. "How can people be so nasty? That's what I want to know. He thought we weren't fit to look after animals, can you believe it? He wanted to know how we could possibly let this happen. He even implied that we were sponging off public money."

Tears suddenly welled up in Sarah's eyes and she ran out into the yard.

"I'll go," I said to Ross as he made to follow her.

I found her leaning on the gate, looking out at the empty field.

"It's not fair, Mel. It's just not fair."

"The paper's only just come out," I said, trying to sound positive. "There's loads of time yet."

"You're forgetting one thing . . . Not everybody reads the local paper."

The phone didn't ring for the next hour. During that time Sarah made a momentous decision.

"I'm going to see James."

We were all stunned. "Are you serious?"

"Absolutely. I should have done it days ago," she said, marching up and down the kitchen with some of her old spark showing through. "James will know what to do."

"Thank heavens for that," Ross said, when Sarah set off in the car. With any luck she would catch James before he started his afternoon surgery. "Those two are made for each other," Ross said. "I just wish they could see it."

"Maybe they need a bit of a shove," I suggested.

"You might be right," Ross murmured.

And already an idea was forming in my mind.

Chapter Eight

I had just gone into Boris's stable to give him his powder. The only way we could get him to take it was to dig out the core of an apple and pour it inside. When we tried to mix it in his feed, he just scooted it all over the place and stomped around the stable with his lip curled up in the air.

Ross was still in the tack room – I had left him pinning up posters of native ponies – and Katie and Danny were in the house, watching a special horse programme on television.

It could have been any ordinary afternoon . . .

I was bent down in the stable, spraying some antiseptic lotion on Boris's knees where he'd been scratched by the thorns from the hedge.

It all happened so fast. The motorbike was there before I had a chance to think. I just froze on my hands and knees in the straw and couldn't move.

I heard Ross come rushing out of the tack room. Bazz was whooping and shouting, going round and round in circles with another lad riding pillion behind him. Boris was getting more and more nervous. I scrambled for the door.

Ross was looking straight at me. "Get down!" he mouthed, waving his arm in a downwards motion.

I dived below the door just as Bazz screeched the bike round to face me. A few seconds later and I would have been spotted. My heart was pounding like a steam engine.

Bazz started laughing. He was circling Ross, tighter and tighter, scuffing up the gravel, revving the engine, sticking his leg out and pushing Ross hard in the back.

Ross held his ground.

The lad on the back wolf-whistled and then giggled hysterically. That's when I recognized him – he was the one who had accompanied Bazz before, the coward who had backed off at the first sign of trouble. But we'd had help then – we'd had Blake, who was tough and used to dealing with thugs. Now there were just the two of us and Ross was out there by himself.

"Look, Paul, it's mummy's little boy," Bazz sneered, switching off the ignition and slowly swinging his leg over the black-and-gold bodywork.

He seemed heavier, broader than before. He had the same pasty skin and cruel eyes, but there was something else – some inner confidence. He had the upper hand and he knew it.

"Got yer now," Bazz jeered. "I'm going to duff up yer pretty little face, what do yer think to that? Fancy a broken nose, do yer?"

I was spying through a crack in the doorframe. The other lad, Paul, turned round and looked straight in my direction. I squirmed to one side and could have sworn he saw me. His pimply face screwed up as if he was thinking and I could see the scar across his right cheek flicker. It was the same lad all right.

"So you've finally got me alone," Ross said in a loud voice, deliberately distracting Paul's attention away from the stable.

Boris was breathing down my neck, nuzzling and pulling at my coat. Please don't let him have a tantrum now, I thought. Queenie and Sophie were standing with their heads over their doors, watching. It was obvious Bazz didn't recognize Queenie.

"Why didn't you kidnap *me*, you creep?" Ross started in fury. "Why take it out on an innocent animal?"

"Oh, that would have been too easy," Bazz snarled, moving a step closer to Ross. "We wanted to see yer suffer, just like me brother is, in prison. We've been following yer. Bet yer din't know that, did yer?" Bazz spat on the ground, a few feet away from Ross.

Boris nudged me in the back and I nearly banged my head against the door.

"Idiot!" Bazz shouted. "You couldn't even find an old nag and yer call yerselves a sanctuary."

He held his hand out to Paul, who giggled and passed him a newspaper which was screwed up under his jacket.

"Nice picture," Bazz leered, enjoying every minute. "Shame about the pony."

Ross belted forward and grabbed Bazz by the collar. But Bazz was quicker. He stuck out his fist and Ross ran straight into it.

"That'll teach yer," Bazz growled. "You're going to have more than a black eye when I've finished."

I had to do something. Think! Think! What would Ross do? I suddenly remembered that Katie and Danny were in the house. Surely they must have heard all the commotion. Would they have phoned the police?

I didn't know. I couldn't say for sure.

Bazz was slowly ripping the paper into shreds and grinding it into the gravel with his heel. Now might be my only chance. I stood up and moved my hand towards the bolt.

"Hey!"

My heart leapt into my mouth. I dived down

into the straw and prayed for a miracle. Paul was walking straight towards me!

"Bazz, look at this horse! It's massive!" He peered in over the stable door and I pressed myself back against the wall.

It wasn't me he'd seen. It was Boris.

He stuck out his hand and I almost cried out to warn him. Boris pressed his ears back flat against his head and, squealing in rage, ran at the door. He sank his teeth into Paul's arm, ripping a chunk out of his leather jacket.

"Bazz, it's bit me!"

I couldn't see what was happening. I didn't dare move. All I could hear were footsteps across the gravel and the door bolt sliding back.

"Let it out!"

"No!" Ross sounded desperate.

"What's the matter, lover boy? Worried about losing another one?"

"Don't let him out," Ross pleaded.

Boris was dying to get out. I couldn't let that happen – he would ruin his leg. I had to do something! I closed my fingers around the spray canister in my pocket and it gave me an idea.

The door burst open and I flung myself forward, blocking Boris's way and catching Bazz off guard. Holding the canister in both hands I sprayed it straight towards Bazz's face.

73

Bazz screamed out and fell backwards. Ross seized his chance and leapt on Paul, but he rolled to one side and Ross clutched at thin air.

"Someone's coming!" Paul yelled out, hearing a car on the drive. "Quick! Gerron the bike!"

Bazz blundered past Ross and leapt on the motorbike, roaring it into life.

"Hey, wait for me!" Paul screeched, suddenly realizing he might be left behind.

But Bazz had no intention of hanging about. He wheeled the bike round and applied full throttle. The tyres scuffed up a cloud of dust and then shot forward. At the same time, Roddy was turning into the yard in his red Mini . . .

"Watch out!" I screamed.

Roddy's face was a picture of horror. He yanked hard on the steering wheel and the Mini careered to the right. Bazz just kept on coming.

"They're going to crash!" Ross shouted.

There was just inches in it. Bazz hurtled past, brushing against the wing mirror.

"What about me?" whimpered Paul.

Roddy fought to control the wheel but it was too late. The Mini crashed head on into the water trough, crumpling the bumper and bursting a main pipe. A great gush of water shot up just as Roddy unfolded his elongated body from the car. He got drenched.

Ross made a dive for Paul, who had set off running, and brought him down flat on his face. They were both rolling around on the gravel when a police car came into the yard.

I was still clutching the spray canister; Roddy came loping across in his designer suit, which was soaking wet; Ross yanked Paul to his feet, revealing his own dazzling black eye; and Danny and Katie came streaking out of the house, carrying a baseball bat and bursting with the excitement of having dialled 999.

"Not you lot again," the younger policeman said.

We were becoming quite well known at the police station.

Ross handed over Paul, who was squealing with excuses and trying to worm his way out of his jacket in an effort to escape. Luckily the older policeman read between the lines and grabbed hold of Paul's collar. "The long and the short of it is, laddie," he said, "*you're nicked*!"

Chapter Nine

"We might as well face it, we're not going to find him." Ross was holding a wet facecloth to his black eye, which was closing up fast.

Roddy was sat in his boxer shorts for the second time in a week, with his suit strung up on the clothes-horse and Katie frantically trying to dry it with the hair-dryer.

"At least we know for definite who stole him," he said lamely, perched on the edge of the armchair and trying to stop Jigsaw from licking his bare legs. "And with any luck that birdbrain they took down to the police station will spill the beans."

"I wouldn't be so sure about that," I said.

Bazz worked on a policy of scaring people. He would have put the fear of God into Paul and the chances of him grassing on Bazz were remote.

"No. If we're going to find Bluey," I said, "it's got to be down to us."

Roddy's Mini wasn't as badly damaged as we'd

first thought. The bumper had fallen off and the wing mirror was bent, but apart from that it was still intact. Roddy said the person he'd bought it from had robbed him anyway and it didn't matter – at least he'd got another lead story and he'd been there at the scene of the crime!

Katie and Danny were ecstatic when he gave them a box of *Weekly Herald* pens, paper, notepads and other stationery. Katie said this was the start of her career as a journalist and Danny said he wanted to be a novelist just like Sarah.

Roddy went back to the office in a crinkled suit and none of us mentioned the fact that we'd had no more phone calls. Up until now the newspaper idea had been a total disaster.

Sarah was devastated. I'd never seen her quite so low. She came back from the surgery looking red-eyed and worn out. I thought she was going to faint when we told her about Bazz and what had happened.

Even Jigsaw couldn't cheer her up, even though he went through his whole repertoire of tricks, from rolling over to sitting up and waving his paw. The poor thing had no idea why we were all so down. Ross and I agreed not to mention James's name until Sarah brought up the subject. Obviously the big reunion had failed to materialize.

I volunteered to make something to eat, while

Ross, Katie and Danny went to feed and water the horses. The house had never been so quiet. Sarah was sitting aimlessly in a chair, watching television with the sound turned down and munching listlessly on a celery stick. Matilda was curled up in her basket; all she seemed to do nowadays was sleep.

I put some sausages under the grill and ended up burning them to a cinder. Ross said we could all pretend it was a barbecue and slapped them between some bread rolls. Sarah came through from the sitting room looking so depressed. I was really beginning to get worried. I quickly pushed Bluey's red headcollar under some papers in case it upset her even more.

We chewed our way silently through the rolls. In the end Ross could stand it no longer.

"We can't carry on like this," he said, leaping up from his chair, looking like he was about to explode with frustration. "If James doesn't want to know us any more, then it's his loss, but we've got to carry on. We can't quit now, too many lives depend on us."

He raked his hand back through his hair and for a moment he reminded me so much of our dad. He had the same strong jawline and dark eyes that showed every emotion. I'm sure Sarah was thinking the same thing too, because a shadow of intense grief passed over her face. None of us had ever really got over Dad's death, but now we had lost James too. We had all thought that James would eventually pop the question and he and Sarah would get married and James would come to live at Hollywell.

There didn't seem much chance of that now. I knew that Sarah found it difficult coping with three children and Danny as well, running a sanctuary and pursuing a career as a romantic novelist. She needed somebody to lean on, no matter how strong she pretended to be.

Tears started rolling down her face and Ross looked mortified. I knew he hadn't meant to upset her; he was just trying to pull her round. I passed her some kitchen roll to wipe her eyes and Jigsaw started whining and rubbing his head on her knees.

"He's gone," Sarah spluttered. "I went to the surgery. I'd got it all rehearsed in my mind as to what I was going to say and everything, but he's gone. Nobody knows where. He's got some holidaytime owing to him and he's just taken off."

Sarah looked heartbroken. I couldn't believe James would just disappear without telling us. He wasn't that sort of person. He was too responsible. Even if he and Sarah had had a humdinger of an argument, he wouldn't just take off. Something must have happened.

"I think he's left me." Sarah started sobbing. "I think he's gone for good. It's just all going wrong," she said. "First Oswald, then that awful Charles Stonehouse. And Bluey and Bazz. We've got no field to put the horses in, no money. People think we're not fit to run a sanctuary . . ."

The list went on and on. We'd gone through testing times before and come out the other side, but nothing quite like this. There didn't seem to be any way forward.

Ross put his arm around Sarah but didn't say anything. What was there to say? For the first time ever, I began seriously to doubt that we had a future.

"Oh, my God," Sarah suddenly said in a numb voice. "We've completely forgotten."

We should have been at the riding centre ten minutes ago. It was Ross's lecture on Hollywell Stables.

"But I can't do it, not looking like this," Ross protested, pointing to his black eye. "What would people think?"

"Well, we can't let Mrs Mac down," Sarah said, quickly drying her eyes and fetching the car keys from the peg. "Mel will have to do it."

"You're joking," I said. "I wouldn't know what to say. I can't stand up in front of an audience. I'd die of embarrassment."

"You stay here, Ross, and stand guard. Any sign of Bazz and call the police. Don't leave the phone. Someone might just ring."

Sarah wasn't leaving me any choice. "You can look at Ross's notes in the car."

I'd need more than notes to get me through this. The last thing I felt like doing was talking to a crowd of pony-mad kids and their parents. "Sarah, I can't do it. I just can't."

Chapter Ten

We arrived at the riding centre five minutes later.
Sarah quickly touched up her make-up and booted
me out of the car. "You'll be fine. Don't panic. I'll
be there in the audience."

"Why can't you do it?" I almost shrieked, my
voice sounding squeaky and hollow.

"You know very well why. It's for people sixteen
years and under. Now come on, you should be
on next!"

We crunched our way across the gravel and I
marvelled at how there wasn't a blade of straw
out of place. All the stables and horses were
immaculate, not like Hollywell, where everything
was always chaotic. It must take an army of
workers to keep this place so clean.

We could hear someone speaking into the microphone, and then a round of applause. A beautiful
bay thoroughbred wearing white bandages and a
double bridle trotted past us and headed into the
indoor school.

"That's the dressage rider," Sarah whispered.

"Apparently she's the area champion. She's doing a display to music."

Suddenly some classical music wafted out of the arena and the audience went quiet. Under normal circumstances I would have loved to watch the performance, but right now I wanted to be a million miles away.

"Sarah, I think I'm going to be sick."

We went into the coffee bar, which was next to the indoor school, and Sarah tried to find out when I was on. I ordered a coffee but my hands were shaking so much I couldn't pick it up. Sarah came back and said I had ten minutes, and why didn't I have some chocolate as it would give me some energy. The last thing I wanted was to eat.

Sarah dragged me bodily towards the entrance of the indoor school, where we spotted Mrs Mac serving on the Hollywell stall. "The mugs and sweatshirts are doing really well," she said excitedly, handing some change to a woman who had just bought a navy-blue extra-large sweatshirt for her husband. "But where's Ross?"

We explained what had happened, and when Sarah said that I was standing in for him Mrs Mac looked horrified. I wanted to say thanks for the vote of confidence, but I knew how she felt. Ross was the articulate one in the family and he was also the riding club heart-throb. All the girls were going to be desperately disappointed when they saw me stand up instead of him. I would be at an instant disadvantage.

"Just do your best, Mel. We can't ask for more than that."

The dressage horse did a perfect square halt from canter and then walked out of the arena on a loose rein. Everyone clapped and then a woman in a striped jacket and black jodhpurs walked into the middle of the arena carrying the microphone. She introduced me as Melanie Foster from Hollywell Stables who was going to talk about cruelty and neglect and what it was like to run a sanctuary.

Sarah nudged me in the back and I stumbled forward, my feet sinking into the deep sand and feeling like I was wearing concrete boots. There was just a sea of faces in the seating area. The clapping soon fizzled out and everyone fell silent. I was left in the middle of the arena, holding the mike and not having a clue what to say.

My brain wouldn't function. My mouth had turned desert dry and my legs were shaking uncontrollably. Someone in the audience coughed. There was a rustle of sweet papers and then two girls I vaguely recognized started tittering.

Ross's words about being strong came flooding back to me. If I could go through the ordeal of seeing one of our cats killed in front of me, having one of our ponies stolen, fighting for my life against Bazz, I could handle this. It was nothing in comparison. Sarah always says you are what life's experiences make you and I wasn't going to let a few peevish teenage girls get the better of me.

I started talking.

Once I began I couldn't stop. It all came pouring out. I talked about Bluey and what it had been like to see for the first time a pony so neglected. I talked about Queenie and Sophie and how we had rescued them. I talked about how you always wanted to rescue every horse in trouble but there were only so many you could take in, and how it never got any easier with each horse you saw in a state of neglect. I talked about fund-raising and how much money we needed to collect. I told them about the new stable block we intended to build and the extra land we desperately needed.

The audience was gripped. I went on to talk about how everybody could do their bit by being extra vigilant. I told them what signs of neglect to look out for – lack of food, water, shelter; what to do if they spotted a horse in trouble. I was actually beginning to enjoy myself.

Then it was time for the audience to ask questions. Everybody was fascinated with the story about Dancer and how we'd had a famous rock star staying at Hollywell. Someone wanted to know how much it cost per year to keep each horse, and then someone asked the inevitable question.

"Have you found Bluey yet?"

My heart missed a beat. What could I say?

"We've seen the article in the paper," a girl shouted out from the back.

I started to describe Bluey. I told them he was twelve two hands and over twenty years old. I explained about his wall-eye and strawberry roan colouring with a black mane and tail.

"What's a wall-eye?" A little girl about Katie's age stuck up her hand.

"A wall-eye is when there is a pale-blue pigment in the eye instead of the usual brown colouring. That's why we called him Bluey."

"And what do you mean when you say strawberry roan?"

"Oh, that's easy," I said. "It's when there are white hairs mingled in with a chestnut coat. It's one of my favourite colours."

"He sounds just like my new pony," the little girl said.

Sarah was at my side within two seconds flat. "What did you say?"

I couldn't believe it.

"How long have you had him?" Sarah was practically shaking the little girl by the shoulders.

Her mother arrived on the scene, looking extremely upset. "I don't know what you're driving at, but we bought that pony in good faith."

"Where's the paper? Has anybody got today's paper?" Sarah was running up and down the rows of seats, practically hysterical.

My heart was pounding and everybody in the arena was chattering and whispering in excitement. Apparently the little girl was called Chloe Taylor and she'd only just got her first pony. She was new to the riding club and her parents had recently moved into the area. They hadn't seen today's paper.

"But our pony's only twelve years old and he's called Red," Chloe murmured, bursting into tears.

Nobody had a newspaper.

"Mrs Taylor, can you tell us who you bought your pony from?" Sarah was in no mood to beat about the bush.

"I can't see how that's really any of your business."

"For heaven's sake, Mrs Taylor, I think you've bought a stolen pony – our pony!"

"I'll have to talk to my husband about this."

"Can you please just let us see him?"

"Don't you think you're being a little unreasonable?"

"Unreasonable?" Sarah was nearly bursting out

of her skin. "Our pony is missing. You've just bought one. It fits our description perfectly. Now don't you think that's more than coincidence?"

We followed Mrs Taylor's car out of the riding centre and along the road towards town. She still wasn't very happy about the situation but at least she was letting us see the pony.

Sarah banged her foot down hard on the accelerator of our old Volvo in an effort to keep up and we whisked round a corner and into a village. All the houses were huge and immaculate, with beautiful gardens, and I could hardly believe it when Mrs Taylor indicated and turned up a long drive with paddocks running on either side.

"Surely if they've got this much money, they wouldn't buy a pony like Bluey," I said to Sarah, who was about to say the same thing. Bluey was a special pony but he was certainly no beauty.

"I get the feeling they don't know much about horses," Sarah said.

We leapt out of the car as soon as we pulled up, frantic to see if our hunch was right. Sarah looked nervous. Now that we were actually here, I was convinced it was all a wild goose chase.

Mrs Taylor led us towards a row of wooden looseboxes with high doors and grids up at the top halves. There was no sign of a pony.

"We're going to have a special door made for

him," Mrs Taylor said, "so he can look out whenever he wants."

Chloe went and fetched a red headcollar just like the one we had at home. A huge lump appeared in my throat when I saw it. Was this an omen? I could barely stand the suspense any longer. Chloe moved towards the middle stable. Mrs Taylor looked nervous and on edge.

I heard a shuffle from inside the stable but I couldn't see anything. Chloe slid back the two bolts, first the top one, then the kick-over bolt at the bottom. I instinctively reached in my pocket for some pony nuts and my fingers closed around Katie's lucky four-leaved clover. It hadn't been taken out since our trip to the scrapyard. I held on to it and squeezed for dear life. Sarah had both her fingers crossed behind her back.

The door swung open.

The pony was standing right behind the door and gave a deep whicker of joy as Chloe pushed her way inside. His forelock had been pulled short and he was wearing a smart red-and-navy rug and red stable bandages to match.

"Well?" Mrs Taylor asked.

Tears sprang up in Sarah's eyes and she could barely speak.

I flung my arms round his neck and started

laughing and crying at the same time. "It's him! It's Bluey! We've found him!"

There was no doubt Bluey knew who we were. He started nuzzling at my face and pushing his way towards Sarah. I couldn't stop hugging him. I didn't want to let go of him for a second. Sarah was ecstatic.

Mrs Taylor looked horrified. Chloe was standing in a corner of the stable, crying over and over that he was her pony.

It suddenly dawned on me that this could turn into a major battle. Bluey could be at the centre of a tug of war. Just who did he belong to?

"We've paid four hundred pounds for him," Mrs Taylor said, looking at a total loss as to what to do next. "You can't just take him away. He's our pony. I won't let you."

Chloe was crying even louder.

"We'll have to call in the police," Sarah said. "It has to be reported. But I think you'll find the law's on our side, Mrs Taylor. Bluey is our pony. He belongs at Hollywell."

When Mr Taylor came home from playing squash, he nearly lost his temper with Sarah. He couldn't believe that Bluey was stolen. Mrs Taylor had calmed down, but poor Chloe was still heartbroken. It was obvious she had fallen in love with Bluey and couldn't bear the idea of losing him.

I didn't know what to say, or what to do, so I just stood there trying to be diplomatic and smiling uneasily.

The police eventually arrived on the scene and we all went inside to answer their questions. Mr Taylor poured himself a large drink and Sarah dropped hints about a cup of tea. I suggested we telephone Ross and tell him what had happened, and Mrs Taylor just flapped around saying what a terrible shock it had all been and why should it happen to them.

It was obvious from Mr Taylor's description that he'd bought Bluey from Bazz. Who else rode round on a black-and-gold motorbike and owned a scrapyard? Bazz had been nosing around Mr Taylor's block of offices, looking for scrap metal, and he'd mentioned that he had a pony for sale. Mr Taylor didn't know one end of a pony from another and Bazz had convinced him that Bluey was only twelve years old.

It was so simple, it was frightening. To think that ponies were being stolen every day and sold to some innocent person within days.

"I just can't believe this is happening," Mrs Taylor said, collapsing exhausted on the settee.

The police had satisfied themselves that Bluey

was our pony and confirmed that we were still the rightful owners.

Chloe ran out of the room in a fit of sobs and I truly felt sorry for her. It must be awful finally to get your first pony and then have it taken away, just snatched from underneath you. Bazz would never know the heartache he'd caused so many people.

"We'll pick him up in the morning," Sarah said.

It was pitch black outside the Taylor's house as we climbed into our car, but the stable lights were switched on and Chloe was looking out at us over Bluey's door.

"Come on," Sarah sighed. "There's nothing more we can do tonight. Let's go home."

We crawled back to Hollywell with Sarah in a trance and me half asleep. The relief at finding Bluey had left us both weak and tired. It was the first time I'd relaxed since Bluey had been taken and now I just wanted to sleep for a week.

Neither of us noticed the strange car tucked away on the Hollywell drive.

We walked into the kitchen unaware and unprepared. Ross was fidgeting around the door, looking wildly excited and shifty. Katie and Danny were sitting under the kitchen table in what looked like a pretend Wendy house with a hoard of chocolate cream eggs, while Matilda played with a cat-nip mouse. Jigsaw was barking non-stop and racing up and down.

The first thing Sarah asked was, "What's going on?"

Ross could bear it no longer. "You've got a visitor," he said, and flung open the door leading into the sitting room.

Someone was standing there holding a massive rhododendron plant which half covered his face and the biggest box of chocolates I had ever seen.

"James!" Sarah whispered.

"Surprise, surprise!" Katie and Danny shrieked out, and James promptly emptied his arms and grabbed hold of Sarah, twirling her off her feet until she was completely out of breath.

"Why didn't you tell me what was going on?"

Ross insisted that James and Sarah needed some privacy and pushed us all out of the sitting room. But it didn't stop us listening behind the door, or Katie complaining that she couldn't see anything through the keyhole.

"Don't you ever shut me out like that again," we heard James say.

"I'm just a pigheaded idiot," Sarah answered.

"It was all my fault," James insisted.

"No, no, it was mine, definitely mine."

93

Everything went quiet. Katie said they must be kissing and wondered if we should time how long it lasted for. I said it was none of our business, but we still couldn't drag ourselves away from the door.

"Shall we agree to disagree?" James finally spoke up.

"To respect each other's opinions?" Sarah half laughed.

"When's he going to propose?" Katie whispered, getting impatient.

Ross accidentally stood on my foot. I yelped out in pain and James whipped open the door. Katie fell head-first into the sitting room, with Danny after her.

"Did you want something?" James asked.

Katie was seriously miffed because there was no talk of weddings and she desperately wanted to be a bridesmaid, but she soon came round when Sarah opened the box of chocolates and we all got stuck into hazelnut whips and toffee creams.

James explained that he'd had to rush off to see his mother, who'd been admitted to hospital with a mild stroke. She lived a hundred and fifty miles away, which was why he'd been forced to take a few days off work.

The first he'd heard about Bluey was when he came home and found the weekly paper stuck in the letterbox. He couldn't believe it, but immediately put two and two together and came up with Bazz.

"I'm just sorry I didn't believe you," he said to Sarah, and Ross explained how none of us had really expected Bazz to go to such lengths.

"He was obsessed with revenge," Sarah added. "He would have done anything . . . The trouble is, he's still out there. He hasn't been caught yet."

We told James about Charles Stonehouse and how he'd ripped up the fencing on purpose and threatened to close us down; how he was never going to sell us any of his land, not in a million years.

"He said what?" James was totally flabbergasted. "So you haven't heard? I'd have thought it would be all over town by now."

"James, what are you talking about?"

"It's Stonehouse . . . Pembroke Properties. They've gone broke. They're finished. It's been on the cards for years – he's been living the grand lifestyle on borrowed money and it's finally caught up with him."

"You're joking?" I could hardly believe what I was hearing. "But why did he still threaten us?" I said. "It doesn't make sense."

"I don't think he can accept what's happening," James explained. "He's had such a good life for so long, he can't imagine anything else. I don't think he can believe that the land doesn't belong to him any more."

"Wow!" Katie said. "This is heavy."

Ross looked totally bowled over and I thought it all sounded like something straight out of a book.

"But you know what this means, don't you?" Sarah said, pushing another chocolate in James's mouth and cramming it full. "It means that all the land will be coming up for sale. All we have to do now is find the money to buy it!"

Finally our luck seemed to be changing. We'd found Bluey; James was back in the fold; Boris was getting better; we hadn't even had to use the thousand pounds reward, which meant we could put up some new fencing in the field. How Sarah expected to raise money to buy the Pembroke land, though, I couldn't imagine. But that would be a long time in the future.

For now our main concern was bringing back Bluey. The next morning we were all on tenterhooks with excitement. Katie and Danny put a fresh bed down in Bluey's stable and filled the water bucket. None of us had been inside since Bluey went missing – it had just been too painful – but now we wanted to make it fit for a prince.

Ross went to turn on the horsebox engine to let it warm up and I popped in through the groom's door and put up a full haynet.

"Don't forget the headcollar," I shouted to Sarah, who was locking up the house. "And his favourite mints."

James was coming with us and arrived with two minutes to spare. He still had a couple of days off work and he wanted to make the most of them.

"Don't forget what we discussed last night," he said to Sarah before we piled into the horsebox.

Ross, Sarah, James and myself had discussed the matter of Bluey until long into the night. For once Sarah had listened to James's point of view and we all knew it made good sense.

"Just remember there is an alternative" was all he added.

"Come on, let's get this show on the road," Ross yelled, and Sarah climbed into the driver's seat. Katie, Danny and myself sat next to her and Jigsaw perched on the back ledge. Ross was travelling in the car with James.

It was one of those brilliant, frosty spring mornings when everything seems to be bursting into life and we had a superb view of the rolling hills. Danny and Katie were counting the new-born lambs and I spotted two shire horses and what looked like a Clydesdale.

Sarah was concentrating on her gear changes, which every now and then sounded like a strangled canary. The driving wheel was huge and there was no power-steering. Katie and Danny started singing "She'll be coming round the mountain when she comes", but I thought it was too early in the morning for so much noise.

Jigsaw started barking as we pulled into the Taylors' drive, with Sarah threatening to knock over a tub of daffodils. James had offered to drive the horsebox but he was hopeless at getting into second gear, which meant we came to a juddering halt half-way up every hill.

We jumped out of the cab and Jigsaw immediately went to make friends with the Taylors' red setter. Ross lowered the horsebox ramp and we went to try and find somebody. Mr Taylor had gone out to a business meeting and Mrs Taylor was in the stableyard, trying to console young Chloe. Her eyes were red and swollen from crying and her face was all blotchy and hot. She was about the same size as Katie, but with blonde hair tied back in a ponytail and a showering of freckles on her nose.

"Before you take him, I just want to say how sorry I am about yesterday. It was all such a shock." Mrs Taylor seemed truly apologetic.

"Don't worry about it," Sarah said, looking

uncomfortable. "We'd have been exactly the same. You can come and visit him whenever you like."

"We've just grown so attached to him, you see." Mrs Taylor's voice drifted off.

"I know," Sarah said. "He's that kind of pony."

"You will take good care of him, won't you?" Chloe's face looked as if this was the end of the world. I couldn't bear to look at her. "He likes you to read to him in the stable, especially if it's about other ponies."

This was ridiculous. I was getting choked up with emotion. Sarah looked mortified. James looked as if he was about to say something, but changed his mind.

"Let's get him in the box," Sarah half grunted.

Chloe went to lead him out and Bluey tottered forward, wearing his new rug and munching on a piece of apple.

Katie and Danny went crazy with excitement. They couldn't stop hugging and patting him. Ross pulled fondly at one of his ears and said he'd never expected to see the old fellow again. Bluey whickered gently and said hello to Jigsaw, who came barging up and started licking the tip of his nose.

Sarah took the leadrope from Chloe and Bluey obediently followed her. Getting him into the horsebox proved a different matter. Bluey hated travelling and I don't think he'd ever been in a big horsebox before, certainly not ours, anyway. How Bazz had managed to entice him away I really can't imagine. Apparently Bazz had dropped Bluey off at the Taylors' in what looked like a pig trailer. Bluey had been sweating profusely and trembling when he came out. Obviously that experience had deepened his fear of travelling, because now he dug in his heels and refused to budge. He wouldn't even be persuaded when Sarah lifted one of his forelegs on to the ramp. Bluey had a stubborn streak when he wanted and he was practically screwing up his face in determination, saying, "No way am I going in that box!"

Sarah was at a loss as to what to do next. James had a go but failed to do any better. I knew Bluey; he would stand there all day if he had to.

Chloe's bottom lip started quivering and then she burst into huge racking sobs and threw her arms around Bluey's neck.

"OK, I give in," Sarah said. "Bluey's made the decision for us."

We had been talking last night about the possibility of letting Bluey out on loan to the Taylors. It was something that most sanctuaries tended to do. It meant that the horses could get more individual attention and also that the sanctuary then had room to rescue other cases. Some homes of rest had over a hundred residents and it was awe-inspiring to think that Hollywell Stables might eventually end up that size.

It would be heartbreaking not to see Bluey's face in the yard every morning, but it would be a dream come true for Chloe. It was obvious Bluey thought the world of Chloe. We could check up on him every few weeks and advise on his day-to-day care. And, of course, he would always belong to Hollywell and he'd spend the last of his days in our fields.

"So what do you think?" Sarah put the proposition to Mrs Taylor.

Chloe looked as if she was about to float up into the clouds. Her eyes suddenly had more sparkle than the whole of the Blackpool illuminations.

"Of course, he wouldn't be able to do a lot of work," Sarah said. "Maybe some light hacking, not much else."

"I think Chloe just wants him as a pet," Mrs Taylor said. "She's not really into all that competing stuff."

"Well, that settles it then," Sarah said. "Chloe, you'd better take your pony back to the stable."

We discussed various feeds and veterinary care, and how much grass Bluey could have, and we arranged to come back in a week's time to see how they were getting on. Sarah gave Mrs Taylor our telephone number and also James's number at the surgery. I gave Chloe the packet of Bluey's favourite mints and told her that he liked one last thing at night.

We left Chloe busy grooming Bluey until he shone and promising to read him another chapter of *Black Beauty*. We trundled out of the drive with an empty horsebox but the conviction that we'd done the right thing.

"Bluey's in seventh heaven there," James said. "And as for you kids, you've got loads of horses back at Hollywell. You've more than enough to keep you busy."

As it turned out, we had more than we bargained for. Charles Stonehouse was at Hollywell and he was after Boris.

"I don't believe it," Sarah shouted, as we turned into the drive and saw the Range Rover and trailer.

Even worse, Stonehouse had Boris out of his stable and was dragging him towards the lowered ramp.

"How could we have been so stupid?" Sarah was boiling over with anger that we'd left no one on guard at the stables. We'd been so caught up with the excitement of finding Bluey that we hadn't given it a second thought. We imagined that by now Bazz would be in police custody or trying to do a runner and we'd never considered the possibility of another visit from Stonehouse.

"Come on, you stupid brute, you're going back to the kennels!"

"You leave that horse alone or I won't be responsible for my actions." Sarah was very, very angry.

Stonehouse turned round to face us. Boris was backing off, tugging on the leadrope, his eyes showing genuine fear.

"You just had to do it, didn't you? You couldn't leave it alone. You had to report me." The muscles in his neck were standing out like cordstrings about to snap and his mouth was turned down in a hard line.

"You deserve everything you get," Sarah hissed back. "Now let go of that horse!"

James was at her side in an instant. "Do as she says, Charles. You're just making a fool of yourself."

"Don't you dare tell me what to do. It's none of your business."

Stonehouse tightened his hold on the leadrope, so Boris's head was yanked down at a painful angle.

"Well, for the record, I've never touched your precious badger set. You're barking up the wrong tree and you're going to look like idiots when the truth comes out."

"Rubbish!" Sarah shouted. "We all know you're guilty. Why don't you just admit it?"

"You seem to have forgotten, lady, that you're up on an assault charge . . . Of course, I could be persuaded to drop it."

"No chance," Sarah said. "Don't even think about it."

Stonehouse took a definite step towards Boris. It was the worst thing he could have done. Boris could stand things no longer. He hauled back on the leadrope, rearing straight up, and came crashing down, all seventeen hands of him, catching Stonehouse on the shoulder with his injured leg and knocking him to the ground.

"Oh, no!" Sarah went as white as a sheet.

Stonehouse sprawled backwards, his head cracking on the concrete with a sickening thud. James shot forward. Sarah stood rock still, not knowing what to do for the best. I dived across to Boris, who was trembling all over, looking shocked and apologetic. I don't think he'd meant to strike Stonehouse – he just wanted to get away from him. Ross helped me lead him back into the stable.

I could hear Stonehouse groaning and trying to get to his feet. At least he was still conscious.

"I think he's dislocated his shoulder," James

104

said. "And there might be concussion. I'll take him to casualty."

"Don't think you're going to get away with this," Stonehouse spat out, glaring at Sarah and leaning on James for support. "That horse is a maniac. He needs putting down!"

James guided him into the passenger seat of the Range Rover and jumped in next to him. "Give it a rest, Charles. It was just an accident."

"Accident, my foot! She's had it in for me from the beginning."

James unhitched the trailer and reversed the Range Rover, while Stonehouse lowered the window on his side and stuck his head out, blood trickling down into his shirt collar and his eyes bulging so he looked like a mad man.

James accelerated out of the yard, but it didn't stop Stonehouse shouting after us, "You're finished, lady, do you hear me? *Finished!*"

Chapter Eleven

"How on earth did you do it? How did you get him to change his mind?"

James had just come back from casualty and somehow he'd managed to perform a miracle. Stonehouse was dropping the assault charge and he was giving up any claim on Boris, who could stay on at the sanctuary.

"So how did you do it?" We were all riveted. What could James have possibly said to cause such a change of heart?

"Let's just say I reminded him of a few things he'd rather forget." James wouldn't elaborate any further.

"But, James—"

"He's just a sad little man looking for someone to blame. Anyway, he's leaving the area. He's moving to Scotland."

"Good riddance to bad rubbish," I said, helping Katie stick together a montage of famous show-jumpers.

"No more Charles Stonehouse, hip hip hooray!" Danny was delighted.

"Of course, the Burlington Hunt will still carry on," James said. "They'll just wheel in a new hunt-master. Hopefully someone a little more popular."

"Talking about the hunt," Sarah said, filling up everybody's mugs with over-stewed tea, "are you still on for tonight?"

If we were going to catch the culprit, it would be tonight, before the meet tomorrow in one of the local villages. James was all for the idea. If something underhand was going on, he wanted to know about it. He was a nature lover just like us, and badgers came high on his list of favourite animals.

Danny and Katie could hardly wait. They'd never camped out all night in a wood before. Neither had I, for that matter.

"We'll need to take plenty of flasks with us," Sarah said.

"And sandwiches," Katie added.

"I hardly think so," Ross interrupted. "We're going on a night watch, not a picnic!"

"I just hope it's not too cold," I added, remembering last time Ross and I had waited in hiding at a racecourse and my toes had nearly dropped off from exposure.

"What about Roddy? It would make the perfect story for him."

"I can see this turning into a coach party with ringside seats," James joked.

"Just as long as we take the torches and the camera, that's all that matters!" Sarah said.

We spent the last few hours of daylight searching through the wreckage of the field fence to see how much could be salvaged. Stonehouse had suggested that we re-erect what was still in one piece, which would be a great saving. I still couldn't believe his change in attitude. Luckily the JCB hadn't damaged too many of the rails, and most of the posts could be repaired, although quite a few had been broken clean in two.

James gave Boris a full examination and thankfully no further damage had been done to his leg. It was still healing nicely. Boris sulked for the rest of the afternoon because he was back in his stable and he didn't think we were making enough fuss of him.

Roddy arrived at dusk, armed with camera, notebook, tape-recorder and a packet of boiled sweets. Thankfully he'd taken Sarah's advice and left the suit at home, but what he *was* dressed in was hardly appropriate for a night in the open air. Sarah threw him a horse rug and said he'd need it.

Roddy wrinkled up his nose and started to sneeze.

"Is everybody ready yet?" Ross chivvied. "At this rate whoever's blocking up the set will have been and gone and we'll be none the wiser."

We finally set off across the field. Katie was complaining that the flasks of tea were too heavy and banging against her leg. Sarah kept wondering whether she'd turned off the electric fire, but it didn't matter anyway because Mrs Mac had arrived to mind the house. Sarah wasn't leaving anything to chance.

"You mean we've got to cross over it? There isn't a bridge?" Roddy was horrified when he saw the stream.

"For heaven's sake, Roddy, there's more water in a puddle! Now grab hold of my arm." Sarah yanked him over the stepping stones before he had a chance to chicken out and he scrambled up the opposite bank.

"I'm not sure this is such a good idea," he said in a tight voice.

Nobody had been near the badger set; it was all as we'd left it. James picked out a spot where we'd have a good view without being seen, and Sarah threw down a blanket for us all to sit on.

"Isn't this exciting?" Danny said.

Katie replied that it was a very serious business, and Roddy said the damp was seeping through the blanket and we'd all end up with chronic rheumatism.

"Can we please have some hush," James insisted, and we all sat as quiet as mice for at least ten minutes.

It was a reasonably mild night, which was a blessing, but there was a strong wind and it rattled through the tree-tops, creating all sorts of weird noises. If we hadn't been in a group it would have been terrifying.

We were in total darkness. We couldn't risk switching on any of the torches – it would be an obvious giveaway – but it was so hard to focus, because everything just blurred into shadows.

An hour ticked by and Sarah decided to pour out some tea. Katie said she wanted to go to the toilet and James said she'd have to wait. Roddy leapt six feet in the air when a spider ran over his hand and Sarah cursed when the tea spilt because she couldn't see a thing in the dark.

An owl hooted directly overhead.

"What if this wood really is haunted?" Katie whispered, showing the first signs of nerves.

"Shush," James hissed. "Listen, over there, to the right! And don't make a noise!"

There were heavy footsteps approaching. Someone was coming towards us.

"What do we do now?" Roddy whispered, sounding terrified.

"Stay quiet. Nobody move a muscle." James was staring intently towards the badger set.

The footsteps were getting louder. Any minute now and we'd see who it was.

The moon must have passed behind some clouds, because suddenly everything went even darker. A twig snapped and a shadow came into focus. Whoever it was, they were carrying a torch and they shone it straight at us.

We all held our breath.

It glanced over us and turned back to the badger set. Then we heard the sound of a spade cut into the earth.

"That's it! Time for action!" James and Ross leapt up, but Roddy was quicker off the mark. He spurted forward on his long legs and within a couple of strides was at the scene and grabbing hold of the dark shadow.

"What does he think he's doing?" Sarah leapt up and ran after him. The last thing Roddy was cut out for was action combat. He could get seriously hurt. "Roddy!"

There was a scuffle and then someone shouting, "Gerroff me." I frantically tried to switch on my torch but my fingers wouldn't work. Sarah tripped in the undergrowth and went sprawling on her hands and knees. Ross grabbed hold of a spade and brandished it in the air.

"It's all right, I've got him! I've got him!" Roddy's voice yelled out in the dark.

"Who is it?" Sarah shouted, fighting off some brambles and struggling to her feet. I ran on ahead and caught up with James, who grabbed hold of my torch and switched it on.

"Don't you move, buster, or I'll break your neck!" Roddy was sitting on top of someone dressed all in black, pinning him to the ground. "I've got him, everyone! He can't move!"

Even so, whoever it was wriggled like fury to escape and Danny and Katie took the initiative and plonked themselves down on his ankles.

"Ouch!" he yelled in a stricken voice.

James shone the torch on the culprit's face. He blinked and screwed up his eyes, cursing from here to high heaven.

"I don't believe it!" Sarah gasped.

"It can't be!" James homed in for a closer look.

But there was no mistaking that familiar goatee beard . . . It was Zac!

"How could I have been so wrong?" Sarah was mortified.

She had truly believed that it was the hunt who

were blocking up the badger set. We all had. But, as it turned out, it had been Zac all along. He was trying to give the hunt a bad name in the most underhand way possible.

"So that's why he came round with his animal rights leaflets, winding us up about the hunt and what they do. He must have known it would be only a matter of time before we spotted the badger set." Ross was as shocked as the rest of us.

"The trouble with Zac is that he's more taken up with the class war and fighting against the establishment than he is with foxes and hunting. He's using them as a vehicle to rebel. He's more interested in his own personal vendetta against Stonehouse."

James's words carried a lot of truth. "The trouble is, it's the odd few like Zac who give the majority a bad name."

"I feel so awful," Sarah said. "I jumped to conclusions without any proof. No wonder Stonehouse didn't know what on earth I was talking about."

"Well, don't lose any sleep over him. He's a bad lot and we're well rid of him."

James insisted that he had to rush off to the surgery, even though it was the middle of the night.

Zac had been taken away by the police. We'd considered letting him go scot free, with just a warning, but the chances were he'd carry on in the same vein. He needed to be taught a lesson.

Sarah was exhausted. Ross's black eye looked even worse. As for Roddy, he was telling Mrs Mac for the umpteenth time exactly how he had tackled Zac and how he was going to write it up as a story. He was covered in mud and bits of twig from head to toe, but he'd given up caring. It was impossible to stay immaculate at Hollywell. There was too much going on.

I collapsed in an armchair, feeling ten years older and twenty years wiser. We'd been through one of the most testing times of our life and I think we'd all learned something from it.

"All revenge does is eat away at your soul. It kills common sense," Roddy theorized.

"OK, Roddy, we don't need a sermon." Sarah threw a sock at him, it glanced off the back of his head and landed in Matilda's basket. "Let's just put it all behind us, once and for all."

The phone call from the police meant we could do just that. They contacted us early the following morning to say that Bazz had been caught. Somebody had tipped them off anonymously, about stealing not just Bluey but also video-recorders, car radios, the lot – you name it, Bazz had taken

114

it. The police did a raid on his house and found a whole treasure trove of stolen goods. Bazz would be going to join his brother in prison and hopefully for a very long time.

"I can't believe that we're finally rid of him." Sarah sighed.

I knew just how she felt. It was like a huge weight being lifted off our shoulders. Now we could get on with running the sanctuary, rescuing more horses, saving more lives. Those were the things that were important.

"Just where has James got to?" Sarah was flinging rashers of bacon into a frying pan and beating the life out of some scrambled eggs.

"We can't have a party at this time of the morning," Ross piped up from an armchair, where he'd spent the last few hours snoring his head off.

"Since when has anything in this house been normal?" I answered, feeding Jigsaw a lump of congealed egg, which looked dishcloth grey and as tasty as cardboard.

"What's all this about a party?" Roddy emerged from upstairs, gummed up with sleep and accidentally bashing his head on the doorframe yet again. He still had a bit of twig or something stuck behind his ear. "Did I really tackle Zac to the ground or was it all a beautiful dream?"

Mrs Mac arrived on the scene carrying a huge

chocolate cake, which we all decided was far more appealing than Sarah's rubbery eggs.

"I've had all these wonderful ideas for the future," she twittered, cutting wedges of cake that were big enough for ten people. "What about forming a Hollywell Stables fan club?"

I disappeared outside to check on the horses and found most of Boris's breakfast scattered outside his door. He was too busy chatting up Dancer, who was looking at him as if he was the equine version of Mr Universe. How do you teach a horse to eat with its mouth closed?

James came racing up the drive in his estate car which was positively heaving with every veterinary appliance imaginable.

"Where are Katie and Danny?" he breathed, looking unusually animated for this time of the morning.

"James, why do I get the feeling you're up to something?"

Katie and Danny came creeping out of the house, looking like two nervous wrecks. James had told them that someone's pet snake had escaped in the back of his car and could they help him find it. Danny's face was a picture of sheer terror.

"Don't worry, it won't bite – not unless it's in a bad mood."

Ross winked at me, but I was still completely in the dark about what was going on.

James flung open the car door and Katie gasped in surprise.

"What is it?" I whispered, unable to stand the suspense any longer.

James reached forward and picked up the tiniest kitten I'd ever seen. It was so small, it just sat in the palm of his hand, and when it miaowed its whole body trembled.

"We found him on the surgery doorstep in a cardboard box," James explained. "Abandoned. I think the poor little chap's had a rough time. He was starving."

"But he's so beautiful," Katie said, gently stroking his tiny body. "How could anybody desert him?"

James was just about to answer when a sudden shrieking noise came from the house.

"What on earth?" James broke off mid-sentence and started running towards the back door.

"I bet I know what's happened," Ross laughed, and we sprinted after James, not wanting to miss the moment.

Roddy was standing on top of a chair, still clutching his piece of chocolate cake and desperately trying to get Sarah to do something. Mrs

Mac was leaning up against the kitchen units looking very faint.

"It's only a mouse," Ross shouted. "It's not even wild."

"Timmy!" Danny yelled, plunging into the magazine rack, where a very fat white mouse had disappeared into a copy of the *Weekly Herald*.

"Mel, do something," Roddy begged, but all I could do was roll around giggling.

"Got him!" Danny shrieked, emerging with Timmy, who looked about the size of a hamster.

"It must have been the chocolate cake," Sarah laughed. "He couldn't resist the smell."

"That mouse needs to go on a diet," James ordered, examining Timmy, who must be the only chocoholic rodent in the country.

Sarah explained to James how Katie and Danny had been leaving lumps of chocolate all round the house to tempt him out, which is why he'd grown so fat.

"Oscar," Katie suddenly shouted out, still holding the kitten, who was watching all the commotion with wide eyes. "That's what we'll call him . . . Oscar!"

Sarah had to be filled in on all the details of our latest arrival. Mrs Mac thought Oscar was adorable and Roddy thought he'd at least be able to keep down the mice. Matilda took one look at him and immediately adopted him as her own.

"How could anybody neglect a little thing like that?" Mrs Mac said.

Oscar would never be able to replace Oswald; no animal could ever do that. He would have his own individual personality, just like all the other animals at Hollywell, like Boris and Bluey and Queenie . . .

James proposed a toast, while Sarah fished out the camera for the family photograph. We always took pictures of the rescue cases, before and after. The difference was incredible. It was impossible to recognize Queenie and Bluey as the same ponies we had originally saved.

"Say 'cheese'," Sarah said, holding up the camera and then changing her mind, deciding to switch on the automatic timer. "Roddy, are you in this picture or not?"

Roddy complained that he was far too dishevelled and couldn't possibly be in a family photograph, but Sarah pushed him forward and he didn't have any choice.

"If we're going to have a fan club, who's going to run it?" Mrs Mac suddenly blurted out.

"Quick!" Sarah said, leaping forward and joining the group.

"I'll be the first member," Roddy shouted, holding up his glass and nearly spilling its contents on Danny's head.

"Smile, everybody," Sarah shouted, just as the flash went off.

If anybody had walked into the kitchen at that moment, they'd have thought we were round the twist. Katie was clinging on to Oscar, who was climbing up her shoulder; Danny on to Timmy. Mrs Mac had her arm round Roddy. Ross was standing there with his black eye and James was waving a bottle of brandy in the air. I was caught with my eyes closed and Sarah was holding a red rose in her teeth.

"So, a fan club it is, then?" James yelled, kissing Sarah on the cheek.

"I wonder how many horses we'll have this time next year?" I mused.

"Oh, hundreds," Katie joked. "But where are we going to put them all?"

"I don't know, but nothing can stop us now!"

Hollywell Stables 1

Flying Start by Samantha Alexander

Piper £2.99

Hollywell Stables – sanctuary for horses and ponies. It was a dream come true for Mel, Ross and Katie . . .

A mysterious note led them to Queenie, neglected and desperately hungry, imprisoned in a scrapyard. Rescuing Colorado was much more complicated. The spirited Mustang terrified his wealthy owner: her solution was to have him destroyed.

But for every lucky horse at the sanctuary there are so many others in desperate need of rescue. And money is running out fast . . .

How can the sanctuary keep going?

Hollywell Stables 2

The Gamble by Samantha Alexander

Piper £2.99

Hollywell Stables – sanctuary for horses and ponies. It was a dream come true for Mel, Ross and Katie . . .

It was a gamble. How could it possibly work? Why should one of the world's most famous rock stars give a charity concert for Hollywell Stables? But Rocky is no ordinary star and when he discovers that the racing stables keeping his precious thoroughbred are cheating him, he leads the Hollywell team on a mission to uncover the truth . . .

Hollywell Stables 4

Fame by Samantha Alexander

Piper £2.99

Hollywell Stables – sanctuary for horses and ponies. It was a dream come true for Mel, Ross and Katie . . .

Rocky's new record, *Chase the Dream*, shoots straight into the Top Ten, and all the proceeds are going to Hollywell Stables. It brings overnight fame to the sanctuary and the family are asked to do television and radio interviews. In one show they get a call from a girl who has seen a miniature horse locked in a caravan, but rings off before telling them where it was. The Hollywell team set off to unravel the mystery . . .

Polly on Location
by Wendy Douthwaite

Piper £2.99

"We think we'll need some extras, sometime next week," he explained. "Some riders and ponies. It will be for a night-time scene. Smugglers coming back from the coast, some riding, some leading pack-horses that sort of thing. And we could do with some horse help, today, too. Interested?"

When Jessica Caswell suggests to her friends in the Edgecombe Valley Riding Club that they audition for the filming, she never dreamt that she and her beautiful Arab mare, Polly, would play the star role!